AF361311

The Museum as Large-Room Pinball Machine

EDITED BY WILLIAM J. BUXTON

THE MUSEUM AS LARGE-ROOM PINBALL MACHINE

A 1967 New York City Seminar
Featuring Marshall McLuhan,
Harley Parker, and
Museum Professionals

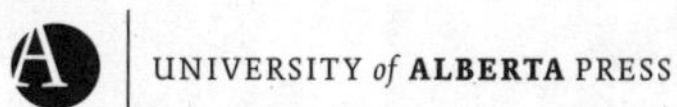

UNIVERSITY *of* ALBERTA PRESS

Published by

University of Alberta Press
1–16 Rutherford Library South
11204 89 Avenue NW
Edmonton, Alberta, Canada T6G 2J4
amiskwaciwâskahikan | Treaty 6 |
Métis Territory
ualbertapress.ca | uapress@ualberta.ca

Copyright © 2026 University of Alberta Press

LIBRARY AND ARCHIVES CANADA
CATALOGUING IN PUBLICATION

Title: The museum as large-room pinball
    machine : a 1967 New York City seminar
    featuring Marshall McLuhan, Harley
    Parker, and museum professionals /
    edited by William J. Buxton.
Names: Buxton, William, 1947– editor
Description: Includes bibliographical
    references and index.
Identifiers: Canadiana (print) 20250159880 |
    Canadiana (ebook) 20250159902 |
    ISBN 9781772128277 (softcover) |
    ISBN 9781772128390 (EPUB) |
    ISBN 9781772128406 (PDF)
Subjects: LCSH: McLuhan, Marshall, 1911-1980. |
    LCSH: Parker, Harley. | LCSH: Museum
    of the City of New York. | LCSH: Museum
    studies.
Classification: LCC AM5 .M875 2025 |
    DDC 069—dc23

First edition, first printing, 2026.
First printed and bound in Canada by
Houghton Boston Printers, Saskatoon,
Saskatchewan.
Copyediting and proofreading by Julie Sedivy.
Indexing by Judy Dunlop.

All rights reserved. No part of this publication
may be reproduced, stored in a retrieval
system, or transmitted in any form or by any
means (electronic, mechanical, photocopying,
recording, generative artificial intelligence
[AI] training, or otherwise) without prior
written consent. Contact University of Alberta
Press for further details.

University of Alberta Press supports
copyright. Copyright fuels creativity,
encourages diverse voices, promotes free
speech, and creates a vibrant culture. Thank
you for buying an authorized edition of this
book and for complying with the copyright
laws by not reproducing, scanning, or
distributing any part of it in any form without
permission. You are supporting writers and
allowing University of Alberta Press to
continue to publish books for every reader.

University of Alberta Press is committed to
protecting our natural environment. As part
of our efforts, this book is printed on Enviro
Paper: it contains 100% post-consumer
recycled fibres and is acid- and chlorine-free.

GPSR: Easy Access System Europe |
Mustamäe tee 50, 10621 Tallinn, Estonia |
gpsr.requests@easproject.com

This book has been published with the
help of a grant from the Federation for the
Humanities and Social Sciences, through the
Awards to Scholarly Publications Program,
using funds provided by the Social Sciences
and Humanities Research Council of Canada.

University of Alberta Press gratefully
acknowledges the support received for its
publishing program from the Government
of Canada, the Canada Council for the Arts,
and the Government of Alberta through the
Alberta Media Fund.

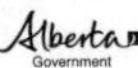

In Memory of Bonnie Buxton and Anne Innis Dagg

Contents

Acknowledgements

THIS IS A STUDY of a largely unexplored *terra incognita* within the galaxy of McLuhan-related scholarship, namely a museology seminar held in New York City in 1967. Not only has it fallen through the cracks of history, but the cracks themselves have left few traces. This has made for a retrieval project rife with intriguing challenges. Given that the seminar was moderated jointly by Marshall McLuhan and Harley Parker, the necessary point of entry for the volume was the dyad they formed; their working relationship can be likened to the two sides of a coin, representing interpretation and practice, respectively, united by a common vision. The seminar cannot be viewed simply as an extension of McLuhan's earlier work; it must be examined *in situ*, as a joint endeavour of the two thinkers. It is by virtue of Gary Genosko's involvement in the project that my effort to treat McLuhan and Parker as a formidable partnership reached fruition. Indeed, I originally became aware of the report because of its mention in an online article that Gary had written. He was well aware of the report, which he described as having "orphan" status within the McLuhan *oeuvres*. I quickly realized that in order to develop the notion of a McLuhan-Parker dyad with any rigour, Gary's involvement in the venture was indispensable. Upon receiving permission from the Museum to republish the volume, I immediately asked him if he would be willing to contribute an essay on the McLuhan-Parker relationship to the new version, which was to be published by the University of Alberta Press. He was happy to oblige. But Gary's contribution to the project did not end there. He informed me that he had other volumes on Parker in the works and was looking for a publisher. Given its commitment to republish the report, the University of Alberta Press was a natural fit. He was able to secure an agreement with the Press to include the two volumes in its catalogue with the understanding that the three works would be published around the same time as a trilogy, an arrangement that would put the idea of a McLuhan-Parker dyad on an even firmer footing.

Equally important in the development of the volume has been the involvement of David Howes. After having learned of my interest in having the report republished, he invited me to present my findings in a lecture series he had organized under the auspices of Concordia's Centre for Sensory Studies. David recognized that the seminar had important implications for understanding the extent to which the sensory dimension had been addressed in museums and agreed to write an essay for the volume surveying developments in this area.

Others have made notable contributions. Michael McLuhan and Margaret Parker have provided support and guidance on behalf of the McLuhan and Parker Estates, respectively. Ms. Parker gave permission to publish an image in her possession of McLuhan and Parker. This image appears on the front cover and shows them in front of Parker's painting *The Flying Children*. Andrew McLuhan kindly included my presentation on the project in the McLuhan Institute's summer school. Terry Gordon and Clinton Ignatov have provided me with valuable assistance in navigating McLuhan's vast collection of unpublished writings. I have drawn on the expertise of Richard Noble to make sense of the art-history backdrop to McLuhan's work. Richard Cavell has helped me better understand McLuhan's debt to Edmund Carpenter. Charles Acland alerted me to some key writings related to the film work of Charles Eames. Owen Chapman informed me about the role played by Tony Schwartz in developing the theory and practice of sound studies. Gerry Fialka raised some interesting issues about McLuhan in a podcast interview with me. I am also grateful for the institutional support provided to me by the Department of Communication Studies and the Centre for Sensory Studies at Concordia University, le Département d'information et de communication de l'Université Laval, and the McLuhan Institute.

In my efforts to annotate the report I have been fortunate to have discovered extensive pertinent material in three archives: the New York State Archives, the Museum of the City of New York Archives, and Library and Archives Canada. I am grateful to the staff of each for their assistance in locating, accessing, and reproducing items from their collections. In particular, I wish to thank the following persons: Mary E. Weber (New York State Archives); Joseph Patzner, Lauren Robinson, Sean Corcoran, and Anne-Marie Walsh (Museum of the City of New York); Aline Landry, Isabel Woods, Anne-Yves Nadro, Diane Abdoulaye, Aisha Idriss, Alison Pier, Anik Laflèche, and Karen Kong (Library and Archives Canada). Material located in the Library and Archives Canada, New York State Archives, and the Museum of the City of New York Archives has been published with permission. My preparation of this text was funded by an Insight Grant (#435-2017-0937) of the Social Sciences and Humanities Research Council of Canada.

I am also grateful to staff from other institutions for helping me clarify particular issues: Daniel Ostroff and Sara McBean (Eames Institute), Deborah Shapiro (Smithsonian Libraries and Archives), and Joanna Rios (Columbia University, Rare Books and Manuscripts Library).

Given the unwieldy character of this critical edition, it is not surprising that it has taken a dedicated editorial village of the University of Alberta Press to bring it to fruition. Its members include Duncan Turner, production editor; Cathie Crooks, associate director/interim director; Alan Brownoff, designer; Elisia Snyder, administrative assistant; Sosthenes Ekeh, PHD student intern; Julie Sedivy, copyeditor; Judy Dunlop, indexer; and above all, acquisition editor, Michelle Lobkowicz, whose leadership of the project has been exemplary. I very much appreciate the extent to which the staff have approached their work in a dedicated and cooperative manner, which has made my involvement with this book a distinct pleasure.

Manon, Océane, and Jesse Lee have always been there for me when I needed to put my absorption with past goings-on in perspective. Finally, the book is dedicated to the memory of two women who passed away during the time that the book was in its final stages: my sister, Bonnie Buxton, and my dear friend, Anne Innis Dagg. Both inspired me with their fierce determination, generosity, and unfailingly good humour.

Québec City, April 23, 2025

Introduction
Towards "Total Museology"

WILLIAM J. BUXTON

WHILE THE WORK OF MARSHALL MCLUHAN continues to attract
considerable attention, one of his most notable contributions has largely
been overlooked. It took the form of the prominent role he played
co-moderating (with Harley Parker) a seminar attended by over eighty
persons examining the communication of museums with their publics
on October 9 and 10, 1967. Under the auspices of the Museum of the
City of New York (MCNY) and funded primarily by the New York State
Council on the Arts (NYSCA), it was held largely at the premises of
the Museum on Fifth Avenue. The report occupies a unique place
within the vast *oeuvres* of Marshall McLuhan.[1] Rather than having
something written or said by McLuhan in isolation from others as its
point of reference, the report is entirely based on McLuhan *in dialogue*
with a broad range of interlocutors; he participated in these dialogues
largely as part of a dyad formed with Harley Parker. Indeed, one could
argue that it was Parker rather than McLuhan who did most of the
heavy lifting for the seminar. This involved not only its planning and
the delivery of its summation, but also picking up the slack when
McLuhan fell ill early on. The report also sheds considerable light on
the state of museology in mid-century America. It was the stated goal
of McLuhan and Parker to disrupt conventional museological practices and to raise questions about the deeply held beliefs of museum
officials. The planners of the seminar believed that those working in
museums could benefit from exposure to the ideas of the two moderators.

But by inviting Jacques Barzun to deliver the final address—largely challenging the views of Parker and McLuhan—this meant that the status quo could largely emerge from the seminar unscathed and that the feathers of the museum elite would largely remain unruffled. A transcript of the proceedings of the seminar was published in 1969. It is unfortunate that the event—and the report based on it—have largely been ignored.[2]

All this changed in 2008 with the French translation of the seminar report by Bernard Deloche and François Mairesse, assisted by Suzanne Nash.[3] Written as an intervention into the then-current discussions in France of new directions in museology, it framed the report as an important, but largely neglected, point of reference. Its title, *Le musée non linéaire*, was intended to capture what the authors considered to be the leitmotif of the seminar.[4] To be sure, they did not claim that there was any direct historical connection between the ideas of McLuhan/Parker and those underpinning subsequent museological thought and practice. But they did suggest that questions posed by McLuhan and Parker (as ably summarized by Kenneth Hudson) resonated with those addressed by figures that had played a key role in defining the contours of a new museology. It is a testament to McLuhan, Parker, and to the other seminar participants that their thoughtful and rigorous engagement with the problems facing the "linear museum" would eventually have reverberations in what was at that time an epoch far in the future.

The present volume builds on the foundations of *Le musée non linéaire* but with different emphases, particularly by delving into the circumstances giving rise to the seminar. To this end, it draws heavily on material located in the Museum of the City of New York (MCNY) Archives, the New York State Council on the Arts (NYSCA), papers located in the New York State Archives, and the Marshall McLuhan Fonds held in Library and Archives Canada located in Ottawa. Given that our text faithfully reproduces the original report, it avoids the misrepresentations that inevitably arise in a translation. Moreover, unlike *Le musée non linéaire*, the images and captions accompanying the report have been included.[5] We have expanded on the introduction to *Le musée non linéaire* by highlighting the important role played by the negotiations between the two moderators and the two institutions.

This text can best be seen as a collective effort to make the report both available and accessible. To this end, the report has been reprinted with extensive annotation. The introduction provides context and background. Given that the work of Parker is much less well known than that of McLuhan, Gary Genosko has contributed an essay to the volume, focusing on Parker's career and his relationship with McLuhan. And since a major theme of the seminar was that of exploring the sensory in relation to museums, David Howes has provided an essay that examines contemporary developments in this area. One can better understand the meaning and significance of the seminar by examining in more detail the two main sponsors of the event, the MCNY and the NYSCA,[6] who worked collaboratively on the venture.

New York State Council on the Arts (NYSCA)

The origins of the NYSCA can be traced back to the election in 1958 of Nelson Rockefeller as governor of New York State. Responding to his leadership, the Legislature established the organization in 1961—the first of its kind in the United States.[7] It was modelled on the Arts Council of Great Britain (ACGB), following a directive of Governor Rockefeller that was read at the first meeting of the NYSCA in 1963. As with its progenitor, the new agency was to supplement rather than replace private support for the arts.[8] The principal areas of endeavour for the Council would be "the Performing Arts Touring Program; the Visual Arts Program, including traveling exhibitions and aid to museums; the Technical Assistance Program…Special Projects Program for arts activities and the Education Program for projects dealing with arts instruction in communities, public schools, and colleges and universities." Council would set up advisory panels for the areas included and would be represented *ex officio* on each.[9] The Council was made up of fifteen members serving five-year terms.[10] In 1965 the legislation named it as a permanent agency,[11] with John Hightower, "an ardent exponent of government" and a protégé of Rockefeller, becoming its director."[12] It is evident that the museums area of the Council benefited from the engagement of Rockefeller and Hightower. It was through

an intervention by Governor Rockefeller in 1964 that Museum Aid
came under the purview of the Council rather than the Department
of Education.[13] And as NYSCA Executive Director Hightower proudly
reported, "In July, 1966, the Legislature of the state of New York…made
law-making history by appropriating at the request of…Rockefeller
$600,000 for aid to museums.[14] By the end of the decade, under the
direction of Hightower, the overall budget had increased to $20,081,000,
with $1,500,000 of that amount earmarked for the Museum Aid Program.
The continuance of this endeavour stressed "public services on a merit
basis with strong consideration of geographical distribution of funds."[15]
The generous funding for museums was in line with the Council's
efforts to "remain sensitive to the needs of the entire population of
the state" and to be "concerned with the equitable geographic distribution of arts opportunities."[16] Indeed, as Barresi notes, the "lists of
performance locations found in NYSCA annual reports (1965–71)
reveal the wide and equitable geographic distribution of Council-
sponsored arts opportunities."[17]

The Museum of the City of New York (MCNY)

At first blush, it would appear that by virtue of its seminar on communications and museums, the MCNY would embody the Council's goals
of spreading arts opportunities equally within the State of New York.
Many of the museum professionals in attendance came from outside
of New York City. Yet because the museum was unapologetically
dedicated to serving as a historical custodian of Manhattan and its
environs, it was almost by definition not in a position to advance the
cause of distributing arts opportunities in an equitable manner. Indeed,
it had established a reputation as an elitist institution, a repository
for items emptied from the attics of New York City's upper class.
Founded in 1923 and "dedicated to preserving the history of the city's
material culture," it served as a "storehouse for the heirlooms of New
York's elite" and a "clearinghouse for the city's history."[18] As commerce
came to dominate Manhattan, "the wealthy fled to the suburbs," leaving
their material possessions behind.[19] From the outset, the Museum, as
a private, non-profit organization, struggled financially. Moreover,
because of its inaccessibility, its attendance figures were perpetually

low, and it had to resort to frequent fundraising schemes to keep afloat.[20] While it "never abandoned its position as a caretaker of elite New Yorkers' largesse"[21] it also carved out a unique role that distinguished it from other museums of history in New York City, coming to be defined as the "museum for every New Yorker."[22] In addition to serving as extra closets for the wealthy, its mission was defined as an educational one, providing the city with a common history and anchoring a common community.[23] To this end, it established a committee on education in 1931, and published a bimonthly magazine (*Our Town*) for children.[24] By virtue of its "Please Touch" program, its offering of a college course, "Museum Methods and Practice in Social Studies," and its opening of the innovative Dutch galleries, the Museum increasingly identified itself as an innovative force in communicating history to the public.[25] Yet its management was of the view that it had largely been forgotten.[26]

Origins of the Seminar

It is not surprising, then, that the Museum sought support from the NYSCA for what it considered to be a seminar, which its director, Miller, felt would be a "major event" during "the museum world year."[27] In the spring of 1967, he spoke with Janice Duff[28] of NYSCA "on the possibility of developing a seminar session on the general subject of museum installation and communication around the talents of Marshall McLuhan and Harley Parker." He noted that they would be spending the next academic year at Fordham University, beginning in the fall of 1967. Miller had already discussed this project with both of them and conveyed that they "had expressed immediate interest" in the event. McLuhan had referred Miller to Father John Culkin of Fordham through whom "preliminary planning details could be channeled."[29]

It was his hope that a "scholastic publication" would result from the seminar. Overall, in his view, the program "would have great appeal to exhibits designers [as well as] directors and curators who are responsible for the visual impact of their particular presentation." Miller wished to have some indication from Hightower about whether the proposed seminar was feasible, as "an operation of this nature cannot be started too soon in order for it to come off in a commendable and creditable way."[30] While Hightower's initial reaction to Miller's project

was a favourable one, he wished to have an opinion about the proposal
from someone with expertise in this area. In the margin of the copy
of Miller's letter, he wrote, "Allon—Sounds intriguing—John."

In line with the practice of Foundation officials, this note most
likely meant that Hightower intended to pass the letter on to a person
named Allon whose judgment he trusted. That person was undoubt-
edly Allon Schoener, a member of the New York State Arts Council's
Board of Directors, who wrote to Hightower providing an assessment
of the proposal.[31] While Schoener thought that "the whole idea [was]
very good," he "had some reservations about Miller and his museum,"
which he felt were lacking in "professionalism and imagination."
Schoener went on to suggest that the project's planning committee
"include people from some of the other major museums where they
do know something about design, communication and presentation."
He suggested representatives from "the Museum of Modern Art,
Metropolitan Museum [of Art], American Museum of Natural History
(Planetarium), [and] the Botanical Gardens." According to Schoener,
of even greater importance to the museum profession for understanding
new communication methods were "designers and filmmakers who
produced world's fair exhibitions." They included, among others, Charles
Eames,[32] George Nelson, and Francis Thompson. He also believed
that "people like Tony Schwartz could add a great deal."[33] Overall, he
was concerned that Miller might not include "these people who have
had the greatest amount of experience and success in this area."
Finally, he was of the view that there was no need for the production
of a "scholarly publication," arguing that "the seminar would not be
addressing a 'scholarly subject.'" Rather, what was at issue was the
advancement of technology and "getting tuned in."

Miller's thoughts on the seminar echoed those of Schoener. He
viewed the seminar as a vehicle for extending the Museum's sphere
of influence in the northeastern United States.[34] To this end, he wished
to make sure that Parker and McLuhan found the seminar to their
liking. Miller stressed to Parker that he and McLuhan could make
changes to it, or even "revamp the entire outline."[35] Perhaps of greatest
importance was to "create an environment in which [he] and McLuhan
[would] be able to work with the group"; the schedule indicated "the

demands upon [Parker's] and McLuhan's time." Miller reminded
Parker of their agreement that they would make themselves "available...for the full two days."

Underscoring the balance that he believed the schedule had achieved,
he noted that the afternoon of the first day (led by McLuhan) would
feature a conversation between Parker and McLuhan; the afternoon
of the second day would be devoted to Parker. The latter would "certainly
sustain the interest and evenly spread the importance of each session
throughout the entire two." McLuhan and Parker would be welcomed
as "guests of honor" to the concluding event of the seminar, namely a
dinner for which Columbia University Dean Jacques Barzun would
be the principal speaker. His remarks "would follow a summation of
the Seminar by either [Parker] or McLuhan." Miller reiterated that an
honorarium of $1500 would be "divided equally between [Parker] and
McLuhan."[36] He also wished to know the thoughts of Parker and
McLuhan on rights of publication as the Council was expecting that
funds would be "available to finance the publication of the findings
and conclusions of the seminar." In his response, writing to Hightower,
Parker affirmed that he and McLuhan believed that "everything seems
to be in order."[37] While they agreed to have the seminar published,
they assumed that Miller had been referring to "transcriptions of the
tape-recorded addresses." Neither he nor McLuhan wished to present
formal papers. He did assure Hightower that they would provide "a
table of contents with appropriate titles for [their] contributions."

The asymmetry in Miller's negotiations with McLuhan and Parker
was noteworthy. Following the suggestion of the Council officers, Culkin
was contacted by the Museum for advice. According to Laurence
Maloy, he was "rather vague about the whole affair" but wished to
make sure that they had "a firm commitment from McLuhan" who
received "thousands of offers." They "should be sure he had said yes
to [them]." He also suggested that Parker be used as their "go between."
He had "reluctantly agreed to do [so]." Culkin was of the view that
"McLuhan would not want to do more than give his address and
answer some questions" but would be available at almost any time.[38]

In planning the seminar, it was evident that Miller indeed deployed
Parker as a "go-between," with McLuhan playing a relatively minor

role in the process. Indeed, Miller arranged to meet personally with Parker when he and two others from the Museum were attending the meeting of the American Association of Museums in Toronto in late May, 1967.[39] As Miller noted to McLuhan in a letter sent at the end of June, the plans for the seminar had become "more formalized" during the preceding few weeks largely through "several discussions" with Parker.[40] Funding from the Council for the seminar was approved, with an official contract signed in June.[41]

The seminar took place as planned on October 9 and 10, 1967. Mirroring the enthusiasm he had displayed in anticipation of the seminar,[42] Miller effusively conveyed his gratitude to the two moderators and the guest speaker in letters written to each on the same day. He lauded McLuhan's "willingness to participate in our recent seminar on museum [which had] electrified the participants and [was] causing an increasing revitalization of thinking among my peers and colleagues." He thanked him for "giving so generously of [his] time and self to this cultural group."[43] He told Parker that he "simply [could not] do justice in words or other forms of communication in thanking [him] for [his] support...and participation." Furthermore, "this all would not have taken place without you. Not only am I in your debt, but in a larger sense, the whole museum profession is also."[44] His comments to Barzun were much briefer, thanking him for his "brilliant participation," adding that it was wonderful having him with them. He noted that Barzun would see the final transcript once it arrived. Most of his letter consisted of an excerpt from a letter that he had received from Mary C. Black, Director of the Museum of American Folk Arts. He expressed agreement with Black's view of "the effect of [his] remarks on the group: Barzun [as the] final speaker [was a] stroke of genius," further quoting Black's opinion that "having been jolted upright by the communication experts, I think he helped give us back to ourselves." If in fact Miller believed Black's assessment of the seminar, it reveals a stance that was much more measured than what he had conveyed to Parker and McLuhan. A similar sentiment can be found in a letter from Ralph Burger to Harry Deutsch, Executive Director of the Associated Councils of the Arts: "I understand that

Jacques Barzun's talk at your Museums Conference really demolished Mr. McLuhan. By any chance, would you have an extra copy around?"[45]

The Seminar at a Glance

Before the seminar began, each of the participants received a tape recording (made by Tony Schwartz) of a wide-ranging conversation between McLuhan and Parker. The first session of the seminar (which took place at 10:00 AM on October 9) began with a continuation of this dialogue followed by exchanges between McLuhan, Parker, and the participants. In his opening remarks, Miller, as chair of the session, emphasized the informality that was planned for the event, with participants having the opportunity to change their places, move tables around, and get coffee. Images accompanying the report conveyed these sentiments along with the flow of the session, from the arrival of McLuhan and Parker to the participants "relaxing between sessions." The section on the museum visit (at 2:00 PM on October 9) begins with a rather striking image of McLuhan, Parker, and Miller gazing at what is described as "one of the exhibits at the American Museum of Natural History."[46] The discussion that took place during the visit to some of the galleries was recorded and subsequently transcribed, revealing the exchanges McLuhan and Parker had with Miller. These were interrupted when McLuhan fell ill and needed to leave. In McLuhan's absence, the discussion opened up to include interventions by a broader range of participants. The report concluded this section by noting the adjournment of the visit at 4:00 PM. This was followed by an image of the participants having cocktails (at 5:00 PM on October 9) in the entrance hall of the museum. By way of introduction into the next morning's visit to the experimental gallery—followed by a discussion (at 10:00 AM on October 10)—the report broke off its text capturing the discussions by including a sketch of the gallery's plan accompanied by an image of Parker and Gerald M. Simon installing "special equipment" in the gallery (observed by Miller).[47] The round-table discussion of that afternoon (at 2:00 PM on October 10) had the visits to the museum and the experimental gallery as points of reference. It was launched by some topics that had "popped up" during the cocktail reception of the previous day, such as how the sensorium could best be studied, and then meandered off in various directions. Initially some confusion was evident as McLuhan was late to arrive and not everyone had been able to visit the gallery. Hence, much of the early discussion involved Parker fielding questions about the nature of the gallery against the backdrop of his experience with museum design. Following the arrival of McLuhan, the discussion veered towards more general issues. Interchanges began to emerge among the participants, who differed widely in their response to the seminar. It featured a presentation on the star system by Letícia Román (Hollywood actress-turned-anthropologist) that led to a wider discussion of popular culture, fuelled by McLuhan's views on the audience as the new star. The President's banquet (at 8:00 PM, preceded by cocktails at 7:00 PM on October 10) was held in the Silver Gallery on the museum's second floor, and began with opening remarks by the Museum's President, Louis S. Auchincloss, followed by comments by Miller, a summation given by Parker, remarks by McLuhan, and concluded with Barzun's address, "Museum Piece 1967." The text for the banquet session, accompanied by an image of the speaker's table,[48] indicated when introductions were made and when applause occurred; it noted that there was a standing ovation following the conclusion of Barzun's speech.[49]

Overall, the report had the aim of capturing and conveying, through text and images, the oral give-and-take of the seminar, largely without recourse to the replication of written material. However, by virtue of its embeddedness in the Museum's *modus operandi*, its purpose went well beyond providing a record of what had transpired at the seminar. Working hand-in-glove with the Museum's *Annual Report* and frequent press releases, it functioned to forge links with the general public, to develop and strengthen its relations with New York City elites, to ingratiate itself with funding bodies, to carve out a niche in the broader cultural scene, and perhaps, above all, to fuel fundraising for what had largely been a very impecunious organization.

Coverage

There is little evidence that the event attracted much attention at the time. To be sure, a press release announcing it was circulated just prior to its occurrence.[50] McLuhan, described as "the foremost exponent of today's methods and media of communication," was given top billing in the release. While Parker's credentials were given mention, a reader of the release would likely have had the impression that his role in the seminar was secondary to that of McLuhan. The release drew attention to the key components of the seminar, including a dialogue between McLuhan and Parker, the museum field trip, a workshop on the alternative museum gallery, and Barzun's presentation. A copy of the seminar's program and a list of participants was included. Arrangements for media coverage were to be made through Mrs. Helen Streeter of the Public Relations Office at the Museum.

At least two local media outlets took up the Museum on its offer. Gregory Battcock reviewed the museum-visit portion of the first day of the seminar[51]—along with an exhibition held at the Riverside Museum—for the *Westside News*. While he did not contest McLuhan's views *per se*, he found them not to be particularly original. He chided McLuhan for not sounding very modern. This was in line with the "crowd" at the event, which, in his view "wasn't the type McLuhan used to attract at places in Brooklyn Heights or at the Jewish 'Y.'" He remarked that in claiming that "galleries or exhibitions...should involve the spectator more deeply than is usual," McLuhan betrayed his ignorance of the approach used in Colonial Williamsburg, where "this sort of involvement [is] artfully managed." And in contending that a "visual sensory bias must succumb to the whole sensorium, including audio and tactile elements," he wasn't really going beyond what one found in Disneyland. He felt that McLuhan's notion of "creating a gallery in which there are 'no answers given, only questions asked'" was "a good idea." But in Battcock's view, this demonstrated that McLuhan was "behind the times" as "the abstract expressionist painter was already thinking along these lines." Battcock's dissatisfaction with McLuhan's views on questions and answers also informed his judgment of the seminar as a whole. He observed that "some questions were not answered at the seminar. They weren't even asked. Perhaps too many jobs were at stake; certainly a lot of comfortable notions were." He nonetheless believed there was some merit to McLuhan's views. This was evident in the second part of his review, in which he assessed the contemporaneous photography exhibit. He noted that "the new show does not meet any of McLuhan's requirements for effective audience participation and meaningful spectator involvement." He judged it to be a failure because it catered to "our visual sensory bias" and "with linear connected spaces…it reads like a book."[52] Arguably, his critique of the photography exhibition could have been written by either Parker or McLuhan.

Richard F. Shepard also attended the first day of the seminar, which he reviewed for the *New York Times*.[53] His article was initially snide in tone and dismissive in judgment. Referring to McLuhan as "the man whose views on media have caused a considerable stir," Shepard claimed that he had advised "the linear laggards of an outmoded visual era to refashion their museums along multimedia lines meaningful to new generations." Having set a skeptical tone for his review, he then proceeded to quote a number of statements made by McLuhan and Parker, thus suggesting that their views should be seen as outrageous impositions on museological practice. He noted at the outset that both McLuhan and Parker were convinced that Western museums suffered from a visual bias; McLuhan dwelt on their obsession with the "world of artifacts," while Parker aspired to create a "museum without labels" as he wanted to get away "from museums organized as books." Shepard seemed to suggest that Parker's ideas were not yet subject to scrutiny, as everything in the "special temporary gallery" was still "under wraps." He also called attention to the $8,000 price tag for the seminar, implying that this was not money well spent. At the same time, Shepard seemed to suggest that there was some value to the urging of McLuhan and Parker that "museums make more use of films, still photographs, voice tapes, and other devices to help place exhibits in a proper environment." Moreover, according to McLuhan, the introduction of computers was bound to enrich the world. Shepard illustrated McLuhan's contention by citing his observation that "the possibility of programming of factory presentations of the forest world is tremendous." The review concluded with a citation from McLuhan suggesting that he was optimistic about the future of Western museums: "The present tendency to involve all of the senses contrasted with an opposite trend in the orient. We're orientalizing with new techniques…

they are westernizing with old techniques." This claim, according to
Shepard, found favour with Shuji Takashina, curator of Tokyo's
National Museum of Western Art.

Grace Glueck covered the second-day museum visit for the same
newspaper with a sardonic tone similar to that of Shepard.[54] She
noted how he "massaged his captive audience with a multimedia
demonstration…intended to show how multimedia techniques could
'orient' museum visitors." Glueck made a point of trying to capture
how the audience responded to the exhibit. She observed that even
though Parker explained that the show had been done on a "time-
and-money shoestring," many visitors still expressed irritation at
what they considered to be "technical imperfections." She reported
that Stuart Silver, manager of exhibits for the Metropolitan Museum
of Art, would not pass judgment and was waiting for "a more sophisticated display." He thought that more time to visit the exhibit should
have been allotted and asserted that "the viewer's primary response
was restiveness, not involvement."

Glueck also remarked on "some lively Abbott-and-Costello byplay
between…McLuhan, Parker and their audience," appreciatively
capturing some of the show's humorous moments:

> McLuhan quoted a line from Eliot in mincing Eliotic voice to illus-
> trate a McLuhan concept of English poetry that he called "a
> sensory bias of levelness, evenness…The English used lineality
> in the equitone way to keep the mob back. It's a strategy of
> self-defence."

She reported that in wrapping up Parker suggested "that the audience adjourn to try a different kind of medium. 'Cocktails,' he said,
walking toward the door."

Not surprisingly, the seminar received a much less searching appraisal
in the MCNY's 1967–68 *Annual Report*. Drawing on the original press
release as an introduction, the publication featured nine photographs
of the seminar, each accompanied by a lengthy caption. The number
of "museum directors and key personnel" who had attended the seminar
was now reported to be over one hundred and the report was at pains

to reveal the lavishness of the affair and to what extent "distinguished guests" such as Commissioner Harmon Goldstone (of the City Planning Commission) and August Heckscher (Administrator of Recreation and Cultural Affairs) were in attendance.

Seemingly inspired by the success of the seminar, Miller followed through on his earlier suggestion that holding an event could be a regular practice of the Museum. Two years later, Lucy Kostelanetz, an officer of the Museum Aid Program of the Council, wrote to Ralph Miller raising some issues about a contract she was preparing for "another museum communication's seminar" to be held by the Museum.[55] As with the 1967 seminar, the Council was willing to "pay towards the fees of Principal Speakers" as well as for the costs incurred in the preparation of a transcription report. She asked that the Museum submit a budget estimate of the anticipated costs. She also wished to know how long it would take to complete the report, whether the contract should be dated to begin on October 1 (extending fifty-two weeks) and what the seminar dates would be. It was her understanding that four speakers would be involved with a fee of $500 each. It is not known whether or not the second Museum seminar actually materialized.

The McLuhan-Parker Dyad

The two had been invited to serve as moderators for the event. That they were chosen to work together may have been because of McLuhan's highly publicized nomination as the Albert Schweitzer Chair at Fordham University for the 1967–68 academic year. At the time of his appointment, McLuhan was well known in New York as a celebrated founding figure in communication studies, whose two major works had become highly influential.[56] A condition of the appointment was that he would be accompanied by a "team," which included Parker. To be sure, Parker's work had in its own right received attention in New York City through a feature article in the *New York Times*.[57] Written by John Lee, Toronto correspondent for the newspaper, it described in some detail one of Parker's major initiatives, namely the New Hall of Fossil Invertebrates, which had opened recently at the Royal Ontario Museum (ROM). The article was largely based on an interview with Parker, "chief of museum display"—identified by Lee as a "McLuhan disciple" who had designed this "new permanent gallery." He described Parker as "51 years old…a tall, thoughtful man with a full head of silvery hair and a yellowish Van Dyke beard." He occupied "an untidy office reached through…furniture galleries." In order to "trace the evolution of lower animals," as Lee reports, Parker claimed to be "creating 'a multi-sensual experience'[that] uses flashing lights, curved spaces, sandy ramps, sounds of gulls and thunder, colour cartoons, slide projectors, literary quotations, small aquariums and fossils people can feel." Nonetheless, Lee reports that Parker claimed that the gallery was "still baby talk" [because] "the monolithic nature of the museum itself—print-orientation and linear sequential patterns" hamstrung efforts to reform it. However, "as a first step," according to Parker "at least it's kinetic, a walk-through, and it stimulates interest. There've been more people in that gallery in the past week than in the whole time since it opened, maybe 20 years ago." He had high hopes for the appointment the following year at Fordham, which he felt would be "Heaven," as it would provide his group the opportunity to "explore audience response, the general environment, [and] sensory riches [as well as] test the differing sensory modalities."

Parker's views were very much influenced by those of McLuhan. A painter who taught at the Ontario College of Art,[58] it appears that he first began to work with McLuhan through the journal *Explorations*[59] and the organization Idea Consultants, founded in March, 1956.[60] In a 1964 letter to Michael Wolff, McLuhan referred to a book he had been working on with Parker, noting that "it is being done with painter and designer (Parker) and is quite a new approach to language and literature and painting."[61] Parker had joined the ROM in 1957,[62] taking a leave of absence for the Fordham year. While working there, he had a cross-appointed position at the University of Toronto's Centre for Culture and Technology, which had been established in 1963 with McLuhan as Director.[63] He did not return to the position at ROM, but joined McLuhan's centre as a research associate, a situation that was marked by friction and tension.[64] He held this position from 1968 to 1975, taking a year off (1973–74) during this time to serve at the Rochester Institute of Technology as that institute's first professor of communications. Parker retired from academic life in 1976, moving to British Columbia, where he focused more on his painting until his death in 1992.[65]

Aftermath of the Seminar

It did not take long for officials of the Museum to put some of the ideas discussed at the seminar into action. A party was planned for November 8 in conjunction with the opening of the exhibit, *New York—The Scene 67/17*. Tickets for the event were fifty dollars each and the proceeds were to be used for the expansion program of the Museum. The party would echo the exhibition theme, namely the contrast of life in the New York City of 1967 to that of 1917.

It was designed by Museum director Miller, who seems to have drawn on his seminar experience in putting it together. He was present at the group tour of the American Museum of Natural History, accompanying McLuhan and Parker as they wandered through various galleries. He heard how they reacted to what they were experiencing, which amounted to a long litany of what was wrong with the Museum, including the use of labels, glass cases, architectural linearity, and an approach grounded in texts and the written word. He also likely benefited from the exchanges among the participants at the seminar, grounded in the Museum professionals' response to the critique provided by McLuhan and Parker. Above all, his new exhibit was very much rooted in Parker's experimental gallery.

It is noteworthy that the exhibition was viewed as "a further extension of *'total museology,'*" a concept first introduced in the Museum's Dutch Gallery. The visitor was invited to go beyond visuality "to achieve a total museum experience." As a "contemporary exhibit...it was a placed in a framework of historical relationship, designed to communicate both physically and perceptually with the viewer." Again, in line with Parker's earlier efforts to reshape the space of the Museum, the environment was reconfigured to receive the new set of artifacts:

> Using the ceiling as an integral part of the installation, posters of the 1917 era from the Museum's vast collection were hung in

contrast with the graphic and psychedelic posters popular today. On the platform extending from the second floor stairway may be seen costumed mannequins and artifacts of both periods in juxtaposition.[66]

The Aliman gallery was transformed into a Palm Court with the auditorium becoming a discothèque.[67] This change underscored the extent to which the exhibit built on Parker's use of the aural. Presenting a juxtaposition of the sounds of New Amsterdam in 1917 with the contemporary (at the time) noise of the streets of New York, the new exhibit featured "simultaneous aural contrasts…eighteenth-century Dutch music, rock 'n' roll, subway noises, children's cries, folk songs, and an offkey Christmas carol."[68] As with Parker's experimental gallery, the new exhibit used projected images as well as the Museum's surfaces in an innovative manner: "Three slide projectors were used in a special gallery to flash, simultaneously, over 200 different views of New York City on the walls."[69]

Miller was also present during tours of Parker's prototype and took part in the discussions about it that ensued. These can be seen as akin to a trial by fire, and they revealed the extent to which leading Museum professionals were receptive to the ideas of Parker and McLuhan. It was evident that Miller had concluded that both the theory and practice of these two experts in relation to museums had merit and could serve as the basis for a new "total museology" making for a "new total museum experience."[70]

The next step was to articulate this approach within the Museum itself through the new exhibit, which opened around a month after the seminar had concluded. This involved working with the Museum committee to plan and organize the opening benefit event. The party not only helped to raise funds for the Museum's expansion, it also served as an exercise in public relations and networking, and in nurturing and strengthening contacts with the broader New York community. In principle, the Museum was for all New Yorkers. However, by virtue of its long history as an *entrepôt* for the discarded objects of New York City's upper classes, those contacted were mostly members of Manhattan's high society. This state of affairs was an artifact of the composition of the organizing committee of fourteen individuals,[71] made up entirely of married women who were members of the Museum.[72] It is noteworthy that all were listed using their married names, with the exception of Mrs. Hart Moss, whose professional name, Kitty Carlisle, appeared in brackets after her married name. By virtue of having a public identity separate from the name of her husband, Ms. Carlisle was a member of a small minority of the committee.[73] However, she was one among others on the committee who were active in arts and entertainment.[74] The other committee members may have become involved by virtue of their marriage to prominent figures within the New York City elite.[75]

Later in the year, the seminar spawned an exhibit in the state capital that had also been inspired by the ideas of Parker and McLuhan. One of its participants, G. Carroll Lindsay (Director of Museum Services of the New York State Museum in Albany) helped put together a special exhibit, entitled *Winter Kaleidoscope: New York*, that was featured during the Christmas vacation period in 1967. As reported in the *Glens Falls Times*, "Designed specifically for school-age visitors [it displayed] the many faces of winter-time New York State from Times Square to Niagara Falls."[76] It was evident that the exhibit had its origins in the Museum's seminar:

> Experimental in Nature and based on ideas from Marshall McLuhan, Expo 67 and the Electric Circus, [it] presents 400 New York winter scenes on some 30 projection screens, but uses only six projectors. Winter scenes appear in a giant kaleidoscope effect.

Perhaps reflecting what had impressed Lindsay at the seminar, the article dwelt on some of the technological aspects of the exhibit:

> Much of the effect comes from a specially designed multi-dimensional "screen" which breaks the images of details seen on different planes. Many of the images assume a unique three-dimensional character, and all appear without particular sequence, following the McLuhan "non-linear" theory...The special screen is "in the round" and may be viewed from many sides simply

by walking through it...[This is an] example of the application
of contemporary technology and design to a particular kind of
museum display.

The article reports that Lindsay was of the view that "the exhibit
represents an important museum venture into the field of contemporary audio-visual technique," echoing the sentiments expressed by
Parker and McLuhan at the Museum seminar. Moreover, he noted:

We must continue to develop new ways of attracting young
people to the museum and communicating to them on their own
terms. In this way we are assuring the interest of the museum
visitor of the future. Frankly the exhibit is a bit turned on and for
this reason I believe it will be exciting for younger visitors.

Intersecting Initiatives

The seminar not only spawned the two exhibits in New York, it also
intersected with some other ventures that drew on McLuhan's ideas
in shaping museological practice. Everett Ellin, who had actively
participated in the seminar, developed the Computer Museum
Network, often referencing McLuhan's ideas.[77] At the time of Ellin's
participation in the seminar, he was in a period of transition. He
had left the position of Assistant to the Director of the Guggenheim
Museum (with Thomas Messer as Director) to become a Division
Director at the Museum of Modern Art (MOMA). As is evident in
the report, Ellin had become disenchanted with the Guggenheim—
and with museum practices in general.[78] After having spent a few
months in Peru, Ellin claimed in an interview to have returned to
the Museum as a "changed person" who was no longer arrogant,
but spiritual. He felt that he was now "in touch with time."[79] He now
found the Guggenheim to be "confining and unbelievably stuffy" and
was "bored to death." He had the revelation that museums [hadn't]
changed in 150 years, since the Louvre." As he put it, "They're still
linear; everything is linear." He noticed that the galleries were "too
crowded" with no quietude. He felt that something had to be done
"to recognize another—other manners of confrontation with art."

He described the process that led him to come up with a different approach:

> And that's when I started reading Marshall McLuhan...the theory of media, media theory...I read several of his books—all of them, as a matter of fact—and they weren't very long...[A] museum is a medium of communication, in the McLuhanist sense. And I went to a roundtable that he was chairing in Manhattan at NYU...[T]here was a discussion period, and I asked him what he thought of my observation that museums are a medium...And I said, "What do you think of that?" And he pondered and he said, "You know, I think you're absolutely right." I said, "Well, don't you think...that museums should be addressing this reality and beginning to function as a medium and understand how they are, because inevitably they will have to square off with mass media, which will be far well ahead of them." He said, "Yes." And I said, "Well, I have this idea for a project called the Museum Computer Network, to bring the electronic age to museums." He said, "Good idea; pursue it." And I walked out of there all glowing, you know, because—like I met Moses and I told him that I—like—I found the tablet, and he says, yeah, go forth. So sell it, you know...[T]hat's when I began to really work out the concept.

Almost precisely at the same time that Miller was seeking funding from the NYSCA on behalf of the MCNY for the *Museum Communication* seminar, Ellin sought support from the same agency for the Museum Computer Network. In this case, he worked through MOMA in conjunction with a group of institutions in the New York City area. Representatives met at the Whitney Museum in early 1967. Echoing the views of Ellin, those present at the meeting recognized that it was not at all surprising that museums were largely not interested in computerization. However, they believed that the "network concept" was the key for using the computer as the main tool for humanities research. It is instructive that Ellin, representing MOMA, prepared the summary of the meeting.[80]

In the spring of 1967, Ellin presented a paper on media and museums, largely inspired by McLuhan's work in communications.[81] He had been invited by the director of the Stockholm's Moderna Museet, Pontus Hultén, who had in the previous year commissioned works by Claes Oldenburg[82] and Niki de Saint Phalle[83] that explored aspects of McLuhan's media theory. Hultén, as an enthusiastic exponent of McLuhan's ideas, subsequently became active in the New York City art scene, curating a 1968 exhibit at MOMA that explored the passage from the mechanical to the electronic age using McLuhan's writings as a point of reference.[84] The following year, Allon Schoener, who had evaluated the proposal that Miller had submitted to the NYSCA, curated the controversial multimedia exhibit, *Harlem on My Mind*, at the Metropolitan Museum of Art. Its director, Thomas Hoving, had participated in the Museum seminar. And in 1969, MOMA featured a sequel to Hultén's exhibit, *Information*, curated by Kynaston McShine, which drew on the ideas of McLuhan.[85] McShine had been encouraged by John Hightower, who had become Director of MOMA after having left his position as Director of the NYSCA, the agency that had funded the Museum seminar.[86] Some participants in the seminar subsequently cited McLuhan or Parker in their work.[87]

The Document

From the outset, it was the intent of Miller to "produce a scholarly publication" based on the seminar.[88] He requested that Parker and McLuhan provide him with their "thoughts on the rights of publication as we are expecting to have funds available to finance the publication of the findings and conclusions of the seminar."[89]

Parker conferred with McLuhan about the matter of publication. Both agreed to have the results of the seminar appear in published form. They took this to mean publishing "transcriptions from the tape-recorded addresses." Neither wished to "become involved in the presentation of a formal paper at this time."[90] In accordance with the wishes of Parker and McLuhan, printed versions of their texts were not asked of them. Rather, the version to be published took the form

of a typescript of the seminar in its *entirety*. It consisted of a typescript of all the sessions and included transcripts of the tape-recorded
McLuhan-Parker "dialogue," the visit to the American Museum of
Natural History, as well as Barzun's keynote address. Copies of this
material were sent to McLuhan, Parker, and Barzun shortly after the
seminar, along with a request for comments and for whatever
changes considered to be necessary.[91]

There is no evidence that Barzun ever responded to Miller's
request. However Miller did receive a copy of the report—likely from
McLuhan—that had gone through a process of editing. He notified
Parker that he was "trying to finish and set the seminar manuscript
and get it to the publishers." However, he "noticed enumerable dele-
tions in blue pencil apparently made by McLuhan's son [Eric], in
which are deleted not only McLuhan's and/or your remarks but questions and comments from the audience." Accordingly, he believed that
"[his] and/or McLuhan's comments should be edited and/or deleted."
At the same time, he did not think it was necessary "to delete the
questions or comments by participants." What he proposed was "to
issue the transcript with a paraphrase of Marshall's or [Parker's]
deleted remarks but quote directly the questions or comments by
others." As it stood, according to Miller, "the thing jerks along badly
in spots," If this was agreeable to Parker, he was ready to proceed.[92]

Presumably, the report was revised along these lines and was
published by the Museum in 1969 with the title "Exploration of the
Ways, Means, and Values of MUSEUM COMMUNICATION WITH
THE VIEWING PUBLIC." It was noted that the principal speakers
were Marshall McLuhan, Harley Parker, and Jacques Barzun.
According to the WorldCat bibliographic database, five hundred
copies of the eighty-eight page volume were originally printed.
The cost was $5585 (including the costs of printing, transcription,
editorial work, and photographs).[93] In keeping with the wishes of
McLuhan and Parker, the report was not based on the submission of
written texts; instead it put into written form what had transpired
through oral exchange in the seminar.[94]

The published report reveals that the event unfolded more or less
along the same lines as had been proposed in the application for it.

To be sure, given that Allon Schoener had harboured doubts about the Museum's level of competence, it is not surprising that some of his suggestions were acted upon, albeit sometimes in an oblique fashion. While there is no evidence that a planning committee was ever formed, leading figures from the Museum of Modern Art, Metropolitan Museum of Art, and the American Museum of Natural History (Planetarium) accepted invitations to participate. Beyond that, the seminar deviated in some ways from the application, in part because of unforeseen circumstances. Most notably, the roles envisioned for McLuhan and Parker were reversed. While the former had been designated as the seminar's leading figure, he in fact assumed more of an ancillary role. This might be attributed to the fact that McLuhan had little real interest in (and knowledge of) museums and fell ill during the visit to the American Museum of Natural History, leading to a late return to the session of the following day. Conversely, Parker's role in the seminar became a more dominant one. This was not only because he was obliged to step into the breach occasioned by McLuhan's illness, but because as a designer with hands-on experience at the ROM, he was very conversant with practical issues related to the mounting of exhibitions; his "experimental" gallery became an important point of reference for the seminar. Parker felt he could have done more had he been given a larger budget. It is instructive that Parker, rather than McLuhan, bore the responsibility of providing a summation of the seminar during the final banquet session.[95]

The report contained a list of all those who had participated in the seminar, along with short descriptions of their positions and places of work. While the original proposal anticipated that "fifty key museum people from all over the state of New York would be invited,"[96] this estimate proved to be wrong in a number of respects. The program listed eighty-five participants, a number of whom did not come from New York State.[97] Moreover, while most of those who attended were indeed "museum people," a good number of them worked in areas that were not directly museum-related, but rather were concerned more with the arts in general,[98] or were government officials.[99] It is also noteworthy that a number of participants were not museum directors but rather museum staff and trustees.[100] This more expansive list of participants was in line with the thoughts on the seminar that Miller had conveyed to Hightower.[101] While over eighty persons attended the seminar, it is evident that the majority did not actively participate. Because of the way the discussions were recorded, it is difficult to accurately gauge which persons took part, the frequency of their interventions, and to what extent the entire group was involved. It appears that the questions and responses were more or less accurately recorded. However for some parts of the sessions, the names of the persons posing the questions were not given. For others, both the names of the questioner along with his/her affiliation were provided. It is apparent that while a fair number of participants were able to pose a question, far fewer had the opportunity to ask multiple questions and have follow-up questions.

Response to the Report

It is likely that the report was destined to receive little attention. As a transcript of a seminar, self-published by a lesser-known museum, it did not readily conform to the conventions of the book world. With no authorship, there was little incentive for those involved to make the text better known to the public. A price was not listed for it; likely it was never available for purchase. There is no evidence that the Museum ever did anything to promote it.

The tepid response to the volume can also be explained by its timing. After having peaked in 1967, McLuhan's reputation was on the wane by 1969 and his ideas were increasingly greeted with skepticism, if not derision and disdain, as is evident in a review written by Kenneth Marantz, Coordinator in Art at the Graduate School of Education, University of Chicago.[102] Judging that "the McLuhan verbal steam roller now exists primarily in reproduced Tootsie Toy form," Marantz viewed the seminar report as just another miniaturized version representing a "lingering love affair with his original utterances." Referring to McLuhan and Parker as "the Man and his travelling crony," he was of the view that "for those of us who have puzzled over the validity of McLuhan's instant success, this record helps confirm the very clay-like composition of his feet." However, he felt that there was "considerable positive value in this entertaining report because it does raise questions which few other books consider." And while he found the answers provided by McLuhan and Parker to be largely inadequate, "the manner in which they are raised and (when permitted) developed generate lines of thought which are most productive for art education." Finally, he believed that Barzun's brief address was "a delightful and stimulating piece" that "contrasts strongly with the previous presentations." He felt that its tone was that of "a Marc Anthony type funeral oration in its cutting down of the extreme anti-intellectual postulates of McLuhan" and was surprised that the latter allowed it to be printed.

Kenneth Hudson, an expert on museums of international renown, was similarly disparaging about the report.[103] While he believed that the seminar had addressed some important issues, he was quite taken aback that its main "protagonists," McLuhan and Parker, "disagreed strongly with nearly every one of the ideas cherished by the museum establishment." Quoting verbatim from the report, he then went on to "set out their major statements as a catalogue of notions guaranteed to make the director of the British Museum reach for his gun." He believed that there was no need for them to be "set out or interpreted in any order. The effect [they had was] cumulative." According to Hudson, their overall message was that "impressions, participation, rhythm, audience reaction, whatever these may mean, are good. The storyline, the label, words, a wish to instruct, are bad." Echoing some of Barzun's sentiments, it was Hudson's hope that if and when the type of museum preferred by McLuhan and Parker become the majority in the world, "a new type of quiet, orderly, restful museum will arise to meet the needs of the minority who are deafened, blinded and exhausted by the new-style attempts to make museums meaningful."

Beyond the two initiatives in New York State in the waning days of 1967, there is little evidence that the ideas generated during the seminar had a discernible impact on museology for several decades.[104] Given that its circulation was extremely limited and that it was lacking in advocacy (not even championed by McLuhan and Parker), were it not for the publication of *Le musée non linéaire* in 2008, the report may well have been consigned to the dust heap of museum history. While it would be fanciful to claim that our text might help redefine the contours of museology, hopefully it will shed light on the role played by McLuhan, Parker, Ellin, Miller, and others in catalyzing the museological ferment of the late 1960s.

Notes

1. It is not even listed in a bibliography of his works; see *Writings of Marshall McLuhan*.

2. When I inquired about it in 2022, an official of the Museum told me that she was not aware of its existence.

3. McLuhan et al., *Le musée non linéaire*.

4. A recent study has drawn on the seminar report, by way of its French translation, to examine the "embodied visitor experience" in museums; see De Caro, "Moulding the Museum Medium." This involved testing "the malleability of the medium in conversation with museum practitioners." The inspiration for this work came from the claim made by Parker and McLuhan at the seminar that museums had a "modular" quality: "The museum was presented as a flexible medium of which we can change the rules; and that is, by its very nature, a means of access to the sensory and intuitive perception of all things"; see McLuhan et al., *Le musée non linéaire*, 15.

5. Some additional images from the MCNY Archives have been added. They capture scenes from the Museum photographed around the time of the seminar.

6. Hightower, "Are Art Galleries Obsolete?"

7. Barresi, "History and Programs," 32. The approach to arts funding of both the New York State Legislature and the NYSCA was based on a statement made by Rockefeller:

   > The arts…are for the many. The values of the arts are universal. Everyone can feel the impact of cultural experiences once his eyes and ears have been opened and his mind sensitized. There is no reason why anyone in…our society should be denied the opportunity for the same experiences, the spiritual exhilaration that the arts can offer. (Barresi, "History and Programs," 97.)

8. Barresi, "History and Programs," 55.

9. Barresi, "History and Programs," 68.

10. Barresi, "History and Programs," 87.

11. Barresi, "History and Programs," 87.

12. Barresi, "History and Programs," 89.

13. Barresi, "History and Programs," 102.

14. Hightower, "Museum Aid Program," 8.

15. Gent, "Arts Council Outlines Plans for Grants."

16. Barresi, "History and Programs," 157.

17. Barresi, "History and Programs," 158.

18. Page, "A Vanished City," 34.

19. Page, "A Vanished City," 61.

20. Rossetti, "Perceptions of Success."

21. Page, "A Vanished City," 60.

22. Rosetti, "Perceptions of Success," 72.

23. Page, "A Vanished City," 59.

24. Page, "A Vanished City," 68–69 and 72.

25. "Dutch Galleries," *New York Times*.

26. Miller, "Letter to the Editor."

27. Ralph Miller to John Hightower, April 14, 1967. MCNY Archives.

28. Janice Duff was the Museum Program Associate of the NYSCA.

29. Ralph Miller to John Hightower, March 15, 1967. New York State Archives.

30. Ralph Miller to John Hightower, March 15, 1967. New York State Archives.

31. Allon Schoener to John Hightower, March 27, 1967. New York State Archives.

32. Together with his wife, Ray, Charles Eames produced an influential documentary film on communication. C. Eames and R. Eames, "A Communications Primer."

33. See note 170 of the *Museum Communication* seminar report in the present volume.

34. He hoped it would be feasible "to extend invitations to certain key museum people in the New Jersey, Delaware, Eastern Pennsylvania area." He was of the view that "widening our borders and 'sphere of influence' has great interest for the profession." Such an event could serve as a prototype for an annual MCNY seminar for which "out of state representation should be encouraged." (Ralph Miller to John Hightower, April 14, 1967. New York State Archives.) He described to Parker the plan to "invite fifty key museum people, from all over the state of New York." It was hoped that "this exposure [would] result in a better understanding of the techniques of communication between a museum and its visitors." This, in turn, would "raise the standard of museum installation throughout the state." The event, in his view, could be better understood as a symposium rather than a seminar: the participants would still be considered to be students, as they would be "coming to learn." (Ralph Miller to Harley Parker, April 27, 1967. MCNY Archives.)

35. Ralph Miller to Harley Parker, April 27, 1967. MCNY Archives.

36. Barzun was paid $500 for his contribution. "Communication and the Viewing Public Seminar, Revised Budget." New York State Archives.

37. Harley Parker to John Hightower, May 2, 1967. New York State Archives.

38. Laurence Maloy in a memorandum to Ralph Miller and Carlin Gasteyer, April 19, 1967. MCNY Archives.

39. They met at the Royal Ontario Museum at 3:00 PM on May 30. There is no mention in the correspondence of McLuhan having attended the meeting. Ralph Miller to Harley Parker, May 11, 1967. MCNY Archives.

40. Ralph Miller to Marshall McLuhan, June 27, 1967. MCNY Archives. That Miller spoke frequently with Parker during the latter's time in New York is evident in a letter he wrote to him in the fall of 1967, after Parker had returned to Toronto: "Hope you are having good success relocating to Toronto…funny not to have you any more at the end of the phone down here." Ralph Miller to Harley Parker, September 28, 1968.

41. Ralph Miller to Janice Duff, June 23, 1967. New York State Archives. The funding received by the Museum was not confined to the seminar. Overall, within the ambit of the Council's Museum Aid program, it had been awarded $18,296. The bulk of it was used to pay for a departmental assistant and a research assistant.

42. For instance, in a letter to Parker he expressed his enthusiasm for the seminar and the pleasure he experienced in realizing that both Parker and McLuhan would be available. He believed that the seminar would prove to be of "immense value" for the museum profession in the State of New York.

43. Ralph Miller to Marshall McLuhan, November 3, 1967. MCNY Archives.

44. Ralph Miller to Harley Parker, November 3, 1967. MCNY Archives.

45. Ralph Burger to Harry Deutsch, November 16, 1967. MCNY Archives.

46. Surprisingly, the identity of the exhibit appears not to have been revealed to the visitors on the tour. Nor does the image in the report provide the explanation that it was the "Transparent Woman," described earlier in the press as "a representation of most of the other equipment of a woman—the major systems, organs and bones…complicated networks of colored wires…light up various organs of the model, as it revolves slowly on a pedestal." Had the visitors been aware of what the exhibit was, they might have responded differently. ("'Transparent Woman' in Museum Is Short on Secrets and Illusion." *New York Times*, January 14, 1954.)

47. See page 128 in the *Museum Communication* seminar report in the present volume.

48. Barzun is shown speaking with Corinne McLuhan, McLuhan is shown drinking, and Parker is nowhere to be found.

49. Miller appears to have believed that in his speech Barzun had refuted the arguments made by McLuhan and Parker on how reliance on written texts contributed to the linearity rampant in muscums: "Barzun made a strong plea for the retention of the written word as 'the thin black line of communication.' [His speech was a] stimulating and provocative conclusion to the seminar." Annual Report of the MCNY, 1967–68. MCNY Archives.

A letter written by Barzun to McLuhan the day after the banquet provides some insight into how they reacted to each other's contributions. Evidently, aside from his presence as the banquet speaker, Barzun's participation at the seminar had been limited to attendance at the 2:00 PM session on Tuesday and visiting the experimental gallery. He reported that he enjoyed meeting McLuhan again, hearing him in the afternoon, "seeing the film, and also having the pleasure of a delightful conversation with your wife." The remainder of the letter was taken up with Barzun's effort to heal a rift with McLuhan that he thought had developed at the seminar:

> It is true that I took in your comment "Bloody awful!" after my speech to the museum directors, but I think you and I should cancel out that heartfelt remark, for it was simply lack of opportunity that kept me from uttering it in reverse after the two o'clock session…I enjoyed your performance…it gave me a better view of your inner workings than one can gather from books.
>
> I'd like to take you up on your rash invitation to come to Fordham sometime [and] meet Mr. Carpenter…It is just possible that you and I have something to say to each other and not only to the world. You're a poet, I'm a mathematician, but we have common ideas as social observers; and as I think I showed last night, a good half of what you say is also what I say.
>
> …[No] matter how strongly I put my disagreements, objections, and rebuttals, I never translate them into hostility to the person. My record in this regard is spotless…I don't find it hard to keep it so which is going Voltaire one better. I loathe what you've just said, and like you immensely. [Barzun to McLuhan, October 11 1967. Marshall McLuhan Fonds, Library and Archives Canada.]

It is not clear whether McLuhan responded to Barzun's letter, or whether an arrangement was made for Barzun to meet with McLuhan and Carpenter at Fordham. Hence, one can only speculate on the nature of the exchanges that might have taken place between the poet, the mathematician, and the anthropologist.

50. Press Release, Museum of the City of New York, "Marshall McLuhan to Lead Seminar on Museum Communication to be held at the Museum of the City of New York, September 11, 1967." MCNY Archives.

51. Battcock, "Failure of McLuhan."

52. Battcock, "Failure of McLuhan," 9.

53. Shepard, "McLuhan Message Goes to Museums."

54. Glueck, "Museum Experts."

55. Lucy Kostelanetz to Ralph Miller, July 2, 1969. New York State Archives.

56. McLuhan, *Gutenberg Galaxy*; McLuhan, *Understanding Media*.

57. Lee, "McLuhan's Views."

58. In a 1955 letter to Wyndham Lewis, McLuhan referred to "an able young painter here (Harley Parker) who has got very interested in your writings." Molinaro et al., *Letters of Marshall McLuhan*, 248.

59. Parker designed the cover and typography for Issue 8 of *Explorations*. He was also responsible for the layout design for the second version of McLuhan's book, *Counterblast*.

60. Gordon and McLuhan, *Marshall McLuhan*, 168.

61.   Molinaro et al., *Letters of Marshall McLuhan*, 304. The book was eventually
      published as McLuhan and Parker, *Through the Vanishing Point*. The two authors
      were later featured together in a film; see McLuhan and Parker, *Picnic in Space*.

62.   Genosko, "The Designscapes of Harley Parker."

63.   Gordon and McLuhan, *Escape into Understanding*, 193–95.

64.   Marchand, *Marshall McLuhan*.

65.   The relationship between Parker and McLuhan is discussed in greater detail in
      Gary Genosko's essay "Trailblazing Follower," which follows this Introduction.

66.   Annual Report of the MCNY, 1967–68. MCNY Archives.

67.   Annual Report of the MCNY, 1967–68. MCNY Archives. The auditorium currently
      bears the name of Ronay Menschel Hall. The Palm Court is a large atrium
      decorated with ceiling-high palm trees and potted plants usually located in a
      prestigious hotel. The one created in the MCNY was likely modelled on the Palm
      Court Tea Room (later restaurant) of the nearby Plaza Hotel. It was designed
      by Henry Janeway Hardenberg and built between 1905 and 1907, with the Palm
      Court of London's Carlton Hotel as its point of reference. Its inclusion in the
      MCNY's exhibit was likely meant to convey the elegance of New York's high
      society in the 1920s. Given that participants in the seminar were quite familiar
      with night clubs (including the proto-discothèque, Electric Circus (1967-71)), it is
      not surprising that the organizers included one in the exhibition.

68.   Glueck, "Museum Experts."

69.   Annual Report of the MCNY, 1967–68. MCNY Archives.

70.   Annual Report of the MCNY, 1967–68. MCNY Archives.

71.   "Benefit Party," *New York Times*. The photograph in the article included the
      Museum director, Ralph Miller. While he had designed the exhibit, he was not
      actually a member of the Committee.

72.   I have been able to identify thirteen of them, with the exception of Mrs. Duncan
      McGregor. The important role played by volunteer women until recently has
      received little attention; see Hill, *Women and Museums*; Mihalache, "The Absent
      History."

73.   The others were Mary Healy (Mrs. Peter Lind Hayes), Elizabeth Bryant, a.k.a.
      Betty Bryan (Mrs. Maurice Silverstein), and Nancy Joan Guild (Mrs. Ernest Harold
      Martin).

74.   In addition to Healy, Bryant, and Guild, these included Ethel Redner Scull.

75.   These included Mrs. Randolph B. Marston (Edna Andersen Marston), Mrs. Edgar
      Bronfman Sr. (Ann Margaret Loeb Bronfman), Mrs. Alfred Gwynne Vanderbilt Jr.
      (Jean Harvey Vanderbilt), Mrs. Winthrop W. Aldrich (Harriet Crocker Alexander
      Aldrich), Mrs. William C. Cahan (Mary Arnold Sykes Cahan), Mrs. Osborn Elliot
      (Deirdre Marie Elliott), Mrs. John R. Fell (Marjorie Clendenin Fell), Mrs. Roswell
      (Madelin Thayer Kudner Gilpatric), and Mrs. Gardner Cowles Jr. (Jan Hochstrasser
      Cowles).

76.   "State Museum to Display," *Glens Falls Times*.

77. Ellin, "An International Survey of Museum Computer Activity."

78. See pages 172–76 in the *Museum Communication* seminar report.

79. Everett Ellin interview by Liza Kirwin, "Oral History Interview with Everett Ellin, 2004, April 27–28." Archives of American Art, Smithsonian Institution. An excerpt of the interview can be found at: https://www.aaa.si.edu/collections/interviews/oral-history-interview-everett-ellin-12188

80. Everett Ellin, "Computer Network Project," February 26, 1967. New York State Archives (MOMA).

81. Ellin, "Museums as Media"; West, *The Exhibitionary Complex*.

82. His "happening" Massage was staged at the Museet from October 3–7, 1966 as part of the artist's solo exhibition. See Kitnick, *Distant Early Warning*, 95.

83. Her sculpture, *Hon: A Cathedral,* was created with Jean Tinguely and Per-Olof Ultvedt during the summer of 1966. Kitnick, *Distant Early Warning*, 93–94.

84. The exhibition, titled, *New York: The Machine, as Seen at the End of the Mechanical Age,* was presented at the MOMA from November 1968 to February 9, 1969 (https://www.moma.org/calendar/exhibitions/2776). See also Kitnick, *Distant Early Warning*, 101.

85. The *Information* exhibit was presented at the Museum of Modern Art in New York, from July 2 to September 20, 1970 (https://www.moma.org/calendar/exhibitions/2686).

86. Kynaston McShine interview by Carolyn Lanchner. MOMA Oral History Program. Excerpts from the interview were compiled in 2010–11 by David Frankel and can be found at: https://www.moma.org/momaorg/shared/pdfs/docs/learn/archives/mcshine_final_access.pdf.

87. Fleming, "Artifact Study"; Ellin, "Computer Horizons."

88. Ralph Miller to John Hightower, March 15, 1967. MCNY Archives.

89. Ralph Miller to Harley Parker, April 27, 1967. MCNY Archives.

90. Harley Parker to Ralph Miller, May 2, 1967. MCNY Archives.

91. Ralph Miller to Harley Parker, November 15, 1967; Ralph Miller to Marshall McLuhan, November 14, 1967; Ralph Miller to Jacques Barzun, November 14, 1967. MCNY Archives.

92. Ralph Miller to Harley Parker, September 20, 1968. MCNY Archives.

93. Carlin Gasteyer to Lucy Kostelenetz, July 9, 1969. New York State Archives.

94. Harley Parker to John Hightower, May 2, 1967. New York State Archives. McLuhan and Parker edited the report, sometimes deleting "some of their remarks"; see the preface of the *Museum Communication* seminar report.

95. This represented a continuation of the leading role Parker had played in negotiating the terms for the seminar.

96. Ralph Miller to Harley Parker, April 27, 1967. New York State Archives.

97. The places of origin included Newark (New Jersey), Washington D.C., Hartford (Connecticut), Winterthur (Delaware), Bloomfield Hills (Michigan), Omaha

(Nebraska), Boston (Massachusetts), Prague (Czechoslovakia), Williamsburg (Virginia), and Tokyo (Japan).

98. These included participants from the academy (e.g., John Culkin, a colleague of McLuhan and Parker at Fordham).

99. These included Harmon H. Goldstone and Mrs. Randolph C. Guggenheimer from City Planning in New York as well as August Heckscher, Commissioner of Recreation and Culture in New York. The planning documents included a "Director's List" that contained the names Goldstone, Heckscher, as well as Miss Alice Winchester (*Antiques Magazine*), Mr. Marshall Davidson (*Horizon*), and Mr. Rosenblatt. "Director's List," New York State Archives.

100. Seven of them were affiliated with the MCNY.

101. Ralph Miller to John Hightower, April 14, 1967. MCNY Archives. He envisioned that the seminar would be "a major event in the museum world year" and "should stand to generate considerable publicity and enhance its inherent prestige." He wondered if it "might be feasible to extend invitations to certain key museum people in the New Jersey, Delaware, Eastern Pennsylvania area." He noted that "the widening of our borders and 'sphere of influence' has great merit for the profession and I am sure that the interest and desire to attend exists." Indeed, he mused about the possibility that "an annual Museum of New York seminar [could] become a reality."

    In fact, it appears that two years later another museum communication seminar was in the works. It was to follow the same format as the 1967 seminar, with principal speakers attending and with the preparation and publication of a final report. A contract was being finalized and a request was made for additional information, including a more detailed budget. Lucy Kostelanetz to Ralph Miller, July 2, 1969. New York State Archives.

102. Marantz, "Review of *Exploration of the Ways, Means, and Values*," 57.

103. Hudson, *A Social History of Museums*, 92.

104. An exception to this can be found in Glusberg and Benedit, "Cool Museums and Hot Museums."

Bibliography

Barresi, Anthony Leonard. "The History and Programs of the New York State Council on the Arts." PHD diss., University of Michigan, 1973.

Battcock, Gregory. "The Failure of McLuhan: Or the Whites Won." *Westside News*, October 19, 1967.

"Benefit Party to Open City Museum Show on Nov. 8." *New York Times*, October 18, 1967.

Century, Michael. *Northern Sparks: Innovation, Technology Policy, and the Arts in Canada from Expo 67 to the Internet Age*. MIT Press, 2022.

De Caro, Laura. "Moulding the Museum Medium: Explorations on Embodied and Multisensory Experience in Contemporary Museum Environments." *ICOFOM Study Series*, no. 43b (2015): 55–70. https://doi.org/10.4000/iss.397.

"Dutch Galleries to Open at Museum." *New York Times*, October 17, 1965.

Eames, Charles, and Ray Eames. *A Communications Primer*. 1953. https://www.youtube. com/watch?v=kaDQlyXilSw.

Ellin, Everett. "An International Survey of Museum Computer Activity." *Computers and the Humanities* 3, no. 2 (1968): 65–86.

Ellin, Everett. "Computer Horizons in the Museum World." *MUSE Museum International* 23, no. 1 (1971): 6–10.

Ellin, Everett. "Museums as Media." *ICA Bulletin*, no. 169 (May 1967).

Fleming, E. McClung. "Artifact Study: A Proposed Model." *Winterthur Portfolio* 9 (1974): 153–73.

Genosko, Gary. "The Designscapes of Harley Parker: Print and Built Environments." *Imaginations: Journal of Cross-Cultural Media Studies* 8, no. 3 (n.d.): 153–64.

Gent, George. "Arts Council Outlines Plans for Grants." *New York Times*, April 2, 1970.

Glueck, Grace. "Museum Experts Given a 'M'Lu-in': Seminar Sees a 19-Minute Multimedia Demonstration." *New York Times*, October 11, 1967.

Glusberg, Jorge, and Luis Benedit. *Cool Museums and Hot Museums: Towards a Museological Criticism*. Buenos Aires: Centro de Arte y Communicación, 1980.

Gordon, W. Terrence, and Marshall McLuhan. *Marshall McLuhan: Escape into Understanding: A Biography*. Basic Books, 1997.

Hightower, John B. "Are Art Galleries Obsolete?" *Curator: The Museum Journal* 12, no. 1 (2010): 9–13. https://doi.org/10.1111/j.2151-6952.1969.tb01759.x.

Hightower, John B. "The Museum Aid Program of the New York State Council on the Arts." *Curator: The Museum Journal* 10, no. 1 (1967): 8–12. https://doi.org/10.1111/j.2151-6952.1967.tb00868.x.

Hill, Kate. *Women and Museums, 1850–1914: Modernity and the Gendering of Knowledge*. Manchester University Press, 2016.

Hudson, Kenneth. *A Social History of Museums: What the Visitors Thought*. Macmillan, 1975.

Kissiloff, William. "How to Use Mixed Media in Exhibits." *Curator: The Museum Journal* 12, no. 2 (1969): 83–95. https://doi.org/10.1111/j.2151-6952.1969.tb01192.x.

Kitnick, Alex. *Distant Early Warning: Marshall McLuhan and the Transformation of the Avant-Garde*. University of Chicago Press, 2021.

Lauder, Adam. "A Clash of Spaces: Harley Parker's Reconceptualization of the Museum as a Communication System." *Amodern 5*, 2015. https://amodern.net/article/a-clash-of-spaces/.

Lee, John M. "McLuhan's Views Shape Museum: Fossils Can Even Be Felt on Display in Toronto." *New York Times*, February 26, 1967.

Marantz, Kenneth A. "Review of *Exploration of the Ways, Means, and Values of Museum Communication with the Viewing Public. A Seminar*." *Studies in Art Education* 11, no. 2 (1970): 57.

Marchand, Philip. *Marshall McLuhan: The Medium and the Messenger*. Vintage Books, 1990.

McLuhan, Marshall. *Counterblast*. McClelland and Stewart, 1969.

McLuhan, Marshall. *The Gutenberg Galaxy*. Mentor, 1962.

McLuhan, Marshall. "Man and Media." In *Understanding Me: Lectures and Interviews*, edited by Stephanie McLuhan and David Staines. McClelland & Stewart, 2003.

McLuhan, Marshall. *Understanding Media: The Extensions of Man*. Mentor, 1964.

McLuhan, Marshall, and Harley Parker. *Picnic in Space*. Bit Works, 1967. https://www.youtube.com/watch?v=tSfxX93dGnM.

McLuhan, Marshall, and Harley Parker. *Through the Vanishing Point: Space in Poetry and Painting*. Harper & Row, 1968.

McLuhan, Marshall, Harley Parker, and Jacques Barzun. *Le musée non linéaire: exploration des méthodes, moyens et valeurs de la communication avec le public par le musée: texte du séminaire tenu au Musée de la ville de New York les 9 et 10 octobre 1967*. Lyon: Aléas, 2008.

Mihalache, Irina D. "The Absent History of Female Volunteers at the Art Gallery of Toronto." In *Museums, Sexuality, and Gender Activism*, edited by Joshua Adair and Amy Levin. Routledge, 2020.

Miller, Ralph. "Letter to the Editor." *New York Times*, December, 29, 1961.

Molinaro, Matie, Corinne McLuhan, and William Toye, eds. *Letters of Marshall McLuhan*. Oxford University Press, 1987.

Page, Max. "'A Vanished City Is Restored': Inventing and Displaying the Past at the Museum of the City of New York." *Winterthur Portfolio* 34, no. 1 (1999): 49–64.

Parker, Harley. "New Hall of Fossil Invertebrates, Royal Ontario Museum." *Curator* 10, no. 4 (1967): 284–96.

Rossetti, Evelyn. "Perceptions of Success: A Case Study of the Museum of the City of New York." PHD diss., Columbia University, 2005, ProQuest (3160590).

Shepard, Richard F. "McLuhan Message Goes to Museums: Urges Multimedia Exhibits at a Seminar Here." *New York Times*, October 10, 1967.

"State Museum to Display Many Faces of New York from Manhattan to Niagara." *Glens Falls Times*, December 1, 1967.

"'Transparent Woman' in Museum Is Short on Secrets and Illusion." *New York Times*, January 14, 1954.

The Writings of Marshall McLuhan: Listed in Chronological Order. Wake-Brook House, 1975.

West, Kim. *The Exhibitionary Complex: Exhibition, Apparatus, and Media from Kulturhuset to the Centre Pompidou, 1963–1977*. Södertörn Studies in Art History and Aesthetics 4. Södertörn University, 2017.

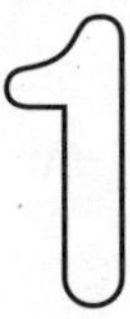

Trailblazing Follower
Harley Parker's Role as Museum
Exhibit Designer, Collaborator, and
Stand-In for Marshall McLuhan

GARY GENOSKO

AMONG THE VERY FEW REVIEWS that appeared in the wake of
the original publication of the seminar report (which will henceforth
be referred to as the "*Museum Communication* seminar report"),[1]
Kenneth A. Marantz's short notice displays the struggle to be heard
through the mediatic noise that Marshall McLuhan faced by the end
of the 1960s. The post-*Understanding Media* period (from 1964 to the
end of the decade more or less) brought McLuhan both celebrity status
and the demands associated with it from a fandom hungry for more
and more of his *aperçus*, along with a critical mob eager to mow him
down while confirming his fading stardom amid a burgeoning population of hangers-on and would-be hagiographers. Marantz aspires to
join the so-called critical mob, but relies on too many analogical criticisms of a limited sort to really gain any purchase on the subject. In
the space of less than a page, Marantz feebly deploys a local Chicago
diecast metal toy as a diminution of McLuhan's status—"Although the
McLuhan verbal steamroller now exists primarily in reproduced Tootsie
Toy form, the widespread distribution of these miniature versions
indicates a lingering love affair with his original utterances"—and an
insult to Parker, "the Man and his traveling crony (Harley Parker),"
not to mention the Man's clay feet: "This record helps confirm the
very clay-like composition of his feet." Marantz may have appreciated

the questions raised about museum curation, but the answers were at best marked by avoidance, fuzziness, and naïveté. Ultimately, he is delighted by invited speaker Jacques Barzun's erudite dismissal of McLuhan and Parker, describing his address as "a Marc Anthony type funeral oration in its cutting down of the extreme anti-intellectual postulates of McLuhan. And it, too, ends with several suggestions for significant research couched in the form of rhetorical questions. I am surprised McLuhan let it be printed."[2] Why Marantz thinks that McLuhan had such a veto is anyone's guess.

I want to focus on only one aspect of this cultivated patchwork of insults, diminishments, and comeuppances, for it holds a key to understanding this important period of post-*Understanding Media* for the intertwined fortunes of McLuhan and Parker. The designation of Parker as McLuhan's "traveling crony" is of course a ridiculous and overperformed gesture. Yet the choice of "crony" contains in it a characterization of coziness between the two men, and that McLuhan is the cause of this situation, because this is the kind of relationship he encourages as alpha to beta, and the kind of behaviour he rewards. McLuhan displays favouritism to those who spread his word, and this, Marantz suggests, leads to the kinds of failures on display in the seminar dialogue. Cronyism in this respect is no different than what supporters of a person or mode of thought typically do, and it is in this context, according to Marantz's review, that Barzun's summative counter-discourse plays such a significant role in the proceedings, as it disrupts the potential effects of cronyism. Barzun, it is worth noting, receives a standing ovation at the end of the event. But the idea that Parker is purely a crony, that the only reason he appears at the seminar is through his connection with McLuhan and that he lacks any qualifications, is patently ridiculous and a gross misrepresentation of Parker's credentials in the arena of museology. It is as if Parker's history and training in the field did not matter; it is as if Parker's construction of an experimental gallery at the host museum did not take place. A crony, as I will show below, would have no means to carry the day. But this negative proof does not yet explain the precise nature of the relationship in the late 1960s between two collaborators who had worked together since the mid-1950s and who would, by the end of the decade, publish two books together.[3] Here, I take on the challenge of characterizing how during this period McLuhan and Parker worked together, yet apart. I maintain that Parker was a trailblazing follower of McLuhan's ideas, and he applied medium theory to museum exhibition design in order to found multi-sensory museological practice.

Since McLuhan and his team, including Parker (on leave from the Royal Ontario Museum), planned to be in New York at Fordham University in the fall of 1967, this made the planning of the two-day-long seminar in October a matter of convenience for its main participants. McLuhan would be the main attraction and lead speaker, and Parker would bring his experience with museum display and artifact installation to the event (both are called "moderators"), earmarked for the second day, which would connect directly with the assembled museum people in the audience. As it turned out, McLuhan was late on the morning of the second day and Parker ably directed the discussion and fielded questions from unnamed participants about his own somewhat hastily installed multi-media orientation gallery, until McLuhan arrived and had an opportunity to visit the gallery with the last of the guests. His previous day's collapse and arrival are duly noted, even joked about by Parker, while McLuhan offers an apology. Upon McLuhan's return, many but not all of the questioners are named in the transcript, as if a sense of order had been restored. This is not too far-fetched, as organizer and host Ralph Miller announces mid-morning once McLuhan arrives that "we're ready to go *officially* [my emphasis], Dr. McLuhan has seen the experimental gallery with the last group."[4] One might say that the criticisms of Parker's installation could officially begin, as its reception was prickly to say the least, with the exception of Everett Ellin, formerly Assistant to the Director of the Guggenheim Museum, a curator who spoke fluent McLuhanese.[5] Ellin was an early advocate for digitalization of resources within the museum and his work with the Museum Computer Network in New York circa 1967 advanced an understanding of the cooperative informational dimension of such institutions, within the broader Computing in the Humanities movement, that cohered with McLuhan and Parker's views of museums as media. Ellin understood that the information environment would create an all-at-onceness and nonlinear organization, reshaping the human sensorium. His nuanced reframing of McLuhan and Parker's characterizations of the Renaissance through linearity (printing, detached viewership), which went against the grain of what many participants in the seminar would have understood about this period's modes of display—"a museological commonplace, however, [is] that in the cabinets and *studioli* of Renaissance princes, scholars or merchants, the organization of artworks and artifacts was in fact anything but 'linear'"[6]—allowed Ellin to eventually positively regain the term "Renaissance" for his own explorations of the contemporary electronic information environment. Despite these divergences, Ellin's voice in the seminar transcript comes through as that of an adept. Indeed, it is Ellin who confesses to his own experimentation with regard to getting to know audiences, for instance, by repairing his car in front of the Guggenheim Museum and listening to visitors' comments, and acknowledges that at the Guggenheim they know very little about "the people who come off the chute at the bottom,"[7] and that it is a mistake to use box office receipts as a measure of success.[8]

Parker's seminal contribution to the *Museum Communication* seminar was his experimental orientation gallery, understood as a sensory training facility, that not only assisted visitors in the selective decoding of artifacts (bringing to light the sensory biases of their creators and users) but that also, in its concentrated use of sound and light, transformed artifacts into art by changing their definitions. Museums do not yet know, Parker assumed, that they are involved in the training of perception, with the power to dislocate and advantageously challenge visitors. By challenging assumptions (i.e., of cultural superiority) and provoking a "sentient stance," he argued, "A museum presentation which makes available to the senses another sensory orientation is effectively raising into consciousness a rich and strange modality of being. The effect of raising new modes into perception will be a necessity of re-evaluating our own."[9] This making strange of the familiar and given, coupled with the need to adapt, implies a deep sentience about self and other. The goal of such a gallery is to bring perception to consciousness, dislodge assumptions, and expose biases where necessary by using multi-media design to produce an interface between visitor and artifact that builds empathic understanding and contributes to highly refined self-awareness.

Choreographing visitors to his multi-media display (which was held in the Dutch Gallery of the MCNY and contained historical views of New Amsterdam contrasted with contemporary New York scenes—though imbalanced in favour of the contemporary, Parker acknowledges, based strictly on "expediency"[10]) is easier under experimental conditions than it is on an everyday basis. Parker insisted on visits by small groups, and briefed only some of his professional visitors about where to stand, given the narrowness of the gallery space and the lowness of the slide projectors. With children and university student groups, he modified his instructions. However, neither Parker nor McLuhan had a plan to analyze responses. Instead, they used anecdotes about classroom experiments and utilized a familiar tool to distinguish between responses based on various kinds of lines (story- or party-).

A ten- to fifteen-minute tour of an "orientation centre" is always a "prelude," Parker believed; indeed, it would "precede and not supplant" a visitor's entry into a museum proper.[11] The concept of an orientation gallery was Parker's contribution to museological thought. By "orientation," Parker meant a space and its contents that would assist visitors in their adjustment to the museum environment. Executed with multi-media, such an intake space would be ideally adjacent to the main museum building, but it could be contained within it. Parker thought in terms of how multi-media could be utilized to recalibrate the sensoria of visitors, and by changing sensory orientations, prepare visitors for the kind of exhibits they would encounter in sensorily-designed museum galleries.

Much of the Tuesday afternoon session of the seminar was devoted to understanding audiences, beyond visitor numbers, through the use of surveys and other related tools of social-scientific inquiry. The generally accepted view among participants was that not enough was known about audiences, whom Parker thought of as key parts of any museum environment. His approach was guided by the need for feedback, unspecified to be sure, but a measure that would result in gallery refinement. His idea for a gallery without labels was proposed as a way to get feedback which would provide guidance on writing labels, and then generate more feedback along the way. The task of bringing to consciousness unexamined assumptions and given stances figured the audience as potentially receptive, but essentially unprepared. In the case of those who were already attuned, such as the countercultural youth he sought to attract to the ROM (even if only a few ever trickled in), the task of orientation would be that of reinforcement and heightened reflexivity, although he does not assume in advance that a group that lives in depth in a highly mediated world is fully cognizant of its implications. Parker's general belief was that "by heightening consciousness you heighten perception."[12] It is in a state of heightened perception and reflexive sensibility that audiences are moved through orientation galleries, which constitutes an "interim period," Parker noted, into the exhibits proper and thus into different worlds. Yet this moving through is a logistical problem with no easy solution and may require bigger budgets, multi-screens, and multiple (re)orientation centres in the case of large museums.

The use of multi-media technologies within an orientation gallery reflected Parker's belief that commercial multi-media events are viable models for museum presentations. McLuhan underlined this by claiming "we live very much in an 'entertainment world.'"[13] This opened for Parker a pathway towards "rapprochement with the audience of today." He stated, "I would regard multi-media shows as being very highly realistic in a sense that they tend to correspond to the general orchestration of sensibilities."[14] Audiences must first understand their own world before being able to understand those on display in museum galleries. Parker's experimental gallery was inspired by the light show at the Electric Circus discothèque in New York's East Village, by the IBM Pavilion at the 1964–65 World's Fair in New York, and by the National Film Board of Canada's *Labyrinth* at Expo 67 in Montreal. These models of nightlife and large-scale fairs and expositions were selected in order to push museums towards exhibits that were short on didactics and high on impact; "chaos" was a term Parker was pleased to accept because it "very nearly approaches the normal human sensibility."[15] As the morning

discussion unfolded, however, the argument became bogged down
in a monumental dichotomy between multi-sensorial nonlinearity as
opposed to linear, rational, visual presentation.

Parker collaborated on his Dutch Gallery with Tony Schwartz,
a sound engineer and an advertising and political consultant. For
the occasion, Parker borrowed from Schwartz sound recordings
and films. It was Schwartz who recorded the "pre-seminar" tape of
a Parker-McLuhan dialogue that was distributed in advance to the
museum professionals participating in the seminar. In the Preface
to the *Museum Communication* seminar report, this preparation was
considered to be "an unusual one in the interest of nonlinear communication."[16] Parker shared with Schwartz (and with McLuhan) the
idea that multi-media technology could be used to massage the
sensorium, bringing to consciousness existing habits and tendencies
as well as reorienting them. That the pre-recorded tape was "special"
is a given, but why it is so is never explained. It was likely an open-
reel magnetic tape (used in a reel-to-reel tape player) or perhaps a
cassette. Whatever the format, the portable auditory acoustic space
gave listeners something in which they could momentarily wrap
themselves.

In his book *The Responsive Chord*, Schwartz developed an effects
theory of communication built around the concept of resonance,
similar to the idea that McLuhan had borrowed from organic chemistry to apply to tactile contact, but focused on sound metaphors. By
"resonance," Schwartz understood a non-symbolically encoded experience stored in memory that has not undergone transformation, in
other words, a percept that has not been semio-linguistically encoded,
and is thus not retrievable by means of a further linguistic prompt;
instead, such encodings may be evoked by stimuli that "resonate with
information already stored within an individual and thereby induces
the desired learning or behavioural effect. Resonance takes place
when the stimuli put into our communication evokes meaning in a
listener or viewer."[17] By "striking a responsive chord" through evocation,
Schwartz displaces the message, as the content of the communication
process does not come into play until the end of the process, given
that meaning arises late or not at all. The encoded information may

be evoked, for instance, by breaking anticipated patterns, especially in the case of manipulating the intervals between sounds, and adjusting the speed and volumes of repetitive sounds. Parker shared the same view, since for him making visitors aware of their sensory biases by bringing perception to consciousness was the first step in adjusting it, breaking habits of linearity, and preparing visitors for new sensory mixes that gallery design could then deliver and reinforce, with the active participation of visitors if they were given some control over lighting, temperature, placement of objects, etc.

The *Museum Communication* seminar report provides one of the most comprehensive statements by Parker about his theories of installation, the role of perception in museum experience, as well as his goals for the further study of audiences. It augments the existing body of published works, including important statements about his Hall of Invertebrate Fossils gallery at the ROM, and his theorization of the iconic.[18] On those occasions when McLuhan required someone to stand in for him, as opposed to stand with him, he did not choose just anyone from among his many followers and acolytes. He consistently promoted Parker in his place during a period when he was inundated with requests. So, while we have seen how Parker ably stepped in on Tuesday morning when McLuhan was late arriving after a medical incident the previous evening, his presence did not require a formal request, and hence differs from the logic of substitution to which I will now turn.

Intellectual fame demands screening mechanisms. Without them, it is impossible to parse the invitations and requests that arrive from all quarters and threaten to overwhelm. This was the situation post-*Understanding Media* that McLuhan faced. As one remedy, McLuhan promoted Parker as a substitute, and for at least some five years tried to send him in his place to a wide variety of events, mostly in the United States. It is difficult to precisely determine how well this strategy worked, as the archival record is spotty, but McLuhan's passing observation about how busy Parker had become—but not as busy as McLuhan!—suggests it was, over time, a winning-enough strategy. As a substitute, Parker was a skilled interpreter of McLuhan's ideas as well as a long-time collaborator, and beyond performing this service, his own intellectual interests and formulations could also take shape. Substitution went beyond trust and entered the realm of endorsement of Parker's abilities and insights. McLuhan settled into a standard promotional language regarding Parker, often stating in letters to suitors that he had a "clear head" and was an "able speaker."

The role of a substitute is well known. It is quite different than that of the crony. As McLuhan's right-hand man, Parker was a trusted interpreter and representative. He was Little John to McLuhan's Robin Hood. The logic at play in the "instead of" relationship involves the same substitute every time. It is in this way deeply repetitive, but would not have been experienced this way by those issuing the invitations, unless they shared the outcomes of their efforts at the time or shortly thereafter. From McLuhan's perspective, this stability must have been beneficially predictable and thus sameness provided both control and continuity.

Within the logic of substitution there are affective contours at work within an intimate relationship that surmounted professional distance and collaborative management of McLuhan's research profile, not to mention the juggling of the two men's respective calendars. McLuhan almost always underlined that Parker was close to him, and that his many virtues would make any suitor's event a success. Indeed, Parker possessed a skill set that McLuhan found very valuable: typographer, painter, graphic designer, exhibit designer. Ultimately, the diverse efforts by McLuhan to smooth the choice of Parker reveal a familiarity that sometimes collapses substitution itself, shaking out possibility in all the carefully crafted modal phrases McLuhan used to get the job done, not by *anyone*, but by a special *someone*. Admittedly, McLuhan was not always kind to Parker, and had a reputation for dealing with him impatiently (indeed, at McLuhan's Monday Night Seminars, Parker was somewhat of a dogsbody, performing boring tasks like setting up the record player, showing films, etc.), but within the familiarity of any relationship, one expects that not all sailing will be smooth.

The type of connection under consideration here is the operation of substitution. It works, as far as the evidence suggests, only unidirectionally, since McLuhan does not substitute for Parker in his absence. A bidirectional logic of substitution would at minimum require an equivalent level of busyness between the two men, thus creating a need for reverse substitutions. Even without such conditions in place, it may be said that unidirectional substitution, if successful, should provide the substitute with useful evidence of his actions. When there are three people involved, as in McLuhan-Parker-Schwartz, the latter two still occupy a secondary position, unless their role is elevated through an analysis of McLuhan's extensive and vital support network that remains understudied in the literature. Although Father John Culkin once jokingly called Harley "Hardly," a good baseball name, as a pinch hitter (a substitute batter) Parker would have evidence in abundance of his stand-ins. Consider Parker's report of his activities for 1970 in the ROM's "President's Report," falling at the edge of the period under consideration.[19] Though none of the material can be verified as substitutions, it appears that the list of thirteen different talks, delivered throughout Canada and the US (as well as one in South Africa and another in Italy) at universities, colleges, and non-academic events, strongly indicates that the logic had benefits at the level of popularity or status, not to mention stipends and honoraria. One talk, delivered at an undisclosed location to the Design Society of America, is vintage epigrammatic Parker. Titled "Good Taste Is the First Refuge of the Witless: A Refugee Camp for Philistines," the derogatory term "witless" here joins forces with the refuge of good taste as a retreat from culture for those who insist they can live without it. The title is in bad taste, but almost any traditional institutional environment could qualify as such a camp. Throughout his career, Parker recycled the epigram "good taste is the first refuge of the witless" and wielded it like a weapon against what he called "good taste" in design, which he considered a degenerative condition, like conventional manners, characterized by conformity to prevailing standards, lack of creativity, and insecurity—all symptoms of bourgeois numbness.

There is, however, a well-defined collection of surviving correspondence among McLuhan, some of his many suitors, and Parker that addresses a set arrangement between the two thinkers and friends stretching over almost five years in the middle and late

1960s. The arrangement was that whenever McLuhan was unable
or unwilling to accept invitations to speak, write, or otherwise make
a personal contribution to one cause or another, he would nomi-
nate Parker in his place. It was a set role that Parker played as a
long-time associate of McLuhan's Centre for Culture & Technology.
The surviving archival examples of this correspondence are almost
all from the US. Although it is not always clear whether Parker was
accepted as a substitute for his friend, the instances where he did
step in do provide insight into how these occasions enabled him to
expand his network of influence, especially in corporate quarters, and
with regard to his interpretation of the concept of an ideogrammatic
icon. In one instance, the correspondence also permits a more precise
examination of the nature of Parker's contributions, as an unpublished script survives, dated June 18, 1964.[20] It is, in addition, curious
to note McLuhan's phraseology of nomination as it morphs over the
years, curls back on itself during playfully rhetorical moments, and
occasionally becomes rote like a form letter—not so much a boil-
erplate rejection letter, but what I like to think of as a substitution
letter.

The primary example of substitution is from the spring of 1964
pertaining to the Greenbrier Management Conference in June of that
year. This period corresponds to McLuhan's "TV Effect" research
of 1963–64. McLuhan writes to his contact there that he is sending
Parker in his place, and this is acceptable to the organizers. Parker
delivers a paper that makes a strong impression on the corporate
audience and engages in follow-up correspondence with the Director
of Advertising of Underwood Ltd. of Toronto, explaining to him the
basic theses of *Understanding Media*, but noting Parker's interest in
establishing sensory typology tests for populations experiencing
television for the first time, specifically in Greece: "I am on my way to
Athens to attempt to study and set up pre-TV sensory typology tests,
to be followed by post-TV typology tests."[21]

In his Greenbrier presentation, Parker recounts his collaboration
with McLuhan on an article about the effects of television on children,
in which they argued that the nowness and immediateness of the
medium replace a future orientation, and shrink near-point reading

distances as children try to replicate with print the involvement
demanded by television. The initial effort of Parker when he joined
McLuhan's Centre in 1963 was with regard to the television research
into synesthetic perception and the hypothesis that this is a factor in
making children highly precocious.[22] Specifically, the "Sensory Profile"
study began in Toronto and was aimed at understanding the transformation effected at the population level by television. McLuhan thought
he would then replicate the approach in a number of cities around the
world. His ambition was to make the results available to the entertainment industry, advertisers, and manufacturers. His approach was
highly behaviouristic and reductionistic, since he thought that "once
you know the sensory profile of a people, how much intensity they
allow into their visual life or their auditory life, you can just read it
off as a percentage of their whole sensorium…Then you can exactly
program the environment…in that area."[23] His willingness to provide
media corporations with recipes of how to manipulate audiences
placed him at odds with critical television and cultural studies tradi-
tions, and gave rise to a highly acrimonious literature that allegedly
exposed the dangerousness of his ideas, specifically with regard to
television.

Parker also addressed the transition from the illustration (visual
bias) to the icon (synesthetic sense) as a way of understanding the
predicament of magazines in the post-literate age that typically
include both elements. In the untitled typescript of his address at
Greenbrier (attached to his letter to the Director of Circulation for
Hearst Magazines in New York), he predicted, despite his reluc-
tance to engage in forecasting, that "the magazine under the impact
of electronic media will tend to become more iconic. There will be
a tendency to break up large masses of grey type with more head-
lines. The type of writing will become increasingly non-sequential.
Thoughts will be dealt with in clusters instead of sequentially. There
will be an increasing use of phototype and other distorting devices to
move the written word closer to its sound. In fact, I see the complete
obliteration of the contemporary mode of typesetting."[24] Parker
could have been describing the trajectory of his own work as a typographic designer throughout the 1950s and 1960s, including his use

of photographic typography in McLuhan and Carpenter's journal *Explorations* and for the *Counterblast* book's layout and design.

In the spring of 1964, Parker became involved in the planning of Expo 67 in Montreal as a communications consultant. McLuhan's invitation to speak at the "automation conference" of the World's Fair organizing team arrived in the fall courtesy of Commissioner General Leslie Brown.[25] McLuhan was asked to address the changing roles of technology in Canadian society, but wrote to Brown with an idea: since he worked closely with Parker and the latter possessed the requisite skills, Parker was "fully competent" to participate in the conference. It is not clear that McLuhan's suggestion was taken up by Brown and other members of the Canadian Government Participation unit, but it marks the third time in 1964 that he would promote Parker (the second was a State University of Iowa invitation). Once the ball began to roll, there was no stopping it. Parker did play a role as a design consultant in Expo 67 and he eventually wrangled some funding to bring his entire design team from the ROM to Expo to study "new display techniques, many of which are far in advance of our own."[26] As indicated above, Parker hoped that he could transfer some of the design accomplishments from the fair to the museum (an example of such an innovation was *Labyrinth*, the National Film Board of Canada's experimental theatre that used, in the second of the building's two viewing chambers, an array of five film projectors and five screens in a cruciform shape, in addition to prisms, flashing lights, etc.).

In early 1965, just as McLuhan and Parker were starting to put together the joint volume *Through the Vanishing Point*, McLuhan suggested that Parker take up in his place an invitation from the School of Library Science at Columbia University, and then from the American University in Washington, DC. McLuhan referred to Parker as his "right-hand man." To Earl Brill at the American University, McLuhan even suggested of himself and Parker: "We are so entirely conversant with each other that we can give a joint lecture as if by one man."[27]

In 1966, McLuhan deferred to Parker ("a fine presence") with regard to invitations from the American Association of Advertising Agencies in New York, the University of California at Santa Cruz,

Look magazine, the University of British Columbia, and *Architectural Design* magazine. To John McHale at Southern Illinois University, McLuhan quipped in good humour: "So far he [Parker] is not quite as busy as I am."[28] McLuhan would provide many more opportunities for Parker, sending his way the chance to write on the art of Christmas cards for *The Canadian*,[29] to speak at the American Federation of Arts, at Stanford University, the Philadelphia College of Art, the Connecticut Arts Association ("I strongly recommend Harley Parker as a stand-in"[30]), at Auburn University, and the Eastern Arts Association in Philadelphia ("quite able to 'carry the torch'"[31]). In 1967 the pattern continued with the American Craftman's Council and the Massachusetts College of Art.

What is remarkable is that the *Museum Communication* seminar rehearsed the structure of complementarity that Parker's "orientation gallery" was designed to facilitate: it began with a pre-recorded "pre-seminar" between McLuhan and Parker sent to participants prior to the event. The pre-seminar was then followed by the seminar proper, opening on Monday morning of October 9, 1967. Such orientation, whether in the form of a taped conversation, courtesy of sound and film documentarian Schwartz, or the adjacent gallery space, would help visitors and participants to adjust to the environment in which they would shortly find themselves, namely, in a seminar or in a museum's main galleries. Parker underlines the interim and multi-media characteristics of his orientation gallery, as well as its role in adjusting perception. The pre-seminar supports this task by discussing the use of multiple screens in exhibit spaces and staging the post-pictorial space of nonlinear presentation (perhaps merely antilinear) in which the "audience is the surround…the new environment for the artifact,"[32] one defined by touch that encourages audience participation and is defined by the "suddenness of discovery."[33] The sensory reorientation of audiences that the experimental gallery was supposed to provoke is discussed in somewhat reductive terms in the pre-seminar tape, through the dichotomy between linear, literate, storyline on the one hand and nonlinear, non-visual, interconnected (interfaced disciplines, non-sequential patterning) on the other. McLuhan summarizes the proposal, and sets up the practical project (what Miller called the "workshop"), which Parker attempts to model experimentally with the limited means available to him: "I think we could really provide orientation centres for museums for specific areas so that the person doesn't just walk in directly from the highway or off the streets of our cities, and you suddenly confront him with a tenth-century Chinese vase. He won't know what to do with it, so you have to provide him with some kind of presentation centre and this, I think, is where the light shows could come in as fast methods of orientation."[34]

The coordinated dialogue of the pre-seminar and the practical experiment in the Dutch Gallery by Parker, which modelled Parker's ideas about orientation galleries, helped to expose the intimacy and fluency of McLuhan and Parker's collaborative style, while displaying the latter's hands-on skills, especially when he considered examples from his work at the ROM with Indigenous artifacts. Parker stepped up on the second day of the seminar and carried the discussion during McLuhan's absence,[35] emblematic of the kind of working relationship that had developed between the two in the late 1960s, during which time Parker regularly stood in for McLuhan. The purpose here is to dispel the bogey of "cronyism," but also to explain in detail some of the ways in which McLuhan and Parker actually worked together, often apart from one another. By considering McLuhan's rhetorical flourishes encouraging substitution in his unpublished correspondence, we can come to understand the substitute as a plastic concept with a range of manifestations.

The logic of substitution begs the question of equal value. Any decision to decline the offer of the substitute rejects the implied equal-value proposition, while any decision to accept the substitute implies an acceptance of equal value, if only in the context of the event in question. Notwithstanding a degree of resignation that might accompany any failure to bag the big speaker, namely McLuhan, for one's event, surely the acceptance of Parker as a substitute would also in some instances have pleased an organizer because he saved their event by delivering McLuhanism directly from the heart of the Centre.

There is an important affective dimension on display on the first day of the seminar during the afternoon field trip to the American

Museum of Natural History. After the seminar visitors retired to the
auditorium, Parker took the floor and explained sympathetically
in personal terms why McLuhan had to leave. It might be said that
Parker stepped up because of his expertise in matters of museum
exhibition design, which would be accurate, but he also added an
important dimension about how substitution worked. That is, it
worked as a form of protection of and care for the one who is substituted by the one who substitutes. This element of care cannot be
lost in the relation of substituter and substitutee. At the same time,
substitution opened the door for the development by Parker of his
so-called "pet theories" while at the same time applying McLuhan's
ideas to the museum as a unique multi-sensory medium. As noted
earlier, when McLuhan returned the following morning, it was then,
and only then, that the "official" proceedings began, despite the fact
that they had been under Parker's able direction for some time. The
question of equivalence is here given a definitive answer by host
Miller: Parker is relegated to an unofficial leadership role and that
substitution has an internal value dimension of inequivalence. This
did not collapse into charges of cronyism. Rather, it exposed just how
difficult Parker's working conditions were in constructing his experimental gallery, which became a magnet for unconstructive criticism.
Parker was open about his limitations in this regard—his lack of
time, budget, and materials, the favours he called in—a fact that was
repeated when attendees noted just how "awful" his gallery was, as
Mary Black (Director of the Museum of American Folk Arts in New
York) stated, acknowledging, in spite of the known conditions, its goal
of "jog[ging] us into saying more."[36]

A further key factor in Parker's difficult working conditions was
that his experimental gallery was a compromise of his own concep-
tion of what an orientation centre for audiences would look like in
the best of all possible worlds: a flexibly constructed "newseum"
located adjacent to a prestige museum in which the process of exhibition design was explored for the purpose of reorienting the perception
of visitors within the context of a fully elaborated sensory museology. The Dutch Gallery experiment took place in an existing
gallery inside of the museum; Parker's temporarily modified space

dealt with the same historical materials around New Amsterdam that the gallery had contained before his work on it began, but this would not have been familiar to all of the participants in the seminar. In the prelude to the evening session of the second day of the seminar, Parker clarified that his purpose was not to foreground technology for technology's sake, but instead, to heighten reflection on given assumptions and trigger the process of seriously questioning them. For him, that would be a sign of success. His astute qualifications were, however, delivered just prior to Barzun's closing speech, which not only diminished Parker's experiment as "some little play" and bandwagonism[37] when it came to rejecting linearity, but no time was allotted for a proper retort by either McLuhan or Parker, or their supporters.

While the complexity of the lengthy working relationship between McLuhan and Parker warrants further attention, it is helpful to consider Parker's remarks in a profile published in what appears to be a neighbourhood newspaper in Toronto in 1970. Titled "Fronting for McLuhan," Parker explains that fronting is what he does: "I front for Marshall." The unidentified interviewer interjects: "This seemed a shame, an indignity, for a 50-year-old man of many talents." To which Parker replies: "Oh no...I have my own dignity, and doing things for Marshall doesn't affect it. Because, you see, we also do things together." Since they had a personal relationship dating back to 1950 and engaged in occasional collaborations throughout the 1950s before settling into a steady working relationship from 1963 into the mid-1970s (when Parker decamped from Toronto to the Slocan Valley in British Columbia), it may be concluded that the displacements of secondariness are acceptable as long as they leave one's dignity intact. Despite Parker's industry, ingenuity, conviviality, and insight into the museum as a medium, the setup of the *Museum Communication* seminar proved to be a challenge when it came to his own integrity and status as a researcher and practitioner, as well as in protecting McLuhan's human dignity under difficult personal circumstances. Nevertheless, Parker seized the opportunity provided to him by the event and demonstrated what an evocative, multi-media gallery space could conjure within the constraints of the given subject matter and existing gallery. In this way Parker may be said to have blazed a trail by embedding McLuhan's ideas into the heart of the Museum of the City of New York.

Notes

1. Originally published as: Marshall McLuhan, Harley Parker, and Jacques Barzun. *Exploration of the Ways, Means, and Values of Museum Communication with the Viewing Public: A Seminar, New York.* Museum of the City of New York, 1969.

2. Marantz, "Review of *Exploration of the Ways, Means, and Values*," 57.

3. Parker designed McLuhan's *Counterblast* and co-wrote *Through the Vanishing Point* with McLuhan. Parker and McLuhan also engaged in a dialogue about space and time in a pastoral setting for director Bruce Bacon's art film *Picnic in Space* (1967). However, it has been suggested that Parker met McLuhan as early as 1947; see McLuhan, "Letter to Harry J. Skornia." By the mid-1950s, Parker was contributing page layouts and cover designs for the journal *Explorations*.

4. *Museum Communication* seminar report in the present volume, 139.

5. Ellin had left his post in the spring of 1967 and took up the position at MOMA as founding Director of the Museum Computer Network. See Fox, "Everett Ellin."

6. West, *The Exhibitionary Complex*, 133.

7. *Museum Communication* seminar report, 174.

8. *Museum Communication* seminar report, 175. Ellin said: "I don't measure response by the box office." He considered success by this measure as "an index of how successfully the exhibition has been promulgated as a news phenomenon." He was more interested in how visitors were being reached than by how many had passed through the turnstiles.

9. Parker, "The Museum as a Perception Kit."

10. *Museum Communication* seminar report, 158.

11. *Museum Communication* seminar report, 140.

12. *Museum Communication* seminar report, 182.

13. *Museum Communication* seminar report, 140.

14. *Museum Communication* seminar report, 182.

15. *Museum Communication* seminar report, 152.

16. *Museum Communication* seminar report, 56.

17. Schwartz, *The Responsive Chord*, 24–25.

18. Parker, "New Hall of Fossil Invertebrates." However, Parker does not mention his unpublished book manuscript, *The Culture Box*, the publication of which was announced for 1972. It would not appear. I recently uncovered the "lost" manuscript, and an edited and introduced first edition was published by University of Alberta Press in 2025; see Genosko, "When a Lost Manuscript Turns Up."

19. Bissell, *President's Report for 1970*. In the same document, McLuhan stated in his Director's Report, "The very large demand for speakers for the Centre has been met in part by Centre Associate Harley Parker" (Bissell, *President's Report*, 86).

20. Harley Parker to Wm. S. Campbell, June 18, 1964. Marshall McLuhan Fonds, Library and Archives of Canada. (Attached to the letter is an untitled and unpublished manuscript of seven typed pages.)

21. Harley Parker to R.S. Hardy, June 12, 1964. Marshall McLuhan Fonds, Library and Archives of Canada.

22. McLuhan, "Humpty Dumpty."

23. McLuhan, "Television in a New Light," 102. In the aforementioned unpublished manuscript (see n. 20), Parker claims (on page 2) to have written "Why the TV Child Cannot See Ahead" with McLuhan for the University of Toronto Press. A section of the same title appeared in McLuhan's *Understanding Media*, on pages 290–92 in the "Television" chapter. The essay was published posthumously and attributed to McLuhan.

24. Essay attached to letter from Harley Parker to Wm. S. Campbell, June 18, 1964. Marshall McLuhan Fonds, Library and Archives of Canada. (The essay is dated "18.6.64" by Parker.)

25. Leslie Brown to Marshall McLuhan, November 26, 1964; Marshall McLuhan to Leslie Brown, December 3, 1964. Marshall McLuhan Fonds, Library and Archives of Canada.

26. Bissell, *President's Report for 1967*, 288.

27. Marshall McLuhan to Earl Brill, September 8, 1965. McLuhan Fonds, Library and Archives of Canada.

28. Marshall McLuhan to John McHale, January 5, 1966. McLuhan Fonds, Library and Archives of Canada.

29. Marshall McLuhan to Anna Gorman, July 5, 1966. McLuhan Fonds, Library and Archives of Canada.

30. Marshall McLuhan to A. Thurm, August 17, 1966. McLuhan Fonds, Library and Archives of Canada.

31. Marshall McLuhan to D.J. Irving, September 29, 1966. McLuhan Fonds, Library and Archives of Canada.

32. *Museum Communication* seminar report, 66.

33. *Museum Communication* seminar report, 68.

34. *Museum Communication* seminar report, 74.

35. In the month following the seminar, McLuhan underwent what was described in press reports as a "brain operation" in November, 1967, and Parker and Edmund Carpenter took over his classes at Fordham. Cole, "McLuhan: Out for Christmas."

36. *Museum Communication* seminar report, 169.

37. *Museum Communication* seminar report, 204.

Bibliography

Bissell, Claude. *President's Report for 1967*. University of Toronto Press, 1968.

Bissell, Claude. *President's Report for 1970*. University of Toronto Press, 1971.

Cole, Arthur. "McLuhan: Out for Christmas." *Toronto Telegram*, December 8, 1967.

Fox, Margalit. "Everett Ellin, 82, a Pioneer in Computerizing Art Catalogs." *New York Times*, October 16, 2011. https://archive.nytimes.com/query.nytimes.com/gst/fullpage-9C0CE7DB1E31F935A25753C1A9679D8B63.html.

Genosko, Gary. "When a Lost Manuscript Turns Up." *University Affairs*, June 7, 2023. https://www.universityaffairs.ca/opinion/in-my-opinion/when-a-lost-manuscript-turns-up/.

Marantz, Kenneth A. "Review of *Exploration of the Ways, Means, and Values of Museum Communication with the Viewing Public: A Seminar*." *Studies in Art Education* 11, no. 2 (1970): 57.

McLuhan, Marshall. *Counterblast*. McClelland & Stewart, 1969.

McLuhan, Marshall. "Humpty Dumpty, Automation, and TV." *Varsity Graduate* 10, no. 4 (1963): 24–28.

McLuhan, Marshall. "Marshall McLuhan to Harry J. Skornia, March 9, 1965." In *Letters of Marshall McLuhan*, edited by Matie Molinaro, Corrine McLuhan, and William Toye, 320–21. Oxford University Press, 1987.

McLuhan, Marshall. "Television in a New Light." In *The Meaning of Commercial Television: The Texas-Stanford Seminar, 1966*, edited by Stanley T. Donner. University of Texas Press, 1967.

McLuhan, Marshall. *Understanding Media*. McGraw-Hill, 1964.

McLuhan, Marshall, Harley Parker, and Jacques Barzun. *Exploration of the Ways, Means, and Values of Museum Communication with the Viewing Public: A Seminar*. Museum of the City of New York, 1969.

Parker, Harley. *The Culture Box: Museums as Media*, edited by Gary Genosko. University of Alberta Press, 2025.

Parker, Harley. "New Hall of Fossil Invertebrates, Royal Ontario Museum." *Curator* 10, no. 4 (1967): 284–96.

Parker, Harley. "The Museum as a Perception Kit." *Explorations* (January 1972): 54–59.

Schwartz, Tony. *The Responsive Chord*. Doubleday, 1974.

West, Kim. *The Exhibitionary Complex: Exhibition, Apparatus, and Media from Kulturhuset to the Centre Pompidou, 1963–1977*. Södertörn Studies in Art History and Aesthetics 4. Södertörn University, 2017.

2 Exploration of the Ways, Means, and Values of Museum Communication with the Viewing Public

A Seminar,
Museum of the City of New York, 1967

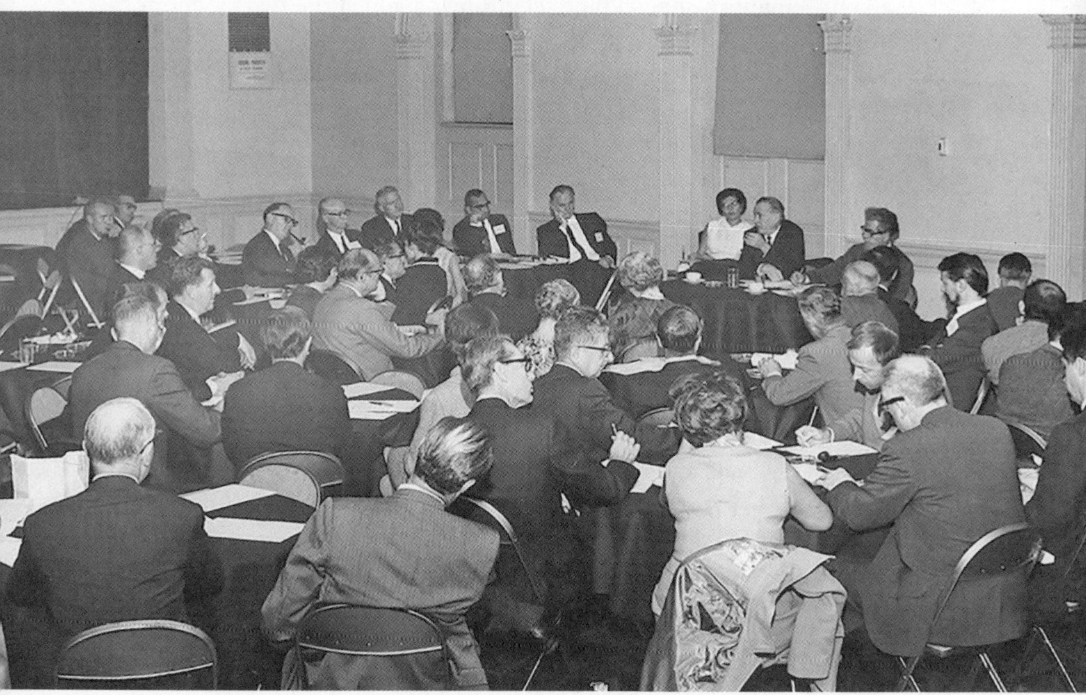

This image of the opening session of the seminar served as the cover art in the original publication. McLuhan and Parker can be seen seated at the top right table. (Photo by Werner J. Kuhn, courtesy of the Museum of the City of New York, Institutional Archives.)

Preface

In the spring of 1967, Ralph R. Miller, Director of the Museum of the City of New York, approached the New York State Council on the Arts with the idea of holding a seminar for museum directors to discuss ways of increasing the effectiveness of their exhibition program and its communication with the viewing public. He met with encouragement and financial support, without which the seminar could not have taken place.

Mr. Miller was fortunate in securing as moderators the controversial communications theorist, Marshall McLuhan, and his colleague, Harley Parker. As a counterbalance, he asked Professor Jacques Barzun of Columbia University to be the principal speaker at the banquet which closed the sessions. The preparations included an unusual one in the interest of nonlinear communication:[1] that of sending in advance to all participants a special tape recording on which the two moderators discussed some of the subjects to be considered at the seminar. Special thanks are due to Tony Schwartz[2] for making this recording.

Arrangements were made for a "field trip" to the American Museum of Natural History,[3] whose director, Dr. James A. Oliver,[4] agreed with courage as well as kindness to let his institution serve as a guinea pig and target for criticism. In addition, a special multi-media "orientation" gallery designed by Harley Parker was temporarily installed at the Museum of the City of New York as a workshop example of the Parker-McLuhan practical application. The electronic equipment for this room was supplied by Sound and Light Productions, Inc. and installed by Gerard M. Simon. Tony Schwartz was again kind enough to lend some of his films and tapes for the occasion.

Many other persons contributed to the success of the seminar: among them, Louis S. Auchincloss,[5] President of the Museum of the City of New York, and the Trustees, who helped to finance the banquet; also Carlin Gasteyer,[6] Laurence Maloy,[7] Hazel Shah, Elizabeth M. Conger,[8] and other members of the staff of the Museum; and, not least, the museum people of New York State, whose enthusiastic participation resulted in lively, and occasionally heated, discussions.

The cover picture and other photographs in this transcript were taken by Werner J. Kuhn, except where other credit is given.

The following pages present a transcript of the pre-seminar tape and of the proceedings of the seminar and the concluding address by Jacques Barzun. It should be noted that Dr. McLuhan and Mr. Parker have edited, and occasionally deleted, some of their remarks. In addition, there is a list of the participants, the complete program, scale drawings and description of the orientation gallery, and a subject index.[9]

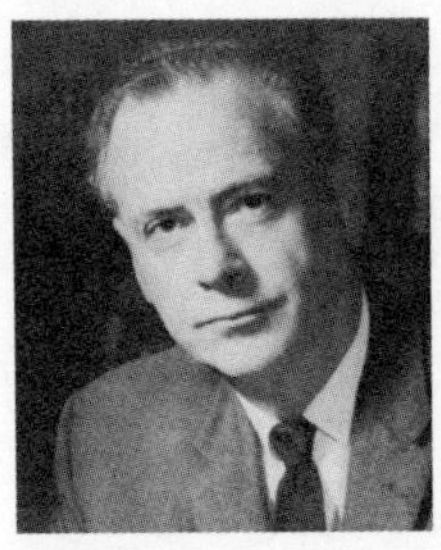

Author of such trailblazing books as *The Gutenberg Galaxy*, *Understanding Media*, and *The Medium Is the Massage*, DR. McLUHAN is Director of the Centre for Culture and Technology[10] at the University of Toronto. Born in Edmonton, Alberta, Canada, he studied at Manitoba University and Cambridge University, where he received his PHD in English Literature.[11] He has taught at the University of Wisconsin, the University of St. Louis, and Assumption University, and in the fall of 1967, was appointed to conduct a seminar on communications media at Fordham University in New York.[12]

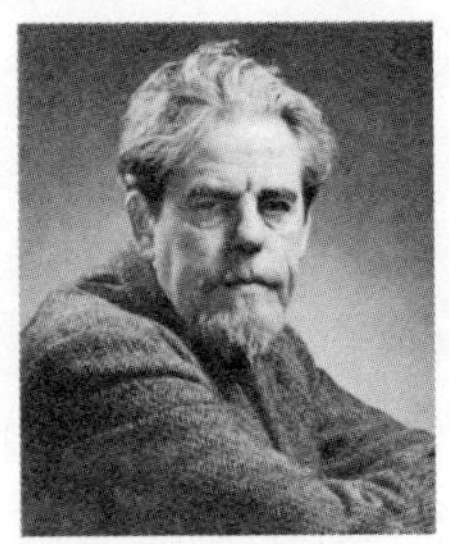

HARLEY PARKER is a founding member of the Centre for Culture and Technology at Toronto, and a close collaborator with Dr. McLuhan. He was born in Fort William, Canada[13] and studied at the Ontario College of Art[14] and Black Mountain College,[15] North Carolina, where he worked under Joseph Albers.[16] For the next twelve years he taught at the Ontario College of Art, where he inaugurated a course on Bauhaus art.[17] Following that, he became Head of Exhibits Design at the Royal Ontario Museum[18] in Toronto. He went to New York in 1967 to collaborate with Dr. McLuhan on the Fordham seminar.

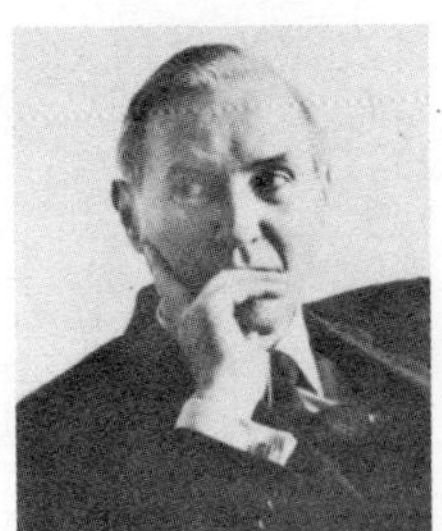

JACQUES BARZUN came to the United States from France in 1919 and received his PHD from Columbia University in 1927. He has taught at Columbia since that year. In 1945 he was appointed Dean of Graduate Faculties, and in 1958 was made Provost of the University. In July of 1967 he became a University Professor, Columbia's highest teaching position, and Special Advisor on the Arts to the President of Columbia. Dr. Barzun's many books include *Berlioz and the Romantic Century*, *God's Country and Mine*, *The Energies of Art*, *The Modern Researcher*, and *The House of Intellect*.

Program of the Seminar

MONDAY, OCTOBER 9

9:30   Registration, 104th Street Lobby Coffee, Fire Gallery
10:00   Dialogue, Marshall McLuhan and Harley Parker, followed by
         roundtable and group discussion
12:30   Lunch, Fire Gallery
2:00   Field Trip, American Museum of Natural History, followed
         by gallery discussion
5:00   Director's Cocktail Reception, Museum's Davies Gallery

TUESDAY, OCTOBER 10

9:30   Coffee, Fire Gallery
10:00   Workshop: Viewing of the experimental gallery set up
         as orientation area for the Dutch Gallery, followed by
         discussion, Marshall McLuhan and Harley Parker,
         moderators
12:30   Lunch, Fire Gallery
2:00   Roundtable Discussion, Marshall McLuhan and Harley
         Parker, moderators; special guest, Miss Letícia Román
7:00   President's Banquet, Museum of the City of New York

Cocktails, 7:00 PM, Main Hall
Banquet, 8:00 PM, Altman Gallery

Summation of Seminar, Harley Parker
Informal Remarks, Marshall McLuhan
Guest Speaker, Jacques Barzun

< Top to Bottom: Marshall McLuhan. (Photo by Ashley & Crippen.) Harley Parker. (Photo by Conrad Waldinger.) Jacques Barzun. (Photo by Werner J. Kuhn.)

List of Participants

John Anglim
Smithsonian Institution

Louis S. Auchincloss
President,
Museum of the City of New York

Mrs.[19] Mildred Baker
Associate Director,
Newark Museum

Albert K. Baragwanath
Senior Curator,
Museum of the City of New York

Mrs. Mary Black
Director,
Museum of American
Folk Arts

Charles Blitzer
Director of Education,
Smithsonian Institution

George Bowditch
Adirondack Museum

Thomas S. Buechner
Director,
Brooklyn Museum

Joseph Chamberlain
Assistant Director,
American Museum of Natural
History

Edward Chandless
Exhibits Director,
Newark Museum

Mrs. Elizabeth Conger
Director of Education,
Museum of the City of New York

James C. Crimmins
Chairman Junior Council,
Museum of Modern Art

John Culkin, S.J.
Fordham University

Mrs. Ferdinand Davis
Trustee,
Museum of the City of New York

Mrs. Jane des Grange
Director,
Suffolk Museum and Carriage
House

Fred J. Dockstader
Director,
Museum of the American Indian,
Heye Foundation

Walter S. Dunn
Director,
Buffalo & Erie County Historical
Society

Elisha Dyer
Trustee,
Museum of the City of New York

John Eastman
Junior Council,
Museum of Modern Art

Everett Ellin
Assistant to Director,
Solomon R. Guggenheim
Museum

James Elliott
Director,
Wadsworth Atheneum

Miss Sara Faunce
Curator of Artistic Properties,
Columbia University

Miss Helen V. Fisher
Director,
Brooklyn Children's Museum

E. McClung Fleming
Education Division,
Henry du Pont Winterthur
Museum

Mrs. Carlin Gasteyer
Assistant Director,
Museum of the City of New York

Harmon H. Goldstone
City Planning Commission,
New York

Robert Goldwater
Chairman of Administrating
Committee,
Museum of Primitive Art

Wilder Green
Director, Exhibitions Programs
Museum of Modern Art

Mrs. Randolph C. Guggenheimer
City Planning Commission,
New York

Robert T. Hatt
Director,
Cranbrook Institute of Science

August Heckscher
Commissioner of Recreation
and Culture,
New York

James Heslin
Director,
New York Historical Society

John Hightower
Executive Director,
New York State Council
on the Arts

Mrs. Edwin I. Hilson
Mayor's Representative on
Cultural Affairs,
New York

Thomas P. F. Hoving
Director,
Metropolitan Museum of Art

Mrs. Jacob M. Kaplan
Trustee,
Museum of the City of New York

Eugene Kingman
Director,
Joslyn Art Museum, Omaha

Richard Koke
Curator,
New York Historical Society

Robert F. Kolkebeck
Assistant Director,
New York Botanical Garden

Thomas Kyle
Assistant Director,
Museum of Contemporary Crafts

Frederick M. Lehman
Director and Chairman
of Displays,
Wantagh Historical Museum

G. Carroll Lindsay
Director,
New York State Museum Services

Robert Luck
Assistant Director,
American Federation of Arts

Laurence Maloy
Assistant to Director,
Museum of the City of New York

Richard B.K. McLanathan
Museum consultant, writer,
and lecturer

Marshall McLuhan
Director,
Centre for Culture and
Technology,
University of Toronto

Keith Martin
Director,
Roberson Memorial Centre

Mrs. Randolph B. Marston
Trustee,
Museum of the City of New York

Ralph R. Miller
Director,
Museum of the City of New York

Roy Moyer
Director,
American Federation of Arts

Thomas D. Nicholson
Chairman,
Hayden Planetarium

John Noble
Curator,
Museum of the City of New York

Harold C. Palmer
Board of Directors,
New York Cultural Foundation,
Inc.

Harley Parker
Head of Exhibit Design,
Royal Ontario Museum, Toronto

Harry Parker III
Chairman of Education
Department,
Metropolitan Museum of Art

Jere Patterson
Trustee,
Museum of the City of New York

Edward Pearce
Museum of Science, Boston

Sam Pearce
Curator,
Museum of the City of New York

Paul N. Perrot
Director,
Corning Museum of Glass

George O. Pratt
Director,
Staten Island Institute of Arts
and Sciences

Harris K. Prior
Director,
Rochester Memorial Art Gallery

Saverio Procario
Information and Publications,
Sleepy Hollow Restorations

Arthur W. Rashap
Director,
Brooklyn Institute of Arts and
Sciences

Frederick Rath
Vice-President,
New York State Historical
Association

Gordon Reekie
Chairman of Exhibitions,
American Museum of Natural
History

Norman S. Rice
Director,
Albany Institute of Art

Mrs. Reginald P. Rose
Trustee,
Museum of the City of New York

Arthur Rosenblatt
Deputy Administrator,
Department of Parks, New York

Allon Schoener
Director of Visual Arts,
New York State Council
on the Arts

Jiri Setlik
Editor-in-Chief,
Výtvarná Práce National Gallery,
Prague

Mrs. Hazel Shah
Executive Secretary,
Museum of the City of New York

James Short
Division of Interpretation,
Colonial Williamsburg

Stuart Silver
Assistant Manager of Exhibits,
Metropolitan Museum of Art

Paul J. Smith
Director,
Museum of Contemporary Crafts

Miss Margaret Stearns
Curator,
Museum of the City of New York

John Still
New York Historian's Office

H. J. Swinney
Director,
Adirondack Museum

Shuji Takashina
Curator,
National Museum of Western
Art, Tokyo

Jarold O. Talbot
Director,
Old Museum Village of
Smith's Clove

W. Stephen Thomas
Director,
Rochester Museum of Arts &
Sciences

Joseph S. Trovato
Assistant Director,
Munson-Williams-Proctor
Institute

Robert G. Wheeler
Research Director,
Sleepy Hollow Restorations

James Whitehead
Curator,
Franklin D. Roosevelt Library

Philip Yenawine
New York State Council
on the Arts

Pre-seminar

[Tape recording sent in advance to seminar participants.]

DR. McLUHAN: We were just remarking a few moments ago about
the word "class." Something having real class. As a nice example of
an old-fashioned, corny, passé word. And somebody else popped
up and said, "Well, isn't our type of classification equally passé?"
As an entrée for the whole problem for the museologists or the
curators might it not be useful to point out that the museum as a
retrieval system for classified objects is not going to be acceptable
very long. People now feel the need to have a sense of the total
surround of these objects and the total environment that produced
them. And the sort of culture that produced them. They like to
see them in their setting in the sort of form in which they originally existed, and, as it were, in action. Do you find the tendency
towards that developing, Harley?

MR. PARKER: Well, I think that to do that, however, we need the
help of a great number of things. We need the help of sound and
we need the help of film, in order to place these objects in their
context. Because I don't think that the old business of creating an
environment, that is, putting proper chairs in the proper rooms…

DR. McLUHAN: It is just a setting?

MR. PARKER: It is just a setting. This won't work.

DR. McLUHAN: Merely pictorial.

MR. PARKER: I would even suggest that we move into the whole
area of sound and light, with simultaneous projections of films
and stills and possibly multi-tape-recorders to give an immediate
sense of this.

DR. McLUHAN: I suppose the advantage of film is that it is the ideal
way of showing a process of development in any field. Because the
very nature of the sequence of shots in a film is naturally geared
to show development in any form. In biological form, in artistic
forms…

MR. PARKER: But when you couple this, of course, to multiple projections, you add a whole new dimension to it, so that it is immediate
apprehension. A very short-form apprehension.

Rather than the lineal and sequential development which might occur.

DR. McLUHAN: You mean a multi-screen approach does that? It tends to sort of telescope the developmental into a single instant.

MR. PARKER: That's right, it's a mosaic. An immediate mosaic. I think that, *apropos* of this business of creating the environment, it is very necessary to take into consideration one other thing and that is, that museums for a long time have been object-oriented. You can talk to any curator in any museum and his whole interest is in the object. It is in very few cases that they have been the slightest bit interested in the audience.

DR. McLUHAN: There is nothing wrong with being interested in the object. However, in the historical regard, every kind of object tends to create a new environment. If it is moccasins or skis or snow-shoes or canoes or railways or motor cars—no matter what the object is historically, it creates for itself a new environment, it enables people to enter into totally new relationships to space.

MR. PARKER: Yes, but this is dependent upon getting the objects out of those glass cases which allow you to stand back and look at them...you know...

DR. McLUHAN: Oh, yeah, but all I'm suggesting is that there is nothing wrong with being obsessed by the importance of the arti-fact or the object...

MR. PARKER: No.

DR. McLUHAN: Provided one is aware of what it does to environments.

MR. PARKER: That's right, what it does to the audience also.

DR. McLUHAN: Ah, well, the effect—again, the affect—on the audi-ence...is an environmental one...the audience is, after all, the environment that the artifact and the museum have to cope with. An audience is the surround. It is the new environment for the artifact.

MR. PARKER: Yes, but this environment constantly changes. You see, as the audience changes...as the audience is changing so rapidly, we can no longer put up with the old methods of presentation. We

have to become aware of our audience, and this is why we have to
become involved in the whole area of testing audiences.

DR. McLUHAN: You remember that scene we have been working on
concerning tactility? The discovery we made that touch does not
create a connection, but an interval.[20] Surely this is very relevant
to the museum world, where a great passion on the part of the
audience is the desire to touch the artifact.

MR. PARKER: Surely.

DR. McLUHAN: You remember the scandal that the sculptures of
Moore[21] created when they went to Germany and the audience
was told not to lay a hand on them? The idea that sculpture should
not be touched seemed utter heresy to the Germans.

MR. PARKER: I even encountered this in the Royal Imperial Museum,[22]
where there is a fossil tree which was about 500 million years old.
It was on display and there was a small boy standing there running
his fingers over it, and the guard came along and said, "Don't touch."
It was around for 500 million years and they would not let him
touch it.

DR. McLUHAN: That theme of touch which is so basic now with the
new TV generation. They, having been X-rayed by the TV image
from early childhood, now feel the need of handling all things in
depth.[23] The old pictorial, external look at things will not serve.
But another peculiarity about touch is this: granted that there is
the natural human desire to touch, the fact that touch creates an
interval involves the audience very much more, the interval has to
be closed. When you create an interval you have to close and it is
the closing of the interval that creates participation and rhythm.

MR. PARKER: I don't know whether you read that article by John
McHale called "The Plastic Parthenon"?[24]

DR. McLUHAN: No.

MR. PARKER: In which he pointed out, you know, that in our age
of technology it is quite easy to reproduce things. So if you have
material which is not expendable in an historic sense, there is no
reason at all why it cannot be reproduced accurately to provide an
expendable item which can be handled and can be touched. But
museums haven't entered that field either, yet.

DR. McLUHAN: But the importance of touch, we now can perceive, is
not to establish connections but participation. Interval for participation. And this kind of relation is surely one that the museums—
having grown up in the nineteenth century, which is so pictorial,
so visual and detached a period—have never really come to terms
with: this human need for involvement and participation.

MR. PARKER: Of course, and pertinent to that line we used before,
that to the blind all things are sudden. Raising into consciousness,
the idea that to the visual man nothing is sudden. It is that interval
in the world of the blind, that is highly involved.

DR. McLUHAN: That is the world of the breakthrough.

MR. PARKER: Yes.

DR. McLUHAN: But, you know, the suddenness of the insight or the
suddenness of discovery, the moment of truth, is closely related to
touch and the interval created by touch.

MR. PARKER: Museums of course in the past have tended—museums
and curators tend today—to also write a story line and then use
the artifacts to illustrate it. In fact, if they were writing a book
they would do exactly the same thing, except that in this case the
artifacts would be photographed and used as illustrations, but
there is no essential difference. In other words they think of a
museum as a book.

DR. McLUHAN: That is one of the peculiarities, and nobody needs to
be told this, in a way, about Expo 67.[25] It is perhaps the first world
fair which had no story line whatever. It was just a mosaic of discontinuous items in which people took an immense satisfaction precisely
because they weren't being told anything about the overall pattern
or shape of it, but they were free to discover and participate and
involve themselves in the total overall thing. The result was also
that they never got fatigued. I remember as a youngster being
familiar with a phrase, which I may have invented, "that museum
feeling," a kind of claustrophobia and exhaustion which settles
upon you as soon as you get inside those straightened avenues and
alleyways. Once you move into a world of continuous, connected
space—visual space—you quickly discover exhaustion setting in,
because there is no means of participation.

MR. PARKER: Also because the artifacts themselves, in many cases,
don't belong in those kinds spaces, so, you have a clash.

DR. McLUHAN: They never came from this kind of pictorial space.
It is that of mechanical man, of highly literate man, so the nature
of the work is totally alien to it. By the way, I have been delighted
to discover since I came to New York that New York is an island
and that like other islands it is characterized by complete devo-
tion to discontinuous, disconnected spaces.[26] Just like England.
The whole of New York, and perhaps other areas adjacent, is
dominated by the need for discontinuous space. Whereas you
don't have to go very far away from New York to enter a rather
completely connected and continuous space, whether it is Kansas
City or Toronto. But it is not only the space of the city that is
discontinuous and twisted and bent into all sorts of little knobs
and nodules, but also the houses, the interior. Now this was not
planned. I have never seen it mentioned and no one told me this.
I simply came here and lived and discovered the actual interiors
of New York houses tend to be like this. You can't just move in a
straight line right through the house. There is no such straight line.
Now this, I think, is of the utmost urgency for the museum world
to know. That if you want audience participation, you get rid of
lineal connected space.

MR. PARKER: Today the emphasis in the museum world is to keep on
building larger and larger museums or more and more museums,
instead of putting the ones they've got into order. I know at the
Royal Ontario Museum[27] they're currently dedicated to building
a new wing. I quipped at one point, that if we wait long enough,
we're all going to have wings, but...

DR. McLUHAN: A wing and a prayer...

MR. PARKER: Yes. But the point is, I think, very important that we
should start organizing the ones we've got instead of...

DR. McLUHAN: But, after all, surely all curators everywhere would
agree that audience participation is desirable...

MR. PARKER: No.

DR. McLUHAN: ...if it's compatible with the protection of the artifact; and you can get this participation to an amazing degree by simply arranging the spaces in which the cases are arranged.

MR. PARKER: One of the problems, Marshall, really is that curators have been in the lineal tradition, literally...literate.

DR. McLUHAN: Literate mould.

MR. PARKER: That's right. They have all been trained in this way. And they believe that they would teach exactly the same way. A curator will spend months or even years trying to find one missing link in his collection. Instead of devoting his time to using the material he has got to say something, he will devote his time to finding that one lost shoe or some such thing.

DR. McLUHAN: It would be a wonderful opportunity to invite the audience to supply that link, to advise them that it is a missing bit. The audience would delight in discovery, and supplying such material. This is the whole charm of detective stories. You carefully pull out the links and connections between the evidence and between the story bits in order to get audience participation.

MR. PARKER: Yeah, well one of the ways. We can talk about the story line, using the artifact as an illustration, and possibly suggest the idea of creating a gallery in which there are no answers given in legal form. But only questions asked. And the answer is inherent in the proper examination of the object, up to the point of the person's understanding. I think this might provide much more audience participation.

DR. McLUHAN: What about....Harley, what about the O.K. Moore "responsive environment"[28] treatment, you know, the typewriter—you touch the letter "a" and it springs at you from the walls and you hear it and you feel it. What about the possibility of designing for artifacts in museum environments that are also responsive, in which the audience could experience this participation? So that when they had recognized the nature of the artifacts, why the bells and buzzers would ring from all over the place! That this kind of recognition, pattern recognition would then be paid off by the environment going into action...

MR. PARKER: Pinball machine?

DR. McLUHAN: Yeah

MR. PARKER: Large-room pinball machine.

DR. McLUHAN: Of course, education by concept is the old way, and
today we are moving into percept. Training of perception—I think
the whole museum world can move around into this stance.

MR. PARKER: Well, the training of perception, I suppose, really
applies to training of the total sensorium, the total human
response, instead of just noticing which category something fits
into.

DR. McLUHAN: You see, I have watched people in museums for many
years and it is rather interesting, both in Europe and America. You
find a person will walk up to an object and look at it casually, read
the label, give it a cursory glance, and walk on. They have not really
looked at anything, because they are data oriented and they figure
that now they've got the answer to that and they know it is tenth-
century this or that, so they walk away from it. So the idea of setting
up a gallery which just asks questions is going to force people to
look at that or touch it if possible but at any rate look at it.

MR. PARKER: Now in the business of creating environments for artifacts: to give an example, in designing an Eskimo[29] gallery, we
designed it in such a way that there were no straight lines in it or
as few straight lines as possible in a rectangular room. We curved
from the floor up to the walls; we curved from the walls to the ceil-
ings, all were curves because, according to anthropologists, this is
the quality of the landscape there.

DR. McLUHAN: A Bucky Fuller Dome[30] might serve for such an
installation.

MR. PARKER: Would be wonderful if you could get hold of one.

DR. McLUHAN: Well, that is the way of tackling the artifact in its
natural habitat. But it's also a habitat that tends to make an Eskimo
world. We know this well enough from Ted Carpenter's instiga-
tions and discourse,[31] an Eskimo world is a pre-visual world. Most
of the exhibits in any museum pre-date the rise of visual culture,
with the Greeks and the Romans. Therefore, the senses that are
relevant to most of the artifacts in the museum are those of what
we would now call an extremely backward country, in which they

used not their eyes in our way, but their whole sensorium. They
would practically live in a world of ESP.[32] When your whole sensorium is in action you don't really use anything except ESP. The
whole skin of man, when it is acting as a perceptive agent, is intuitive. It doesn't need any special message. It gets the message very
quickly from just the slightest change in the environmental
pressure.

MR. PARKER: There seem to be two problems really. One is:
creating—now, first of all it is in a museum, and therefore you
cannot create a natural environment for the object. What you can
do, though is, from the experts, to get some idea of the sensory
components which were most effective.[33]

DR. McLUHAN: Most dominant.

MR. PARKER: What was the bias in any given culture.

DR. McLUHAN: Right.

MR. PARKER: Then you have the further problem of presenting
something to our particular society, which has a different sensory
bias. And this sensory bias varies in children and adults.

DR. McLUHAN: On the other hand we are sort of circling or cycling
back to that pre-visual culture—so that much of the latest culture
of our world is getting very close to the most primitive culture in
terms of the sensory bias. The real gripe we have about the beats,
and the hippies, the teenagers, teenyboppers,[34] is that they are so
primitive.

MR. PARKER: That's right.

DR. McLUHAN: And we are trying to force them back into a literate
context, a sort of "Down, Rover," instead of looking straight at this
development and saying, "All right, what do we do about it, how do
we use it for education?" By the way, an Eskimo igloo is an excellent example of an auditory space. A resonating dome-like structure.
But doesn't it follow in the same way, the new preference or the
new inclination towards Bucky Domes indicates that we are going
on visual, auditory, and tactile lines in our own time?

MR. PARKER: But we need more data on this because—you know it, I
know it, and various others know it—but to convince museum
directors across the nation we need data.

DR. McLUHAN: I wouldn't think it necessary to convince them, so much as to alert them to the possibility of a completely new relation to the public.

MR. PARKER: Well, this is true...

DR. McLUHAN: But I don't think you have to convince them by argument.

MR. PARKER: No, not by argument.

DR. McLUHAN: I don't want to convince them by argument, but I would suggest that I put forward the idea of having a console in a gallery which would allow a person to manipulate the light, high, low, warm, cool, and to choose sounds in relation to things. There would be a feedback on that, and then we would have some data which would be very convincing. There is a problem in museums, of course: the fact that Near Eastern curators don't talk to Far Eastern curators. And Far Eastern curators don't talk to ethnologists. And so you get this fragmentation, and you rarely ever get a chance to bring these various artifacts from different cultures together so they can create abrasive situations alongside each other.

MR. PARKER: Interfaces.

DR. McLUHAN: Interfaces. You never get it, or very rarely except in special exhibitions.

MR. PARKER: The researcher is a man who deliberately creates interfaces in order to make discoveries. He deliberately sets off situations that will irritate one another, until you suddenly get a flash insight. But it is very rarely that...this is a matter of territoriality...Each man is defending his own territory.

DR. McLUHAN: That is again the classification of approach. The old nineteenth-century classified knowledge approach. Alphabetized approaches.

MR. PARKER: To give an example, it only recently occurred to me, as I was beginning to work on some Chinese material. A tremendous flash came to me that the Ming Period of Chinese Culture,[35] which is a rather decadent period, was coincidental with the Renaissance,[36] the High Renaissance.[37] This is a very interesting thing.

DR. McLUHAN: Chronological terms. But you never have any chance, the average person never has any chance to make that discovery. Because he has never seen the artifacts together and had a chance to say, "These co-existed." Any medievalist would regard the Renaissance as decadent. Oh, yes.

MR. PARKER: Just as we, today, regard the Renaissance as decadence.

DR. McLUHAN: We tend in that direction. In other words, we incline to favour the Middle Ages again, too.

MR. PARKER: That's right.

DR. McLUHAN: Which again is a non-pictorial space. It is not a simple continuum anymore. The Renaissance discovered the merits or the advantages of the simple continuum, connected space.

MR. PARKER: Well, of course, these light shows, the Electric Circus[38] and all the rest of the things that are going on, are very indicative of this whole business, of the breakdown from lineality. And the youngsters love it.

DR. McLUHAN: So I think that we have to inject these new techniques into museums and bring them alive.

MR. PARKER: I am not quite sure that we need to foster them, as much as exploit them, in the hope that they will go away quickly.

DR. McLUHAN: No, I don't think so. But I think there is a tremendous potential for education in this, in that particular mode, in terms of pattern recognition rather than data assimilation, you see. I think we could really provide orientation centres for museums for specific areas so that the person doesn't just walk in directly from the highway or off the streets of our cities, and you suddenly confront him with a tenth-century Chinese vase. He won't know what to do with it, so you have to provide him with some kind of orientation centres and this, I think, is where the light shows could come in as fast methods of orientation.

MR. PARKER: I think that is fascinating...

The Seminar

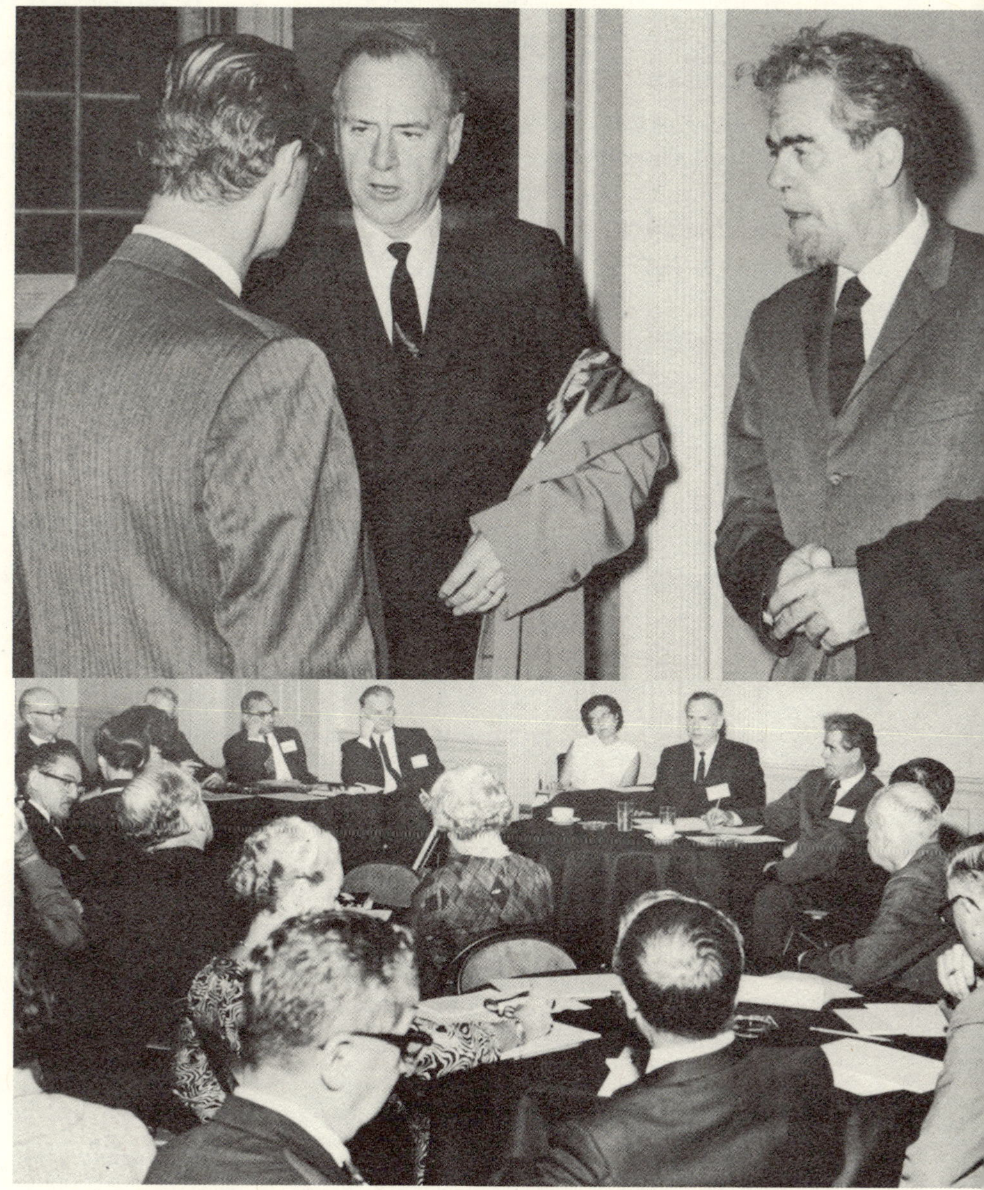

Top: Museum of the City of New York's Director Ralph R. Miller greets Marshall McLuhan (centre) and Harley Parker (right) as they arrive for the seminar. (Photo by Werner J. Kuhn.) Bottom: This image of the opening session of the seminar captures the relaxed, conversational environment the Museum hoped to create, showing McLuhan and Parker seated (top right table) among the various museum directors and trustees in attendance. (Photo by Werner J. Kuhn.)

Monday Morning, October 9, 1967

MR. RALPH MILLER (Director, Museum of the City of New York):
Ladies and Gentlemen: I bid you good morning, and a very warm
welcome to the Museum of the City of New York. I'm not going to
take much time, because there are two gentlemen on my right whose
remarks may be more important than my own. One announcement
that I would like to make is that, if you do get a chance to look at
the Dutch Gallery on the first floor, it might be of advantage to you,
because we have constructed on the second floor of the Museum
for tomorrow's workshop an experimental gallery, based on the
subject of the Dutch period in New York City. So, for contrast, and
to see how it's done one way, or how it might be done another way,
take a look at our Dutch Gallery.

We will now open our seminar, and I will present you to Dr.
Marshall McLuhan, who I'm sure you all know of, or know, and Mr.
Harley Parker.

The whole general idea of this seminar is one of relaxation.
Please feel free to go back and get coffee, move your chairs as you
will, push the tables around if you can't hear Dr. McLuhan and
Mr. Parker. They will carry on a dialogue for a spell, and then will
open the channels for observations, conversation and what-have-
you, comments from everyone here in this room. We will now get
under way.

Gentlemen, the floor is yours.

DR. McLUHAN: I am delighted with the association that comes to
mind with the name Miller. There is a wonderful book called *The
Russians as People* by Mr. Wright Miller,[39] which I have just been
reading; I never heard of it until recently. One of the advantages of
working with a team is that you can sort of pool your bibliographical data, and Ted Carpenter put me onto this one. At the very
beginning of the book, a scene that concerns us all here is help-
fully stressed, namely, the kind of space in which a Russian is born
and raised. I remember, as I read those early pages, being absolutely stunned by the awareness that, at the opposite end of the
visual or civilized spectrum, there is another form of individualism

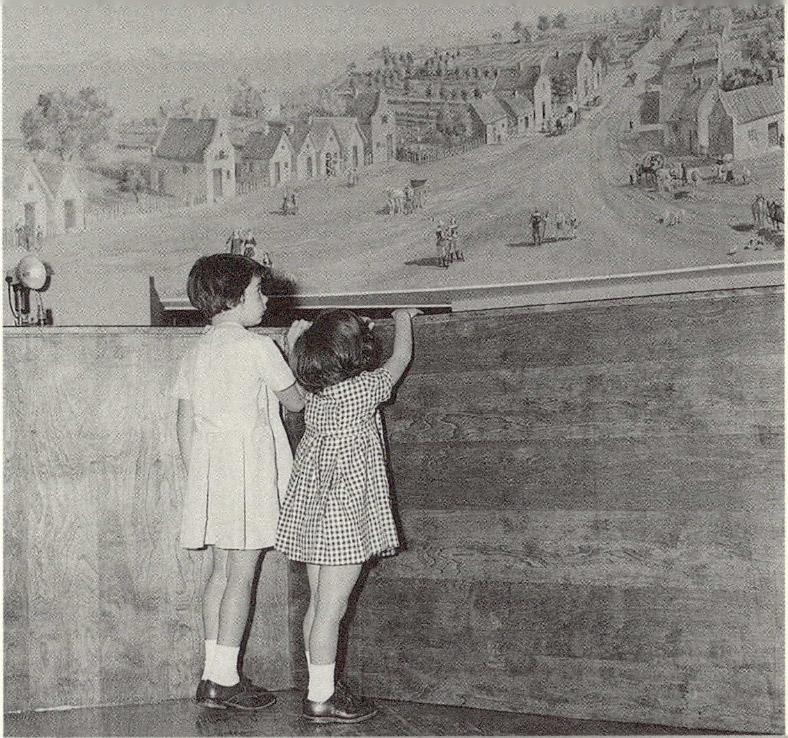

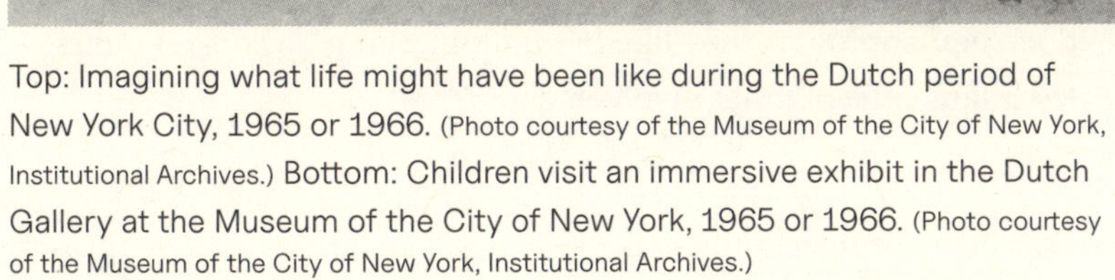

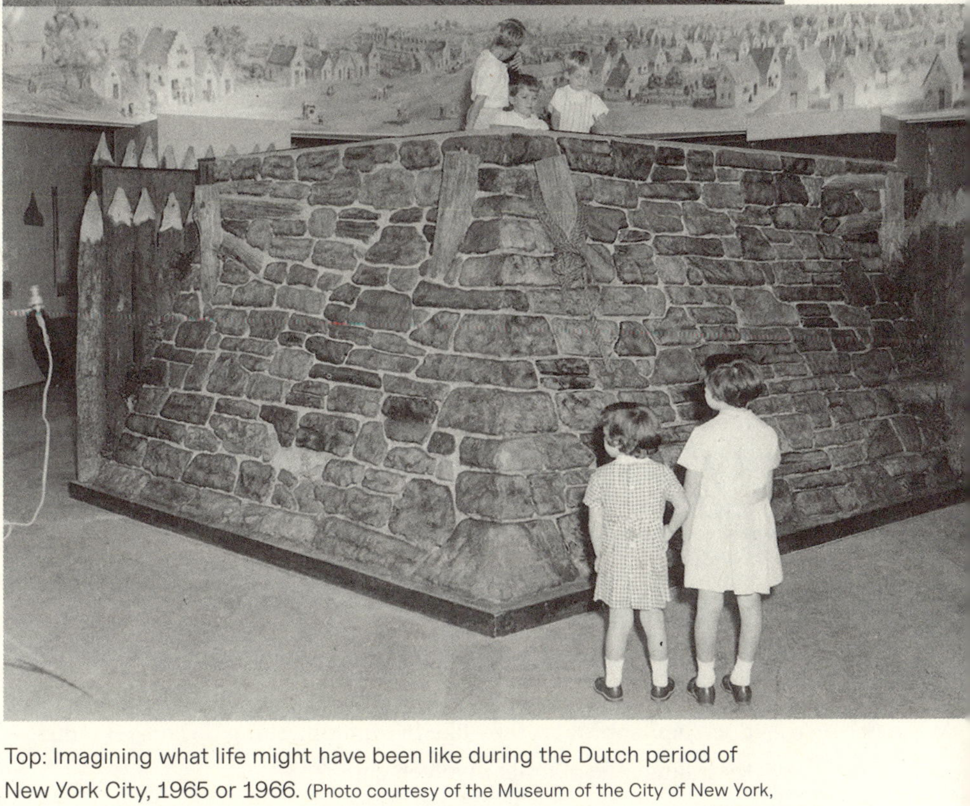

Top: Imagining what life might have been like during the Dutch period of New York City, 1965 or 1966. (Photo courtesy of the Museum of the City of New York, Institutional Archives.) Bottom: Children visit an immersive exhibit in the Dutch Gallery at the Museum of the City of New York, 1965 or 1966. (Photo courtesy of the Museum of the City of New York, Institutional Archives.)

that is totally tactile. It is the result of the monolithic, iconic form of space created by touch.

Harley Parker and I have worked on this a good deal. In fact, I owe directly to Harley the discovery that touch doesn't create a connection, but that instead, it creates an interval. The Russian individualism is that of touch, of interval, the opposite of our visual identity or separatism, or privacy. The Russian is tribal, tactile, involved; we are detached.[40]

Our museums, I imagine, are unconsciously laid out on the visual pattern without awareness of this new electronic age, which acts on us as a kind of incubus. Space, under electronic conditions, is so total and so oppressive that it's a mesh of tactility that is translating our civilized world into a primitive pattern once more.

Our teenyboppers have many of the manifestations of natives and pre-literate types of people. I'm talking about my own kids.[41] Yet people are quite mystified as to why they should be growing their hair and going around barefoot and making these strange stereo noises. The stereophonic is another word for touch.

MR. PARKER: As a postscript to the name Miller, I remember you got a letter from [Romania] in which a doctor pointed out that the word Luhan in a certain language meant "miller." I hope you people aren't in the same position as I am. I haven't heard the tape.

Apropos of the business of tactility and visual spaces, some months ago we ran across, in a book by Alex Leighton the phrase, "To the blind all things are sudden,"[42] raising into conscious thought the idea that to the man with sight, to the visually biased man, nothing is sudden. He has perspective; he can look back and ahead of him. I think one of the salient factors of the hippie stance is the nowness of now.

DR. McLUHAN: Involvement.

MR. PARKER: They're not interested in a future. They're not interested in jokes. But nowness of now I think is the hippie stance.

DR. McLUHAN: The Buddha stage[43] looks good to them because it's involved. It doesn't go outer, it goes inner, and, without benefit of doctrinal approach, they like the Buddha thing because it talks their language of inner involvement.

MR. PARKER: If we relate this to the simple facts of the difference between, let's say, tactile, kinetic, and Old World as opposed to the visual world as Leonardo da Vinci[44] said, "Seeing is believing"—but the whole quotation is "Seeing is believing but to touch is the word of God."

If we begin to extrapolate this kind of idea into the museum world, it raises this factor—that the audience has changed so radically in the last thirty years since the War. I don't think that in the whole history of man there has been such a sudden change in sensibility. So my own position, in terms of museums, is this: certainly, concern with artifacts is a very necessary thing, this is the curatorial job, the curatorial function; but it seems to me that with this tremendous change in audience we must have people within museums who are concerned with audience-audience [*sic*] reaction. We must get feedback, we must find out how to present these artifacts which we are looking after so carefully.

DR. McLUHAN: One of the amazing aspects about all artifacts that concerns all of us is that they tend to create environments. They make their own spaces. The satellite world, for example, is an artifact, a man-made environment that goes around the planet.[45] The planet has now become an object contained in a man-made environment. It is no longer nature. It's an old art form. An old nose cone.

You may have heard about the two mice in the nose cone[46] and one says to the other, "How do you like this kind of work?" And the other says, "Oh, well, it's better than cancer research."

But the planet has now become the content of an artifact. One of the things we don't notice about artifacts is that they do create environments. The motor car creates a special environment. The radio environment is quite different from that of television. The real artifacts made by man are environment, not objects that are contained in environment. When I say real, I mean the real, potent ones. And they are invisible. For some biological, physiological reason, people never see environment, they always see the content of environment.

This is true of the scientist as well as the ordinary human being. The Darwinians[47] thought that the evolutionary process attached itself to the little content of nature, the little biological entity. In actual fact, the evolutionary process has been taking place in the environment itself, and not in the biological thing.

The evolutionary process has leaped ahead eons by electronic means. In fact, it's going so rapidly that we can't help but notice the possibility of programming it, for the first time in human history. The possibility of programming evolution by deliberate means is wide open in the age of the computer, but it also involves a much greater responsibility than any previous age dreamt of.

In order to program any total situation like that you really have to know an awful lot more about welfare, values. A point of view is of no use whatever in programming or evaluating a total environment. By its very definition, a total environment doesn't permit a point of view.

As Burke[48] said about the rebellious American Colonies, "I do not know how to indict a whole people."[49]

In the same way, no value judgments are possible when you're dealing with a whole people. That is, no point of view is possible. Not unless you just wish to appear foolish.

MR. PARKER: To go back a bit, there's possibly one thing which could use a little elaboration, and that is the business of the changing sensory modalities of today.

I came to an analogy for this through long study of colour. Ostwald[50] was a German physicist, a colour scientist of the late nineteenth century, and he said at one point that all sensation is one hundred percent. He could have said all perception is one hundred percent.

He said, in colour it's as if you had a full test tube of colour and you can only change that colour or add something to it at the expense of the initial ingredients. I find that this is a good illustration for the sensory life. Because as you put more, for instance, of the visual into a perception, the other factors, of necessity, must go down, if all experience is one hundred percent. If you raise the tactile, the oral will go down. It's always in a constant flux of orchestration.

Since the Renaissance, and actually since the Greeks, we have had this increasing bias towards the visual, which began to become obsolete, or began to change, I think, in 1837, the time of telegraphy,[51] and developed, in the arts, an increasing tendency away from the visual bias.

So today we find visually oriented audiences walking up to a painting and saying, "Well, what is it?"

DR. McLUHAN: It was Aristotle[52] who pointed out, way back in that period when they were just discovering visual space and values, that any form, any kind of organized form, when pushed to its limits, instantly assumes the opposite characteristics.[53] We have seen this happen in our own time. Culture has become our business.[54] Ours used to be a business civilization with a little culture added. Now, in the age when the knowledge industries have become overwhelmingly dominant, culture has become the primary mark of our age.

MR. PARKER: You lose business at it. Actually, not to be so all-embracing, but to give an example of this change: I myself place, not Cézanne,[55] as the turning point in our history, but Seurat.[56] It's very interesting that Seurat applied the Newtonian concept of the division of light. The impressionists ceased to paint the obvious, they only painted light upon objects; and when Seurat took up divisionism,[57] he suddenly discovered that all the old visual values were no longer appropriate. He could no longer deal with perspective properly, or foreshortening, even *chiaroscuro*[58] became more difficult, and on top of that, he returned to Egyptian imagery.[59] So there was a complete reversal at the point of pushing colour to its ultimate ends.

DR. McLUHAN: Many people have difficulty understanding that the television screen is not a visual form at all, but a world of profiles that are very tactile and very flat. Joyce[60] has a phrase about this: he called the television screen the "charge of the light barricade."[61] The image comes at the viewer. The viewer doesn't look at the screen in television. He is the screen. In movies, you are the camera and you look at the screen.

MR. PARKER: Which is involvement versus the detachment inherent in the visual bias.

DR. McLUHAN: In the movies, our cinema, you're the camera. In television you are being X-rayed at every moment. The light barricade is charging at you. This is involvement.

The movie, on the other hand, doesn't represent involvement. It is detachment. Our only civilized sense, sight, is the only sense that provides detachment. All the other senses create depth involvement. Sight alone gives detachment, and sight alone gives what we consider to be the main qualities of civilized society: continuity, connectedness, uniformity.

MR. PARKER: This is why, in the nineteenth century or earlier, we came to the conclusion that in museums it's quite enough to put things in glass cases and shine sufficient light on them so that they can be seen.

DR. McLUHAN: So long as they are labelled.

MR. PARKER: The other night I walked through the museum after hours. The lights were very low, and I found it an intensely moving experience. In other words, the dimming of illumination was very much an involving thing. Whereas, if you can see everything that you're looking at very clearly, you just stand back and look at it with no sense of involvement.

There's another interesting problem which I raised at an architectural conference. I pointed out that our engineers have decided arbitrarily that every child must have ninety-six or ninety-two candlepower of unfluctuating fluorescent light at his desk level. And yet it doesn't take very much insight to know that the human eye has been developing under constantly fluctuating light, and has a remarkable ability to adapt from five candlepower to five thousand candlepower. You can handle a white shirt in the five candlepower light and you can identify it as a white shirt. As a designer, I know very well that if you continue anything long enough you bore someone. Therefore, looking at museums, let's start moving around into rheostats.[62] Let's start fluctuating our light from warm to cool to dark.

DR. McLUHAN: Related to this is the subject of "near point." Our children have moved very much closer to the printed page than their fathers and mothers ever moved. It hasn't been sufficiently studied, but we are sure that young people will continue to get much closer to the printed page than their parents. This "near-point" business has a great deal to do with involvement patterns and the new impediments to learning. Many reading deficiencies, many learning deficiencies, are the result of this sensory shifting and have nothing whatever to do with intelligence. Abe Kirshner[63] in Montreal has discovered that the trampoline will correct many of the reading difficulties of our children, because it permits a coordination of the senses which is impossible to the television generation, who are being subjected to the old forms of visual experience based on specialism and fragmentation, while also being savaged by the TV image. The trampoline serves to coordinate the senses, and many children with serious visual and learning difficulties have been able to establish a more natural approach to reading by jumping up and down on this gimmick.

MR. PARKER: Isn't it true that in our school system it's the visually handicapped who suffer most? A child can move through our educational system with a complete insensitivity to touch. And he can be an excellent scholar. He can even have hearing difficulties and be an excellent scholar; but if he has sight difficulties, then he's really in trouble.

I would like to elaborate more on this near-point thing. Dr. Art Hurst,[64] who is in New York now, has been doing a great deal of work, in which he discovered that the near-point distance for reading was six inches, and the near-point writing distance was four and a half inches for children in grade three. This is really close. He also discovered that, back in 1942, the near-point reading distance was ten inches. The classical reference is elbow to ulna[65] for the near-point reading distance, and that would be about ten inches for a ten-year-old.

DR. McLUHAN: The school furniture companies naturally are interested in this problem. They had hit upon some mean distance like sixteen inches for the ideal distance from the desktop to the eye of the student, but it's based very much on rule of thumb, and not related to the changes going on in our midst.

MR. PARKER: Marshall and I have postulated that the reason for the child bringing the book closer to him is a rather pathetic attempt to get the same sense of involvement out of the book that he got out of the television screen. I imagine most of you have encountered a small child still in diapers in front of a television screen. You can't walk between him and the screen. I think it's very possible that this is one of the reasons a child misses a sense of involvement when he reads a book.

DR. McLUHAN: We must ask the question, what equivalent means are being provided in the museums or in the art galleries? There's a story about De Gaulle[66] visiting one of the French galleries, escorted by Malraux.[67] He inquired, "What is that picture over there?" "That's a Renoir."[68] "And over here?" "Oh, that's a Miró."[69] And De Gaulle saw a picture coming up and said, "I think I know who made that monstrous cartoon, that must be a Rouault."[70] "Oh, no, that's a mirror."

MR. PARKER: A friend of ours, John McHale, who works with Buckminster Fuller, wrote an article recently[71] in which he pointed out the tremendous technological possibilities of reproducing artifacts. They are available to us today, so that even though we have no expendable articles in museums, it's still possible to make facsimile reproductions which can be handled. I think this possibility of touch can be a very salient factor in terms of involvement.

DR. McLUHAN: One bizarre illustration comes to mind: Twiggy.[72] Twiggy is not a sculptural, not a pictorial object. Twiggy is like Giacometti,[73] tactile. To get abstract art, you have only to take away the story line. What we call story line is connected visual space. Such continuity has been pulled out of the film world and out of the art world and out of the newspaper world, and we continue pulling out the story line in order to keep up with the increasing effects of the electronic surround.

But Twiggy is non-pictorial: that is, the clothing is not intended to complete or to enclose the image. She's an icon—not glamorous; tribal—not civilized. The miniskirts aren't erotic. They're iconic. The erotic consists in specializing, in fragmenting attention. There are a lot of strange aspects to that matter which we need not go into.

MR. PARKER: Let's go into pornography.

DR. McLUHAN: All right, you take that.

MR. PARKER: Pornography is purely the result of visual stress, a fragmentation of all the other senses, and a complete concentration on the visual.

There is a story of the university professor who was crossing the border, and the customs man said to him, "What do you do?" And he said, "I'm a professor." "Have you got any books?" And he said, "I have a few books." "Do you have any pornographic books?" "I don't even own a pornograph."

Visual stress is the one thing that fragments pornography off from a true, healthy sensuality.

DR. McLUHAN: Don't make value judgments.

MR. PARKER: I'm not a voyeur, but a psychiatrist tells me that the voyeur who has fragmented sight off from his other senses and depends upon it entirely is totally harmless. He's the most harmless sex deviate in existence. No involvement.

DR. McLUHAN: But the absence of story line is something that certainly concerns the museum. In order to create involvement you have to take out story line and perspective, and stress process. This is the great discovery of Edgar Allan Poe.[74] In his poetry and stories he discovered that if he pulled out the connections, he could get much higher involvement. The reader becomes co-producer, co-creator.

If you fill in all the projections, the reader can only be a consumer of packaged goods, not a participant. Thus the new teenage bunch aren't consumer oriented, much to the dismay of Governor Reagan, for example.

MR. PARKER: Ted Carpenter[75] was telling us that Governor Reagan has stopped hunting Communists. He's hunting non-consumers. Kenneth Boulding,[76] the economist, made a remark that was very interesting. He said that we had entered the area of operation overload. The amount of data coming in via computers was of such volume that it was impossible for anyone to keep up with it, so he invented this term, "operation overload," and said the answer to it was pattern recognition.

So I applied this principle to galleries. I know that when I designed a gallery of invertebrate paleontology,[77] I discovered that there were three invertebrate paleontologists in Toronto. I decided to design this gallery for children rather than the paleontologists.

If you're going to design a gallery on such a subject, it's obvious that you can't do it in the old linear, sequential way, with Latin names. What do you do? You work for pattern recognition, a broad idea of the concept of this particular discipline.

So I set out to tell the children a few very simple things. One of the first ones was, what is an invertebrate paleontologist and why? I feel if I tell the kids this I will have told them something: that he's important to the oil industry and increases human knowledge. Another important thing to tell them was that all life originated in water. Another was the beauty of shell life, and the simple geometry that lies behind it. This is done, not simply by compiling data, but by giving them meaningful experiences which they will not forget.

If they have those, children who want to become invertebrate paleontologists now have a pattern recognition into which they can fit the specialized data. It raises, in my own mind, the way we teach history in Canada.

I know my daughter[78] used to study the year 1609, the discovery of Lake Champlain,[79] to 1710. The next year she would study from 1840 to 1912. By that time she has already forgotten the 1609 date, and at the end of her public school life she knew absolutely nothing about the history of Canada. She knew no pattern.

The same thing applies to museums. The museum must deal in pattern recognition. Behind the scenes in study collections, that's for the scholars.

DR. McLUHAN: Let's take it from there, for a moment. The French Canadians never had an eighteenth or a nineteenth century. In

Canada, they went from the seventeenth, with nothing in between, to the twentieth. There's a pattern in French Canada and in the same way there's a pattern behind good jokes-grievance.[80]

MR. PARKER: That's why we have so much humour in the Museum.

DR. McLUHAN: There has been a great decline of jokes in recent years, and I don't think it represents the decline of grievance. I owe to Steve Allen[81] the observation that the funny man is a man with a grievance.[82] Given that pattern recognition, you can really have fun with jokes, as a serious form of research. That's another aspect of living in a world of information overload. When the pressure of data creates the need for integral awareness, overload leads to pattern recognition. You can only specialize just so much, then you have to go integral again.

There is the story about the chicken and the pig walking along the highway in the early morning, and they come to a restaurant, and the chicken says, "How about going in there for breakfast?" "Oh no," says the pig "for you it's just a contribution, for me it's a total commitment."

One of the big grievances of our times results from the new depth involvement, since the establishment is not involved, but classified.

But this whole business of pattern recognition is becoming indispensable in the age of systems engineering.[83] I don't know what the computer is going to do to the museum world; I should think it would enrich it considerably, because you can have access to all cultures in the world simultaneously and instantaneously. In the age of the space capsule, you take the planet with you when you go into orbit. You take the whole thing. That's real involvement. Today we take all the cultures with us.

MR. PARKER: In the Museum of Natural History[84] several years back, we began to talk about the Museum, and we came to a conclusion: that to some extent, at any rate, museum fatigue is a result of a clash of spaces. You present artifacts which come from spaces which are not visually organized, and you present these artifacts in spaces which are visually organized, and this generates a kind of psychic clash between these two things.

The object, from a primitive society, will create its own space, but what do we do? We create some kind of a proscenium-arch[85] stage to put the object in. A painter once gave a beautiful description of the way a Renaissance painter painted. He said, "We create the ground, and put something down the sides and we create Renaissance three-dimensional painting,[86] the sky and horizon, and after we have done that, we then put the objects in."

This is typically visual organization of space; three-dimensional Renaissance painting necessitates a single point of view. This is the point of view from which the painter painted. Three-dimensional painting is a cul-de-sac of one time and one space.

The concept of the icon was mentioned earlier. The difference between the icon and the Renaissance three-dimensional painting, as illustration, is the difference between one-time, one-space point of view and many-times, many-spaces, and multi-points of view. We cannot take an icon and place it in a proscenium-arch stage in a three-dimensional, visual organization.

DR. McLUHAN: Expo 67 is a mosaic. There are no connections between any of the parts. It has no story line. Everybody can get into the act. They're not being given any organized image of anything.[87]

There are a few exceptions in some of the pavilions. Most of the pavilions have no products, no exhibits, no projects, except Russia's.[88] They're desperately trying to have a nineteenth century at last, and so they filled their pavilion with products, which is what we used to do in our world's fairs. It was a world of produce, not of process. Expo is a world of process, not of products.

Apropos of pattern recognition, the new learning situation demands that the students become involved in the learning process, and not that they sit there receiving data. The age of lecture and of teacher up in front passing out data is behind us. The students must now become part of the team engaged in discovery. Discovery, not the mere accumulation of data.

MR. PARKER: That can certainly be extrapolated into the museum world. I have been around European and most American museums, and I have so often noticed that somebody will come along to some object, take a casual look at it, very carefully read the label, take another casual look at the object, and move on, because we're absolutely dedicated to the idea that the only information we can get is verbal information. So I have postulated the idea of a gallery with no labels at all, in which the answer to the questions you might ask is inherent in a very good look at the object. You could then, possibly, at the end of that gallery, check the information inherent in the object against the verbal information, if you feel that's necessary.

But I certainly think we have, somehow or other, to get away from the idea of organizing museums as if they were books. First of all, you write a story line and you use the artifacts as illustrations to your labels. That's backwards.

QUESTION: I'm old enough to remember the days of radio, when we listened to varieties of programs, which required our imaginations to fill in the pictorial aspect of the thing, and I can remember that it was difficult to adjust to television because it seemed very limiting. Instead of opening another dimension it did the reverse. It required only that one scene that was there.

DR. McLUHAN: One of the celebrated things about the radio generation was Gertrude Stein's[89] phrase, which Hemingway used as an epigraph for *Farewell to Arms*,[90] "You're the lost generation."[91]

Today people over twenty-one can't adjust. We're all in a "lost generation." That is, in our sensory lives we will never make the switchover. Only those coming up through the nursery will.

MR. PARKER: The focal point is that we have a tremendous tendency to equate imagination with visual imagination. If you have to fill in another sense this is also imagination.

DR. McLUHAN: A famous phrase in *Art and Illusion*[92] says that the whole difference between Western art and Oriental art is the difference between matching and making. The Westerner, a visual man, thinks of art as a repetition. He thinks of language as a repetition. But we're the only culture of which this has ever been true. All the other cultures think of art forms, including language, as making.

MR. PARKER: Western civilization is the only civilization in which the father draws differently from the child. That is, conceptually.

The Chinese artist is much more sophisticated in his rendering
than his child, but nevertheless the concept of the image-making
itself is the same. But in our society the child starts out drawing
like a Chinese artist, or drawing through all his sensory life.

By the time he enters his tenth year, the visual bias has come
along, and now he wants to draw the way his father draws.

DR. McLUHAN: The visual man is always looking for connection. "I
don't follow you." This is the autograph of the visual man.

MR. PARKER: "From my point of view."

DR. McLUHAN: "From where I'm sitting, I can only disagree with you
completely."

MR. PARKER: One of our politicians says, "From these boots it looks
like–."

QUESTION: I wonder whether we're getting terribly intellectual?

QUESTION: I think of us as not intellectual, and I believe you're right
when you say that the museums are a failure. But it's not the fault
of the work of art, it's because we're too intellectual about the
work of art.

MR. PARKER: I didn't hear your words.

QUESTION: I said that you're right when you say museums are failures. They are failures, because they don't give the work of art a
chance, and you're right when you say that it's displayed like a
dictionary.

DR. McLUHAN: We never said that the museum was a failure. The
museum is a magnificent illustration of our Western bias towards
the whole world of artifacts.

QUESTION: But we don't need to have that bias. For instance, you
mentioned primitive art. It's quite obvious that we can't, in a
museum, reconstitute the concept in which an African piece was
made. We can, if we give the piece a chance to speak for itself, but
we can't point it out. We can enable the viewer to rediscover it, but
we can't label it.

MR. PARKER: I'm not certain you're not suggesting that we create a
jungle in which to put it. But we *can* suggest.

I think one of the most salient areas is to so constitute the
spaces and the sensory involvement which lies within the object,

that it reveals the bent of the man who made it, which is probably
a highly tactile pattern-making.

DR. McLUHAN: The simplest poets hit upon the formula, "To suggest,
not to state."

QUESTION: But the same applies for sixteenth-century painting or
fifteenth-century painting. It's not only an organization of space.
There is much more in it.

DR. McLUHAN: There are many other spaces besides visual space.
There are acoustic[93] and tactile and olfactory spaces. They are all
in those paintings, of course. Space is not vision.

QUESTION: There is also the inner space.

DR. McLUHAN: Which is again the interplay of all the senses. Touch
is a form of overlay of all the senses simultaneously. It's integral.

QUESTION: But I don't think you can do too much wrong about that.
I think what can be done is what Mr. Parker does, to try to break
that visual circle and display the works of art so that they can
speak in their own language.

MR. PARKER: I would love to try a gallery, somewhere, with no
labels.

DR. McLUHAN: I'm not afraid of being intellectual, and on the other
hand I'm not eager to be. If you have to be intellectual in order to
be aware—

QUESTION: Aren't you placing yourself in the position of the voyeur
instead of being a viewer?

DR. McLUHAN: Pattern recognition is not visual. There are tactile
forms.

QUESTION: But the pattern is only a way of expression. We're
analyzing things.

DR. McLUHAN: You think we're using metaphors. We're talking literally and physically. We're not talking metaphorically. These aren't
figures of speech.

MISS HELEN FISHER (Director, Brooklyn Children's Museum):[94] What
is the tactility of our television. Isn't that metaphor?

DR. McLUHAN: This is literally, physically true. The thing moves in
on you physically. The television screen moves in on you. You don't
look at it.

MISS FISHER: If you're being literal, what do you mean by saying
that everyone who looks at television is being radioed?
DR. McLUHAN: X-rayed in depth. It's literally true. An X-ray is not a
visual thing.
MISS FISHER: An X-ray, I take it, if you're being literal—
DR. McLUHAN: X-ray is the process of penetrating to many levels.
You can't do that visually. Television is not a visual form.
MISS FISHER: If you project television onto a movie screen, is it the
same as movies?...Or what if a television show originates from a
motion picture?

[Dr. McLuhan says that a movie on television is no longer a movie; it
becomes television.]

QUESTION: I'm simply trying to understand something. A short time
ago I saw this film "8 1/2"[95] in a movie theatre, and I thought it was
just wonderful. It wasn't theatre, it was film. It was film art. I saw it
on television and it was a failure altogether. Why?
MR. PARKER: I can comment on that. The movie image as such is a
high-definition image. A variety of filmmakers are now moving to
low-definition image. The low-definition image requires you to fill
in more, so it's more involving. It's as if you're walking in a wood
and you hear a bird. Was that a bird? So we swivel our eyes around
and find the bird. If he will stay still long enough we will walk up
and touch him. And finally we say it's a duck-billed platypus or
whatever it might be.
    The point is, when we have discovered what it is, we charac-
terize it, file it away and forget it. Isn't this true?
    Television image is a low-definition image, which requires a fill-
in. In that sense it's an iconograph. Therefore, if you begin to take
a highly illustrative thing like a film technique and place it on an
iconographic, low-definition screen, something happens. It doesn't
come across. The best thing I have ever seen on television was
Marcel Marceau doing mime, because he moved into the Egyptian
image.

I know that on a television program in Houston, I said, "That's not a hand, right into the television camera. That's a little better—a fist—but on television that's the best hand-flat to the screen." You move into what I have called the significant profile—that aspect of the image which would be most appreciated by the sense of touch.

And talking about X-ray, we have discovered that doctors, in examining an X-ray, use their eye almost like a finger. They follow the edges, the contours. We checked this through the head camera, and found that they do follow contours just as if they were feeling.

DR. McLUHAN: An X-ray is not a picture.

MR. PARKER: So, immediately, the doctor with this low-definition image pulls the tactile sense in to explore.

DR. McLUHAN: The baseball world is present and handy for checking these points. Baseball on television is committing suicide and is disappearing very rapidly from the sports scene on television, because it's a one-thing-at-a-time game. It belongs to the nineteenth century and to our old, specialist phase of culture.

One thing at a time, perfectly executed; the new world is not like that. It's an interphase world of many phases and many methods simultaneously, and it prefers football or more tactile sports. Skin-diving, anything rather than baseball. Baseball is high definition. It's precise, elegant, finished.

MR. ROY MOYER (Director, American Federation of Arts):[96] I want to say that I think the Renaissance was not visual, not as visual as we have presumed, because I think our concept of visual arts is primarily a late nineteenth-century visual interpretation. Now artists couldn't exist until photography, so it began by comparison of photographs, and it became German *Kunstgeschichte*,[97] which was very scientifically, objectively oriented. The German critics also dealt primarily with public monumental art, rather than with intimate, personal art produced during the Renaissance.

The documents that are used to prove that Renaissance artists were visually oriented really dealt with a completely different matter, and at the time painting wasn't considered a liberal art.

They sought to justify it and, as a consequence, they sought to emphasize the value of the eye.

When nineteenth-century *Kunstgeschichte* people interpreted the Renaissance and came into contact with something like late Donatello,[98] they attributed it to his students. The whole definition of *non finito*[99] objects, particularly Bartholdi,[100] they dealt with not at all, because the artists never produced monumental works, and Michelangelo[101] was considered to be unfinished.

But it was an entire aesthetic of people who did handle things, sculpture, etc., and that's the sixteenth century, with mannerisms which would—

MR. PARKER: Can I state it in another way? I agree with you completely. We think of the Greek work as highly visual, but if you go and look at the models, it's obvious that they are very highly iconographic.

The same thing applies to high Renaissance. I would agree that our categorization of extreme visual bias is nineteenth-century. But I would think of it as something that began with the Greeks, received a great boost in the Renaissance, and developed until the nineteenth century, when it collapsed.

MR. MOYER: I don't think so. I think it happened in a very short time in a small place in Europe and that it very quickly disappeared, and the art of the connoisseur was really *non finito*.

MR. PARKER: I don't think we're trying to insist that the art at any point of the Renaissance was totally visual. But I think there can be no question at all that there is a great deal more visual bias in a Michelangelo than there is in a fourth-century artist.

DR. McLUHAN: Harley and I have a book coming out called *Through the Vanishing Point*. One of our exhibits is Bosch,[102] who gave a powerful dramatization of what was going on in their bosoms at that time. He had one foot in medieval space and one in Renaissance space, and the meeting of the two represented to him pure nightmare. The world of absolute nightmare was the meeting of the medieval and the Renaissance.

MR. PARKER: Such as the meeting of the nineteenth and twentieth centuries in Kafka,[103] where we find a parallel. He takes the common little clerk who lives in his little rooming-house, he creates the whole visual space of the nineteenth century, and suddenly introduces into it a man who turns into a cockroach. I think this kind of thing occurs at the abrasion of two contrasting things, when there is a radical switch between one culture and another.

MRS. ELIZABETH CONGER (Education Director, Museum of the City of New York):[104] May I say this about the involvement that you speak of: it may be a passing stage of the electronic age just as art is a series of waves. You can honestly predict the next interest in art, and when we speak in a broad way of the Renaissance, it has been brought out, of course, there was a progression through that wave. If you look at the process of art, it's as it happens, the light falls on the object, you say this is visual, it's reflected to the retina of the eye, the message is transferred to the part of the brain that recognizes it, it's carried on to the part of the brain that has feelings about it, it's directed to the hands, to the medium, to the canvas. If there is no particular emphasis on any of this process, all of these things are equally emphasized to get the high classical Greek, the balance between geometric design and realism.

But as that does get boring, there is also a reaction against everything that has just been started. People kick against what they have just outgrown, and we get the progress of more emphasis on what the eye—let's start with what the eye has seen. Take Monet.[105] It can be seen in various ways through the history of art.

But then the reaction against just what the eye has seen sets in and you get more interest in form and back again to composition. Then you get another reaction, and feeling must come back, as it did in Expressionism; and finally, if we want to get into our period, we have the interest in the art medium for its own sake—just the splashing of the paint on the canvas—and we all know right then and there that the next phase would be a return to realism.

MR. PARKER: How would you define realism?

MRS. CONGER: Representation as visual, three-dimensional, as we see it. I'm not talking about anything but art.

I can do the same thing in literature. I heard Gertrude Stein[106] give a lecture, taking literature as a medium. She talked about words in the Elizabethan Age.[107] Words were important, and they were lively because they were chosen.

Little by little somebody began to emphasize the phrase. Then Gertrude Stein went on to the rhymed couplet, the epigram. She went on, then, to Addison and the *Spectator Papers*,[108] with the perfect paragraph.

It's a wave, and if you say in your book that we're surprised by all-at-onceness,[109] we have to take it all in. We have little props built inside of us. Our own heart measures time, and somewhere, someone is going to find a way to stop the all-at-onceness and get a little trickle that he himself can comprehend, and even the savages living in a tribal community can have the tom-toms beat and raise their hearts collectively, but then they become individuals again. They get off into the woods to survive.

MR. PARKER: I would certainly bet against the return to visual realism.

MRS. CONGER: I think that there will be a return to individualism out of this tribal swarm of things.

DR. McLUHAN: There are two kinds of individualism, as the Dickens[110] character said, but they are both tribal.

The artist is not a category; it's a function of all of us. Art is probe. The only person who dares to look at the present in any period is the artist. The rest of mankind looks in the rearview mirror. We don't live in the twentieth century, we live in the nineteenth.

The Renaissance didn't live in the Renaissance, they lived in the Middle Ages. More's Utopia[111] was back an age, never the present. The present is hated by all people in all ages. Plato[112] never lived in the New World that he helped create. He lived back in the old, tribal world. His subject is entirely devoted to glorifying the tribal chieftains and tribal structure. He did not live in the new, civilized world. He didn't want to have anything to do with the Socrates[113] character.

In our time people hate this electronic all-at-onceness. But I'm determined to understand this age, because it's the only one I expect to live in. So I probe like an artist. I keep probing the present and what I probe I do not present as a view, but purely as conjecture.

MR. EVERETT ELLIN (Solomon Guggenheim Museum):[114] Making a comparison, your example about television signing the death warrant of baseball is very interesting, I think, because of our own involvement. I think television has killed baseball because television is a very involved medium and baseball is not an activity to allow for multi-level involvement, since it is essentially one act taking place at a time.

Television has very graphically demonstrated this; therefore we find baseball today rather uninteresting compared to the pre-television days. Aren't we likely to find the same thing happening in our own field of activity, because, whether we like it or not, we're deeply in an electronic age, and young people who are coming to museums, will, like the television viewer, expect a multilevel involvement in the museum?

The museum differs from baseball in that our ground rules are far more flexible,[115] and there is no reason why we can't program our own environment to shape it to the expectations and the attitudes of the people who come to us. In this sense we're not a game. We have this difference. Baseball cannot change its rules and make itself multi-level without losing its identity as such.

But I think museums can begin to think nonlinearly. They can begin to reshape the Renaissance phase, which they have lived in for 150 years, and begin to make it possible for the object to come with its own environment, with its own ambience. I think it's very important that we begin to think in these terms, that we give the new world a chance to become involved. That we think about eliminating the story line, the didactic Cook's Tour[116] that we take everybody on.

DR. McLUHAN: It helps to know how you got there, if you're going to change the ground rules, or why they were ever designed in the first place.

MR. ELLIN: I think we're here to think about these rules, and to think about what is happening and to see how, if at all possible, we can

begin to reshape our environment, in the light of what is inevitably
going to happen to us. Why can't we apply some intelligence to
this change?

MR. W. STEPHEN THOMAS (Director, Rochester Museum of Arts and
Sciences):[117] The point has come up for oversimplification of
information as opposed to what I consider initial excitement.

DR. McLUHAN: There is a wonderful example of oversimplification
hanging in a junk yard—a sign that says, "Help Beautify Junk
Yards. Throw Something Beautiful Away Today."

This is a counsel that I think we all understand, and we're all
engaged in. For example, the schoolmarm teaching grammar
is engaged in throwing away most of the beauty of the English
language.

This came up after a recent experience of a Circle Cruise.[118]
The greatest Surrealist gallery in New York is the cruise around
Manhattan Island on the Circle Line.[119] The objects on the shore,
in all their fantastic incongruity, one environment around another—
you never know what will happen next. Great, elegant structures
framing broken-down sheds and warehouses. I never saw any
Surrealist painting to equal the ordinary views you get around the
Island, and of course mingled with them are the most magnificent,
beautiful things.

Manhattan is an island and is a museum. It probably should be
preserved. Like people on other islands, the Manhattan population has taken to living in discontinuous, tribal space. Unlike any
other space I know of except England, the space of Manhattan is
discontinuous, nuclear, and pocketlike. "You can't get there from
here." This is true not only outside, but inside most homes. It's
completely unconscious on the part of the dwellers in this area.

The city also refrains to a large extent from story line. If you
notice the directions on the posts and street signs, they are the
most minimal and suggestive. There is no story line to be found in
New York signposts.

I'm personally strongly in favour of story lines, especially when
you're in a car. But the amount of complicated, non-visual space in
this area is to be matched only by London, and I have never seen a

comment about it by anybody. I never knew about it myself until a couple of months ago.

What we have been saying is "wrong" with the museum (if you can use that kind of value judgment) is that it isn't tribal enough. It's too continuous and connected.

MR. PARKER: Within exhibit areas, this is true. Nevertheless, the museum, generally, has a remarkably disconnected space. As I remarked earlier, I know a museum where the Far Eastern curator won't talk to the Near Eastern curator, or the ethnologist to the archaeologist.

DR. McLUHAN: But that's visual fragmentation and specialism.

MR. EUGENE KINGMAN (Director, Joslyn Art Museum, Omaha):[120] May I ask you to enlarge upon the comment that the artifact needs its environment? Whose environment? The environment of the artifact, or our idea of the museum, or the viewer's idea of it? Whose idea is this, and if the museum implants it, is this a story-line label bias?

DR. McLUHAN: The environment created by the artifact is the one from which it came. In this sense, museums have helped in the recreation of the original environmental process which produced the artifact.

There is no sense in putting an igloo in a heated space. There's no use showing off snowshoes behind glass. Right out there[121] you have *Alice in Wonderland*[122] illustrated by puppets behind glass, as if it were in Macy's.[123] Nothing could be more bizarre. It's more bizarre than anything Lewis Carroll[124] ever thought of.

MR. PARKER: In the book,[125] actually, we have a very interesting thing. We have a facsimile reproduction from one page of *Alice in Wonderland*, the original Dodgson manuscript[126] of it. Then we have the expurgated edition, illustrated by Tenniel,[127] in which all the grammar was cleaned up.

But interestingly, the Lewis Carroll drawing of Alice—this is Alice when she is ten feet tall—starts to distort at the feet. She has little girl's feet, and the attenuation starts and moves right up through the whole figure.

When you get the Tenniel edition set in type, you get a drawing which, if you cover it from the shoulders down, is a perfectly formed little girl. The only attenuation that Tenniel could manage to achieve, was to lengthen the neck and then, rather frighteningly, he raised the collar to hide it. So there was no real sense of the spaces of Lewis Carroll. And of course, the type bears no relationship to the illustrations.

What I'm simply saying is that Tenniel is a highly literate illustrator who was totally incapable of dealing with the mathematical and non-visual spaces of Lewis Carroll.

MRS. CARLIN GASTEYER (Assistant Director, Museum of the City of New York):[128] How do we protect our works if we can't use glass?

MR. PARKER: It's quite possible to make reproductions so the people can handle them. Another thing is air curtains instead of glass. Another is protection by electric eye.

I know there are certain fragile things in which we're forced to use glass. I was faced with this problem of glass in a habitat group of the West Coast Indians. What I did was to produce a case which was almost totally in the round, and you walk into the centre of it. Even though there had to be glass—and I'm still toying with air curtains—but if there has to be glass, people are in a complete surrounding with the round glass. It's all around them. This is one way of breaking through that glass barrier.

MR. ROBERT T. HATT (Director, Cranbrook Institute of Science, Michigan):[129] You made the comment a while ago that the museum tried to be a three-dimensional textbook, but I would like to inquire what an artifact out of place really means. In Montana, the artifacts have some suggestion of the background and sound and light intensity, but if you take one of those artifacts and put it in a shop window on Madison Avenue, it completely divorces itself from other associated artifacts. I don't think there is anything there but the price tag to identify it. I doubt that this can mean very much.

Being a sociologist, and one-time taxonomist, I'm basically thinking in terms of linear arrangements, and such museum designing I have done has been largely based on that. I would like to interpose one story in terms of lineality.

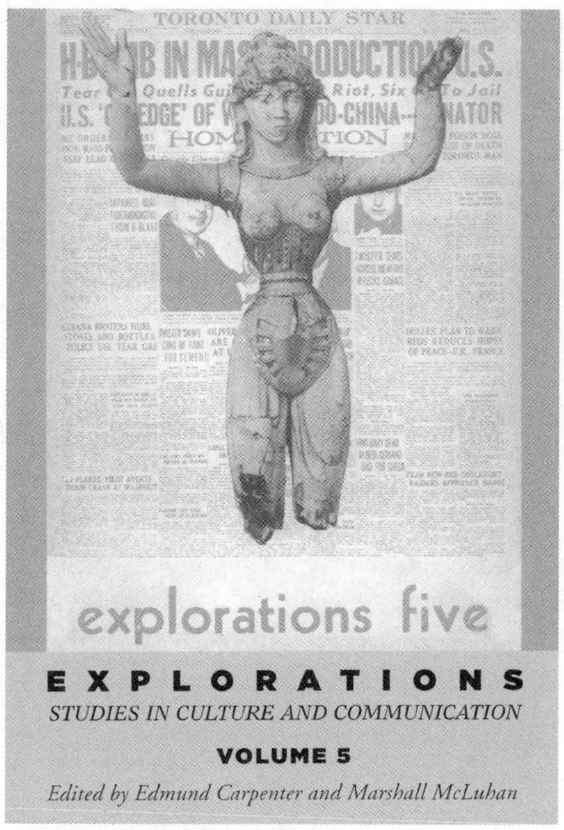

The front cover of *Explorations 5* (June 1955), edited by Marshall McLuhan and Edward Carpenter, featuring the Minoan ivory goddess, an icon of the Royal Ontario Museum collection. (Photo of cover by William J. Buxton.)

We used to say that a young man went to school and got a job and married, and had a family. Today he has a family, goes to school and then gets a job and then gets married.

MR. H.J. SWINNEY (Director, Adirondack Museum):[130] I would like to ask whether the plastic Parthenon[131] has the same virtue as the genuine?

MR. PARKER: The Parthenon is not a good instance. Let's take the goddess of sports of Knossos.[132] It could be possible to make duplicates which, while not as good, would do more than looking at it through glass.

If you could buy a facsimile—[Dr. McLuhan mentions the reproduction of the Parthenon in Nashville, Tennessee.][133]

MR. SWINNEY: But not many more people go to see it than see the original.

MRS. GASTEYER: It's not touched by people.

MR. PARKER: But the feeling via the tactile senses is another source of power.

MRS. GASTEYER: Wouldn't you have to have it reproduced in the same material?

MR. PARKER: I'm not suggesting you're going to get the same feeling. I'm merely saying that it's a good adjunct.

DR. McLUHAN: It came as a great shock, thirty or thirty-five years ago, to discover that the same words spoken to two different people mean quite different things. There is a book called *Seven Types of Ambiguity*.[134] To the literary community, in 1932, when this book came out, it was a great shock to discover that the most clear and simple expressions have totally different meanings to different people when written or printed. Words don't mean the same thing to any two people, and they shouldn't.

It is our job to make sense. Sense isn't something that should be stuffed down your throat. It's something you have to "make" on your own. You know, the whole theory of communication considers it as the transfer of a certain item to a certain area intact. That's for the legal profession, and they're not doing so well. They're having plenty of trouble.

DR. FRED J. DOCKSTADER[135] (Director, Museum of the American Indian, Heye Foundation):[136] If you're going to make sense, you would prefer to have guideposts—going back to your stricture about the museum without labels.

MR. PARKER: I didn't say it was a stricture.

DR. DOCKSTADER: Let me accept it as a stricture. I think it's a failure that any group can draw whatever conclusions they wish when there are no labels, and it's just as easy to draw false inferences. Don't you have a responsibility to point the direction and give some sort of clue?

DR. PARKER: I don't want to repeat the little story of the way people casually glance at something, read the label, casually glance and walk on.

Let's have an opportunity to look at something without reading the label. I have used a general label to identify an object. If you want more specific information, you press a button. The interesting thing is that very few people press the button except children, and they press it to watch the light come on.

DR. McLUHAN: A button could be pressed that would give the instant environment from which the artifact originally came.

DR. DOCKSTADER: You can't do this. You can't give an original environment in a museum.

DR. McLUHAN: You can. For example, the Eskimo igloo is a recent artifact. Eskimos[137] don't live in igloos, they live in stone houses on the seashore, somewhat round in shape. The igloo is a product of the white man's visitations. When the white man showed them the Primus stove, they added that to the snow house and it became possible to live there. Or if they didn't live there, they used it for their trapping lines.[138]

The igloo is not where they reside. I have yet to see a photograph of an Eskimo stone house. They're Stone-Age people. They're Paleolithic.[139] But what we see are these recent artifacts resulting from the white man's visit, which completely falsify the whole image of that culture.

MR. PARKER: To elaborate, I also suggested that, having given the person a real opportunity to explore a certain area, it should still be possible for us to have individuals to answer his question or we could even tape a machine with answers to the thirty most commonly asked questions, which the visitor could easily plug in to correct his mistakes.

I was thinking not of zoological specimens, but rather of objects of art at which I want people to really look. I think that many of the answers are inherent in a good, close examination. That is, within the limitations of a person's culture, background, and knowledge, the kind of questions he would ask are there.

DR. McLUHAN: Somebody said we don't know who discovered water, all we know is it wasn't a fish. One thing a man will never know is his own job, the one that goes around him. You have to cross boundaries to make discoveries. Maybe that's a useful strategy. If you want to make a discovery, you have to cross into the other man's world. You can't stay in your world.

MR. KEITH MARTIN (Director, Roberson Memorial Center):[140] Speaking of museums, what is a museum?

DR. McLUHAN: A museum is a kind of garden of the muses.[141] That's what the word means, and the muses are the various faculties of the human mind, extended out into environment.

Our new computer world is an extension of our nervous system into a total environment, not just around the planets but around the cosmos. What the muse of the computer will be, heaven knows. But the muses are the human faculties, mental, spiritual, sensory, extended out into the environment. A museum is then, presumably, a collection of all of them in a kind of consciousness.

MR. PARKER: I was at a conference at Columbia some time ago, and they were using the word "creative" as if they were playing ping-pong. I challenged people to define it, and there was a blank silence. Then they asked me to define it. This is a good ploy, always.

I hesitated to define it, but I know there is one thing always there, and that is the ability to challenge an assumption. The function of a museum is to set up an environment which allows the challenge of assumptions. This is the field in which creativity can occur.

It is also other things that are obvious. But I think one of the most important things that museums can do today is to help solve one of our biggest problems: our incapacity for intercultural dialogue. The Chinese say something; we interpret it from the Western point of view and scream. Perhaps the Chinese didn't mean what we thought.

One of the big possibilities for museums is to explain one culture to another. I don't think we're doing that very successfully. Because we're constantly feeding it through the strainer of Western thought. I don't think that's the way to go about it.

We have somehow or other to orient people to the particular culture which produces the object that allow us to have an idea of the way it feels about spaces. What its attitude is towards a given statement in politics.

DR. E. McCLUNG FLEMING (Education Head, Henry du Pont Winterthur Museum):[142] I think your suggestion is that information and labels without involvement isn't good enough. This is a very important and acceptable point. I need some help on another point.

It seems some of the time as though your recommendations are for total involvement without this information; but just a minute ago you implied that you would have both. I'm not quite clear how important the information or the label remains in the attempt to get involvement.

MR. PARKER: With so many disciplines, and so many children, if you take any one discipline, you can assume that perhaps four tenths of one percent of the children taking part in a certain museum experience are going to become specialists in that particular field. It's useless trying to give that to everybody. We used to have Latin labels in the past, and the whole linear, sequential thing. This is rather futile, something that most people aren't interested in. When you're talking about ornithology, what it means generally to all people—

DR. McLUHAN: It's for the birds.

One of the things that has become important is leisure. An artist is never at work; it's because he's always at leisure. When he's totally involved in his work, he is not working, it's play, it's leisure.

A gentleman never had any visible means of support because he was supposed to be an integral being. He didn't fragment himself, he was totally involved, always at leisure. A great image of Sherlock Holmes himself.

We're heading that way. Instead of heading into a world of joblessness, we're heading towards a period of creative involvement, which is leisure. Involvement is far more demanding of our energies than any job could be. But when you're totally involved, you're playing, you're not working. You're at leisure.

This is a paradox; but although the creative act is one of intense activity, it's not work. It's leisure, because all of our faculties are engaged.

So you can get a line on the museum, find out how much it tends to engage all of the faculties, and how much it appeals to special awareness and special interests only.

DR. FLEMING: The answer here is both.

MR. PARKER: My only answer is, yes, the information should be available for those people who are specialists, or who wish to become specialists, but for the general public, no. They should be offered an experience which they will remember.

And getting back to the words "pattern recognition," the public gets a broad concept of what it is about and why it is important. How many people walking through the streets of New York now are invertebrate paleontologists? Yet it is important to tell them some of these things.

MR. HARMON H. GOLDSTONE (City Planning Commission):[143] Early this morning you spoke about how little your daughter had obtained from her history of Canada, and this is the way modern history is taught. But I wonder, patterns and perceptions of total patterns of chronology—couldn't they be organized by playing on sequences and simultaneity in such a way that history could be taught more meaningfully by the school or the museums, a museum such as the one we're in, which is endeavouring to teach history? I wonder whether chronological patterns can't be created as a very valid communication of history?

MR. PARKER: I think that the chronology would probably form the perimeter around patterns. For instance, by encouraging a proper understanding of space as it is in poetry and painting, you would arrive at children who could look at a Titian without the foggiest idea of who painted it, but would know it had to happen at a certain point in history because of the broad sense of pattern they had when facing it.

This is the kind of pattern recognition I want. We're not trying to train historians, but they started teaching my daughter the subject as if they were.

DR. McLUHAN: One of the peculiar things about our twentieth
century is that the backward countries have all the advantages.
They don't have to go through the primitive stages that we went
through, to arrive at General Motors.[144] They get the latest. That
was true of the United States in 1770. They started with the latest
technology of the world, and now you museum people are helping
them acquire the early ones. The pre-literate ones are now being
built in. But in a more advanced country we don't get the latest
first. We have to go through all the earlier phases in order to arrive
at the latest.

MR. PARKER: *Apropos* of that, Ted Carpenter was telling us about
the Eskimo who can be trained to fix an airplane engine. He can't
read a blueprint, but if you give him one motor that's running
properly, he will tune the other one to the same pitch.

DR. McLUHAN: At a university in Vancouver they have been experimenting by taking people out of the African jungle and in five
months turning them into proficient mechanics. But they discovered that they were equally good at prescribing particular therapy.
Give them a case history, a sick man, and they can spot the trouble
just as quickly as they can in the airplane engine. Because they
play the total field, they don't have a point of view. They do it with
smell.

The medical profession is completely fragmented, but these
primitives are so electronic that they can cope with this all-at-
onceness without any effort. It's amazing how long it takes for
news like that to travel.

And do you know why? People don't like to hear that kind of
news. It's unpleasant, and upsetting. Most of the important discoveries are so upsetting that they never get mentioned in decent
company.

You talk about "all the news that's fit to print"—that only means
all the news that you can fit into the old printed format. Anything
that won't fit into that kind of motivation is not news. It's left out.

MR. HATT: On your tape you made a point that startled me, because
I think of art works as being largely silent and having definite
visual content.

DR. PARKER: An Eskimo, in a blinding snowstorm, has no possibility
of seeing anything, but he can tell by the direction of the wind, the
kind of snow, the way the snow crunches underfoot, exactly where
he is, and he very seldom gets lost. As for the highly visual element
of the Eskimo culture, I would disagree. It's very, very highly
tactile. Its function is to be made and passed around while the
chap who made it recounts the story of the way he killed the bull.
When it is passed around and he has told his story, it's thrown
away. It's not regarded as an object of art.

Feeling is so very important.

DR. McLUHAN: The Balinese[145] are the same: "We don't have any art.
We do everything as well as possible."

MR. ELLIN: I think there's an interesting point in your Eskimo story.
In your account of how the Eskimo can go through snow, storm,
over terrain, and also paddle a kayak through dense fog for five or
six hours, and by sensing differences in the flow of currents, arrive
at a remote point. Aren't we facing a generation of children in our
own environment who really are Eskimos? Won't they be able to
chart courses without a didactic map telling them how to get
there?

Doesn't the fatigue that we find in the museum environment
when the visitor is given an original, programmed itinerary—I
get tired when I face the task, when I know the exact dimensions
of the task. But when I start out on something that's completely
unprogrammed, and I am able, I can keep at it for twelve or fourteen hours.

I think we're going to find that in our new museum's visitors.
I don't think we can use ourselves as a fair criterion of the type of
person we will be addressing ourselves to. We have a new generation, a whole world of little Eskimos in our own society.

MR. PARKER: I agree completely. I think one of the failures is the
manner in which we make a person study a given subject. Curators
study ethnology; the way they have studied it is via various linear,
sequential methods. So they think that that's the only way to show
it. It may be the only way to show it—I would hesitate to argue—to
a man who is going to be a professional ethnologist.

MR. ELLIN: It may be the only way to show it to somebody who is
used to finding his way only with a linear map. When you're
dealing with another kind of person who has developed another
set of senses and another set of skills, you have to begin restyling
the directions.

MR. PARKER: Therefore I would recommend that the museum begin
to hire a lot of the more alive young people. Let them tell us
something.

DR. McLUHAN: By the way, the same pattern of development is
occurring in our business world at the highest levels. The organization chart is not very necessary anymore. It's no longer of use.
That little series of classified levels and categories, and initiatives,
doesn't obtain in business anymore. The dialogue and interplay
between those levels are so considerable that they have had to
cross out the organization chart these last twenty years.

The business community is not motivated by disinterested
passion for knowledge, but it is desperately eager to survive, and
therefore its motivation in learning is considerable. I have spoken
a great deal to management groups over the past twenty years,
and I have always found them very flexible, very eager to learn,
and they have a lot to learn in our time.[146] They're just as desperately hard-pressed by innovation in new technology as any part of
the community.

You can find a lot in common with their problems. You could sit
down with any group of managers and discuss organization problems and be amazed at how much you have in common with them.
I strongly recommend this, because it's desirable to have dialogue
at all levels of the community.

DR. JAMES HESLIN (Director, New York Historical Society):[147] I was
curious to know why you thought the Renaissance was decadent
and your colleague thought the Ming Dynasty was decadent.

DR. McLUHAN: We never used the word. Did I use the word
decadent?

DR. HESLIN: Metaphorically.

DR. McLUHAN: In terms of censuring. I can't imagine why a change
from the medieval involvement in all the senses, I can't imagine

why that should be decadence. Once you switch into one sense, then you can say decadence; but when you're using all the senses, you can't have decadence.

As we return to all the senses now in the electronic age, we call that decadence because it's a complete lapse of visual culture.

DR. HESLIN: My point is that you said the Renaissance was decadent. May I ask what Renaissance you meant?

DR. McLUHAN: I think we're talking about the fifteenth or sixteenth century, something like that.

MR. PARKER: 1442, the Gutenberg Bible,[148] to the nineteenth century.

DR. McLUHAN: It doesn't refer to the Renaissance as a period.

MR. PARKER: But rather as visual bias.

DR. HESLIN: But you mentioned the Ming Dynasty, which happens to be from about 1350.

MR. PARKER: I understand from the only Chinese scholar I know that it is regarded as a decadent period.

DR. McLUHAN: When the Japanese art treasures[149] visited Toronto about a year ago, Harley was standing in front of one of the items, a sculpture of a beggar, and he said to one of the men in charge, "Did they have phonetic literacy in the eleventh century in Japan?" It was the only "visual" representational item in the whole collection.

So the curator made off to his experts and came back with quite an amazed expression, and he said, "Yes, there was a period during the eleventh century, where Japan had a phonetic alphabet, in the Western sense."

But he said that it isn't generally known. "How did you know?" Well, that's how he knew. This was a realistic statue, and looked like something out of the Western world: eleventh-century Japan.

DR. HESLIN: I don't like to press this, but I don't think my question was answered.

[Dr. McLuhan indicates that he does not believe it can be answered.]

DR. HESLIN: Then I take it that the one Chinese scholar proved that the Ming Dynasty was decadent? Why do you accept what he said?

MR. PARKER: Because it served a purpose.

QUESTION: But you don't know it yourself. You're trying to—

QUESTION: Is it a fact that you don't know it for yourselves?

[Mr. Parker and Dr. McLuhan agree that "decadent" is an unfortunate word, which has outlived its usefulness.]

MR. MOYER: May I ask what you see as the future of the picture gallery in museums? Does a display of paintings out of context on the wall have virtue or value or virtuosity, or aesthetic value, or is it just a display of objects on the wall?

MR. PARKER: My answer to that is that I'm unalterably opposed, in the twentieth century, to fragmentation, and if we're going to show paintings, I would like to see Rembrandts[150] juxtaposed to El Grecos[151] in order that one thing can strike sparks off the other. It's also possible to use other techniques to explain spatial contexts, philosophical attitudes, all kinds of things, by means of film stills, sound, various other methods.

MR. MOYER: Or other art forms in conjunction with paintings?

MR. JAROLD O. TALBOT (Director, Old Museum Village of Smith's Cove):[152] You suggested the plastic Parthenon. Would you also suggest reproductions of paintings?

MR. PARKER: We have them, and very high fidelity ones. Some of them from Switzerland and Czechoslovakia. I don't think any reproduction is the same as the original, but surely there is some value in reproduction.

MR. TALBOT: Is that the value we want to give to children?

MR. PARKER: It's a point worth examining. I don't think you're going to solve that. You know the whole world is flooded with reproductions.

MR. TALBOT: I'm against plastic as used today or modern paintings as a creative thing.

MR. PARKER: The point about it is, having enclosed a piece of sculpture in glass, is it not true that if you provide a person with something, a reproduction of it which he can feel—isn't that a small step towards giving him more information?

DR. McLUHAN: Let's suppose that an object is shown on a video tape, closed circuit, in the act of being made, instead of as the end product—that you actually showed an Eskimo making and enjoying one of these things. This could be done for almost anything in a museum.

MR. SWINNEY: Could that be done equally well by a real projection motion picture?

DR. McLUHAN: I don't know. In India, natives will pay for the privilege of standing behind the screen.

MR. TALBOT: Will the scale be the same?

MR. PARKER: I point out that you're challenging the whole television industry and film industry as vicarious experience. I don't think there is as much validity in watching the film of Vietnam warfare as there is in being there. It's a totally different experience.

MR. TALBOT: You do have a soundtrack sometimes, too, which is untrue.

MR. PARKER: It is just badly designed. It's like the girl on that Circle Line, who talked incessantly, platitudes and pieces of random data, in which I can't imagine anybody really being interested. We were accused of being rude because we weren't listening.

DR. McLUHAN: You put a soundtrack around a pictorial experience like the Circle Line, that's as distorting as putting a soundtrack around a silent movie. It completely alters the whole image, and this barrage of platitudinous data, while we were watching the most thrilling scene—this is a most amazing, surrealist experience.

QUESTION: What would you say of the value of the moving-camera eye interpreting a painting to the viewer?

MR. PARKER: I can tell you one of my own experiences. I saw *The Titan*[153] before I saw the *Pietà*.[154] I found the movie extremely exciting. I found the *Pietà* quite a let-down.

QUESTION: Would this also apply to the use of tape recordings geared to people standing in front of an exhibit?

MR. PARKER: I think it depends upon the demonstrator. I have found some of them terrible, because again, they're working on the basis of data assimilation. Instead of explaining anything about the painting, they're telling you about when the painter was born, etc.

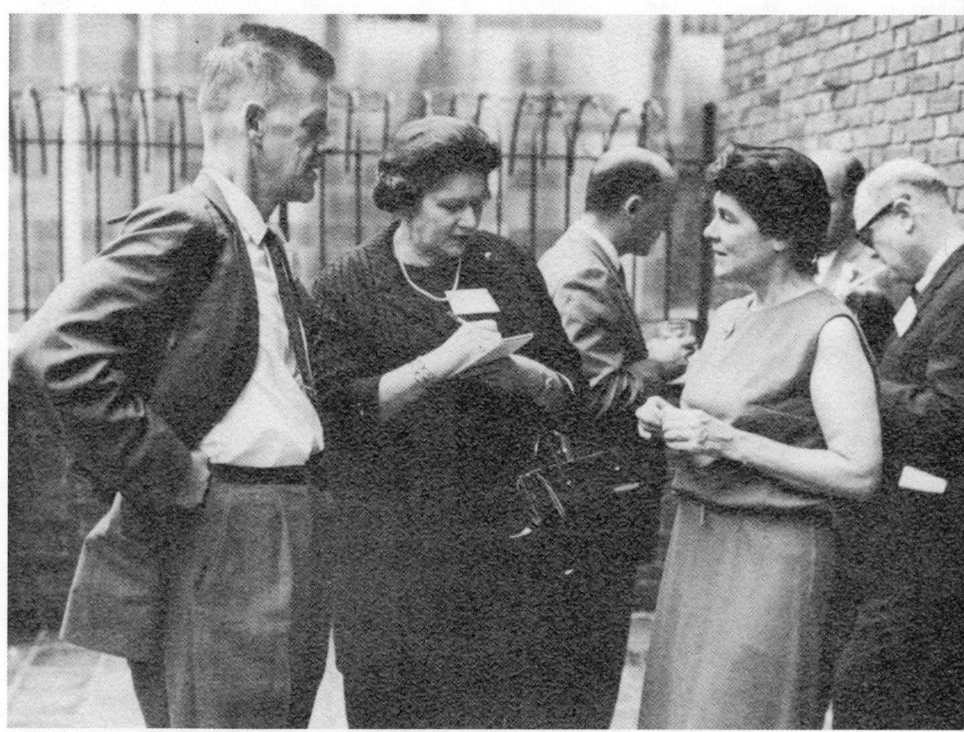

A glimpse of the informal conversations that took place between sessions. From left to right, Eugene Kingman, Director of the Joslyn Museum, Omaha; Mrs. Betty Kingman (1911–2005), who made significant contributions to understanding the archeological past of Rocky Mountain National Park; Norman S. Rice (1926–2021), Curator of the Albany Institute of Art, now called the Albany Institute of History & Art (AIHA); Mrs. Ralph R. Miller; and Robert Wheeler of Sleepy Hollow Restorations, an educational and historic preservation organization founded in 1951 by John D. Rockefeller Jr., now called Historic Hudson Valley. (Photo by Werner J. Kuhn.)

If you did a really intelligent job, and illuminated the object, I think it's an added dimension to the experience.

MR. MILLER: Ladies and Gentlemen, we will serve lunch very shortly, and then we will go by bus to the American Museum of Natural History for a close examination of galleries, with comments by our principal speakers here.

[Adjourned 12:30 PM.]

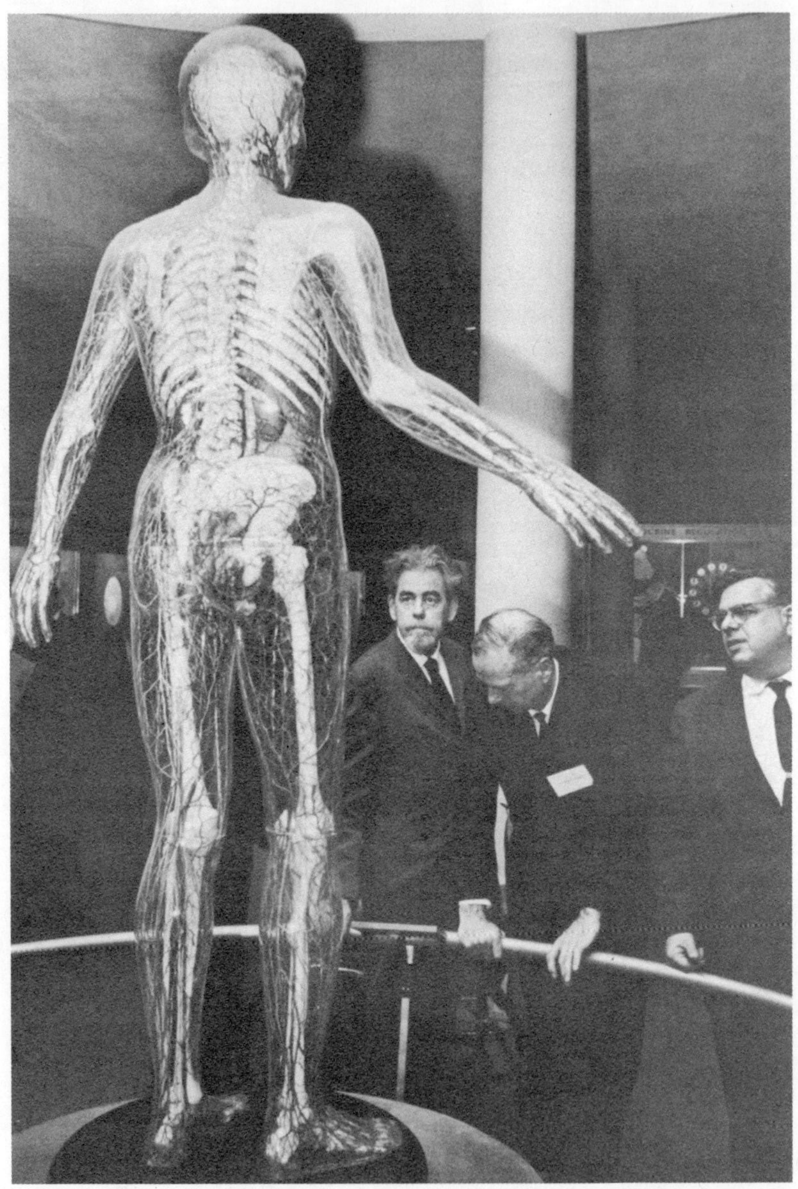

Despite visiting several exhibits at the American Museum of Natural History, this image of McLuhan (centre) and Parker (left) examining a model of the human body (titled *Transparent Woman*) was the only one included in the original publication. (Photo by Werner J. Kuhn.)

[The Monday afternoon session of the Museum Program convened
at the American Museum of Natural History, Mr. Ralph Miller
presiding.]

MR. MILLER: The first thing we're going to do is to wander through
this hall, called the Hall of the Biology of Man,[155] and hopefully
you will all get a general impression, or a more specific one, and
after that we will program further what we will do. This is known
as a play-it-by-ear tour.

DR. McLUHAN: This is the plight of mechanical man in an organic
world.[156]

MR. PARKER: This, to me, is a poor illustration: tissues.

DR. McLUHAN: There they are, ready for use. What tissues do they
refer to?

QUESTION: Does this give the public too much to dwell on? Too
many words and too many pictures?

DR. McLUHAN: It all began with the fall of man. This is the reproduction process in full spate, all this nonsense.

MR. PARKER: Take photographs of all this stuff, put them in printed
form, and you have a book. It isn't a museum. The whole concept is
a written one.

[Standing in front of reproduction of abdominal organs.]

MR. PARKER: There is a nasty sight.

DR. McLUHAN: It gives you pause.
    A name is, in a sense, a numbing of perception. When you're
with a group, I don't know any way of having a private reaction.
That display creates numbness. You can't produce a group reaction
for a private thing. The layout is for an individual, not for a group.

[Walking through Hall of the North American Forests.]

DR. McLUHAN: These are all very pleasing exhibits, but you might
as well be turning the pages of a book.

[Standing in front of cuts of tree.]

QUESTION: I find it very interesting that you would have walked
    past all the ecological groups representing New York State, and
    walked right over here to the tree.
DR. McLUHAN: There's even a piece of bark.
MR. PARKER: What did they use this for, as a building material? This
    is a California redwood.
DR. McLUHAN: We were talking about the news items in the morning
    paper, about their getting frozen seeds out of the ice in Canada;
    once they start exploiting that side of the Canadian icebox, they
    had better beware. It could be quite startling, some of the critters
    that might leap out of the icebergs.

[In response to inaudible question by Mr. Miller.]

DR. McLUHAN: Mostly I see the dimensions still pressing down on
    the individual. People suddenly clam up when they get into this
    area because they feel overwhelmed.
MR. MILLER: Don't you think it can be likened to Gothic architecture?
DR. McLUHAN: No, Gothic is a relatively pictorial world compared
    with these monoliths. Gothic is much more tactile.
MR. MILLER: Did you see the trees in California, the redwoods?
DR. McLUHAN: I have driven through one of them.
MR. PARKER: I would like to hear those birds singing.

[Walking through the Hall of the Biology of the Invertebrates.][157]

GUIDE: This hall is not complete. We have opened up the sections.
MR. PARKER: This is realistic.
MR. MILLER: Is this the new gallery?
GUIDE: This hall is the one that has taken about ten years to conceive,
    and we're now in the fourth year of preparation. There is so much
    here. We think these little displays are special, this tidal zone.
MR. PARKER: It's very interesting.

DR. McLUHAN: It's environmental, as far as you go, particularly environmental—but somehow or other, fragments of environment.

How about odours? In this kind of an environment, the overwhelming effect that balsam and pine and resinous odours have would be great.

MR. PARKER: Salt water.

DR. McLUHAN: I don't think the salt-water odour can compare with the resins.

MR. PARKER: This is a salt-water tidal flat.

DR. McLUHAN: That's driftwood. I think the olfactory is very relevant to that. They could get tremendous involvement through the use of pine odours.

How about the possibility of programming the olfactory in that forest world? It would be tremendous. This would be salt water as well. I think the olfactory is a very valuable factor in this kind of setup.

MR. MILLER: We thought of it in the Museum of the City of New York. We had shops of New York and we got someone to manufacture three brands of drug smells, awful, horrible, and terrible. People would come up and say, "My God, it really smells like a drugstore."

But this is quite possible where it goes on cue. This is an area that the museums haven't touched. In this kind of a museum it's hard to do. The communicative factor—

DR. McLUHAN: In terms of the creature sounds.

MR. MILLER: How about squashing floors when you're going through the forest? You know in the Kodak Exhibit at the World's Fair,[158] this moon thing, they had a surface that was like a path, and you could meander around and about. You were very conscious of the fact that you were on scrunching surfaces.

DR. McLUHAN: Does it attempt to simulate conditions on the moon?

MR. MILLER: I don't think so. They had treated the surface.

[Discussion in Auditorium]

MR. PARKER: It's amusing that everybody sits in these straight lines and the chairs are all laid out in rows. I once gave a program in Wayne State,[159] and we did a fade-out. That is, we photographed a book page with the lines of type and the title, and then we faded that into a classroom, and there was scarcely any difference. There were still lines of type and the teacher's desk was a title. Then we faded that into parking lots where you had all the rows of cars. Then into a supermarket shelf and it was the same thing.

In this way we can see, very definitely, the pervasive lineality of our whole mode of organization.

I have to announce that Dr. McLuhan had to leave for two reasons.

One, he was overtired, and he isn't well. He hasn't been well these last few days.[160] And inasmuch as he's a close personal friend, I feel very responsible for him and I told him to go home. I thought the choice was between keeping him on here and not having him here tomorrow, or letting him go home now.

So if I may carry on as well as I can by myself: I do like the dialogue, because I find that when I forget something, Marshall will give me a lead, and I will remember, or I will say something and it will bring something to his attention.

In going through these galleries, I just have one salient feeling, or two, actually. And they are both related to the visual business.

Apparently, the term "visual bias" is causing some consternation, so I would like to explain that before I go on. The visual bias doesn't have anything to do with bias of ideas. It has only to do with the orchestration of the sensory life. That is, in certain cultures this or that sense goes into high definition.

Certainly, there can be no question at all, looking at it historically, that the impact of the technology of printing in the fifteenth century did give rise to an extreme, supreme interest in the bias of vision. I understand at the end of the fifteenth century, fifty-eight years after the Gutenberg Bible, there were nine million printed volumes in Europe. This constituted a tremendous technological change, and it is at this point—where man is capable of taking the whole, resounding, oral world and translating it into the visual, abstract cycle—that you get these visual biases.

I would say that in many cases, instead of going through this museum, I would find out what the best available book was. I would go to the library, take the book home, sit in an easy-chair, and go to work. I'm sure I would get just as much information out of that book as I do out of this gallery, because it is book-oriented. It follows what I was talking about this morning. First of all, you create a book pattern, a beginning, a middle, and an end. Then you take artifacts, and in the habitat groups, plastic figures, and use them as illustrations to your story line. I think that there is as much validity in doing that as there is in putting movies on television screens. I don't think it works.

The second thing I have to say is that, personally, I think the picture-window diorama[161] or habitat group[162] is a nineteenth-century pictorial form. It necessitates a single point of view, and automatically calls for a kind of dispassionate survey.

There was one we went into where there was a surround, where you had the window in front of you and on each side, so that you had a sense of being surrounded by that tropical rain forest. I think this is an improvement on the picture-window idea.

I think that the exhibits are beautifully designed and executed. But from my point of view, they do not exploit the museum as a medium. I would like to hear comments.

I missed, in that wrap-around diorama, the sounds of birds.

QUESTION: The first point you made about going home and reading a book—personally, I couldn't agree with you more. But what about the people who are not book-oriented?

MR. PARKER: They are not going to read those labels.

QUESTION: I think most of us are aware that we get people in museums who get an educational experience through the visual presentation that they would never get from reading, and this may be the one thing we do have to offer to this generation and the next.

MR. PARKER: Our technology has developed such sophisticated methods of picturing, I think these are archaic. If I wanted to use pictures to tell a story I would go into film.

QUESTION: I was thinking of the actual, three-dimensional objects.

MR. PARKER: I think film, supplemented by three-dimensional objects might work. I'm not against three-dimensional objects. This is the exact quality that a museum has: that it does present actual artifacts. I don't think we should denigrate or move away from it.

MR. HATT: Some twenty years ago, I remember that Margaret Mead,[163] in this institution, wrote an editorial on the fact that the museum was the one place where you could go and deal with reality. So much else in our life is fake or secondhand.

MR. PARKER: I disagree with this as a concept.

MR. HATT: And things made of plaster, where you're not getting reality but a pretty darn good interpretation?

MR. PARKER: I don't think, for example, that if we film an African tribe, it's the same experience as being with the African tribe. We come pretty close when we get the sound, emotion, colour. But it's a different experience.

I would hate to set up a hierarchy of values saying one is better than the other. I would say one is different from the other. I don't think of a film as a secondhand experience. Not at all. It's a firsthand experience of a film.

MR. HATT: Miss Mead said that you could spend five minutes with an elephant in a zoo and get a better experience than by looking at a whole herd of them standing still downstairs. I think this is a very valid point, but there are different ways of reaching your audience.

MR. PARKER: Myself, I believe that museums are a unique communication medium. And I think that we have had too great a tendency to imitate, just as every technique has—the first motor car looked like a horseless carriage. Television is still in its infancy, inasmuch as it is still using film. Film used the book. Everything feeds on the former method.

Museums are still feeding on the book. What I'm asking for is, please let us recognize that this is a unique medium. Explore it and begin to exploit it.

MR. WALTER S. DUNN (Director, Buffalo and Erie County Historical Society):[164] The history of the museum is not of feeding on the book, but feeding on the collection of curios itself.

MR. PARKER: Presentation techniques have been those of feeding on the book. I know the original curiosity cabinet[165] sort of thing had no line at all, but that isn't what it has developed into, these big museums of the nineteenth and twentieth centuries which depend largely, for their methods, upon the book form.

MR. GOLDSTONE: Of the two equally valid museum presentations, one is strictly information, and I agree with you that what you saw in the galleries down here you could get as well, certainly, from reading a book. But there is the other function, which is stimulation and motivation, particularly of children who come into a museum with no motivation whatsoever.

If the whole technique is simply to stimulate with experience and motivate them to learn, are you going to throw out the other aspects of really conveying information, or can you do both?

MR. PARKER: I think you can and should do both, because the museum is a unique institution, and to eliminate the functions of the museum, or to limit its function only to the child who is vaguely interested, is wrong.

I think the study collections are very pertinent. The technique I suggested this morning—pressing a button to get more data if you wish—is probably valid. But I know that nothing you could design would be more capable of alienating the interest of children than some of those galleries.

MISS FISHER: There is, perhaps, an interesting commentary on what we were saying this morning about reproductions. In those galleries downstairs those models, those beautiful glass models, in themselves, could never be reproduced. It's a whole new dimension of reproduction. They can never be reproduced.

MR. PARKER: I think we should exploit this more. We were talking about the voice. I don't know if this is a normal situation in the Museum, but there were some people in that room, when the voice was being fed from the plastic woman,[166] which became an irritation because you really couldn't hear it.

If it's anything like the museums I come from, on Monday, Tuesday, Wednesday, Thursday, Friday you have to look for people. Occasionally you will find somebody wandering around aimlessly. Saturday and Sunday you can't get inside the place. This is an aspect of museums which might bear examination. I know that our museum has the stupidest hours. It opens at ten o'clock in the morning, and closes at five. That means that no one who works can ever get to the museum except Saturday and Sunday, and when you go on Saturday and Sunday you can't get in, or if you get in you can't see anything.

We have ninety-five galleries in our place, and we get as many as eight thousand people in an afternoon, because it's only open from two to five on Sundays.

DR. JOSEPH CHAMBERLAIN (Assistant Director, American Museum of Natural History):[167] I would like to speak on that, because it's not valid in New York. At least, this museum has been open at night for many years. Even though there is a pattern of increasing attendance, the night programs don't attract visitors.

We can attract visitors at any time for a special program of activity, and we do. We have many activities in this museum every night; but opening it to the public in the hope that they will walk in the doors has been tried and proved impossible.

MR. PARKER: I think you do have to have special programs in order to attract people. This raises one of my pet theories. I want to build what I call a "newseum"[168] which consists of a building outside the museum proper, but which draws on the artifacts and material of the museum for its shows. The idea of a newseum is that it is concerned with news, any news in the world which is of great moment, whether it occurs in science or archaeological discovery or what have you, or whether it occurs on the political scene.

I think it would be possible to put on shows of those items which are in the news, and museums can do a unique job. Regardless of what the press can do, or film, we can do something else. We can show the artifacts of that culture. If you're having trouble in the

Congo,[169] let's put on a show about the Congo. I think we can do
that, and I think it would attract people.

MR. CHAMBERLAIN: This is what we're doing in the special program
in this museum. Its being open at night doesn't represent our not
using the other aspects of the news.

MR. PARKER: I didn't even know the hours of this museum, but I
know this is prevalent in most museums: they don't stay open at
night.

QUESTION: Your comment, a moment ago, that this museum is not
exploiting its exhibits downstairs, is I dare say, the first of your
opinions of the day that I might possibly share. However, the
problem concerns me, and I suspect concerns anyone else who is
connected with exhibits in the field of natural history.

Is there any precise recommendation you have for making the
situation a whole lot better? Because we could introduce films and
all kinds of push buttons and gadgets and make the whole place
exciting, and yet as one follows the visitors about a museum that
uses all of these magnificent new electronic viewers, they don't look
at the film or the slide presentation, or the tape lecture any longer
than they look at the labels. They don't get any more from it.

MR. PARKER: They don't get any more from it, you say?

QUESTION: No, because the attention span with the slide or tape-
recorded lecture is quite brief. Just as brief as it is with the label.
We provide two minutes of film, and the casual visitor will pay no
more attention than he does to the label.

MR. PARKER: May I suggest that it's poor design? If you're using a
method of communication and nobody is reading—

QUESTION: Let me suggest that Charles Eames[170] is a poor film
designer.

MR. PARKER: It may not be the film. It may be the environment of the
film. Let's face it quite frankly. If I produce a newspaper that
nobody reads, I have a lousy newspaper.

MR. SWINNEY: But one of the most read newspapers in the United
States, *The New York Times*, is among the most linear.

MR. HATT: At the French Pavilion at Expo, there was a small series
of films which were very inferior, and yet when I was there a good

many people were watching the films, simply because this was one
of the most comfortable places to sit down. At some other films
you had to stand on the hard floor.

QUESTION: I think it's important to recognize that you don't solve
the problem of getting information across simply by taking it out
of the printed format and taping it or putting it on film. When the
thinking is organized exactly the same way, and you just change
the medium, you're not dealing with the problem. But if you start
using images in a fresh way and begin to throw multiple images at
somebody and give them a selection of four sound channels, of
which one, perhaps, has the sound of the forest superimposed with
voice, while the other might have just the sound, you begin to
think in a multi-sensory way, and then you're putting your information across in the new way rather than just transposing the
medium.

MR. PARKER: That's right. I had a very interesting demonstration.
Tony Schwartz,[171] the sound man, taped first of all a young man
commenting about his dating habits. He would rather date in the
summer than in the winter, for various reasons, and so on. Then he
started over again, and made some different comments. Then Tony
put them together and overlaid them, and both your ears sort of
went out like this, you were trying to catch both things at once.
And the sense of involvement was amazing.

As long as there was a single voice, you could just sit back
and listen, but as soon as these two voices began to come out at
you simultaneously, a tremendous sense of involvement was felt.
I'm going to suggest that I didn't see many dissatisfied customers
watching films in the Czechoslovakian Pavilion.[172] I didn't see
anybody being annoyed at *Labyrinth*.[173]

QUESTION: I quite agree. I think the Czech Pavilion and *Labyrinth*
were the finest things. But there are other problems.

Of course, the whole basic idea of the museum is to provide
information in an interesting way. But it wouldn't be possible
for me to reproduce a good deal of what you saw at the Czech
Pavilion. It would be tremendously expensive. It's all right for six
months, but how are we going to stand it for six months? If you

went behind the scenes you could see how many technicians they
have to operate it.

MR. PARKER: I know. I tried to persuade Fordham to buy it.[174]

MR. KINGMAN: I have felt for some time that the exhibition designer
often carries his art too far. His imaginative goes beyond his
gadgetry and projection. The visitor comes in—particularly little
Johnny—and he's intrigued by how it is done. He still doesn't know
what the exhibit is all about. I think our goal should be the
simplest thing possible.

MR. PARKER: I would answer that it's just bad design.

MR. SWINNEY: There's a tendency, in this world, to confuse novelty
with virtue. We ourselves, as museum people, go through new
exhibitions, which may be extremely effective, but are using techniques which are not unfamiliar. At last we spot it in a corner—a
new trick—and we say, "That's a great idea, I never saw that done
before." Whereas, in fact, it may not be as effective as some more
hackneyed devices that were used in the exhibition.

MR. PARKER: While the new, novel twist may be novel to you, your
kids live with it every day. I, myself, am much more concerned
with the young people in a museum. I feel utterly sure that the
archaic methods of museum exposition will remain in sufficient
volume, throughout this country, to satisfy the people who are
over forty, and who are oriented that way. But I think we have to
begin to move in and accommodate this generation which is
growing up.

MR. SWINNEY: I think you mistake my meaning. I'm not saying that
this archaic exhibition satisfies me better. That's not what I equate
with success. I mean that an exhibition which has been installed
with techniques familiar to skilled and sophisticated museum
people may, nevertheless, be found more effective in getting across
to young people, by some objective criteria evaluation.

MR. PARKER: You never throw out anything until you challenge it.
But the main thing I'm after is to challenge the assumptions.

Take a good, close look. If it works, keep it. But don't keep it
just because it's been done before.

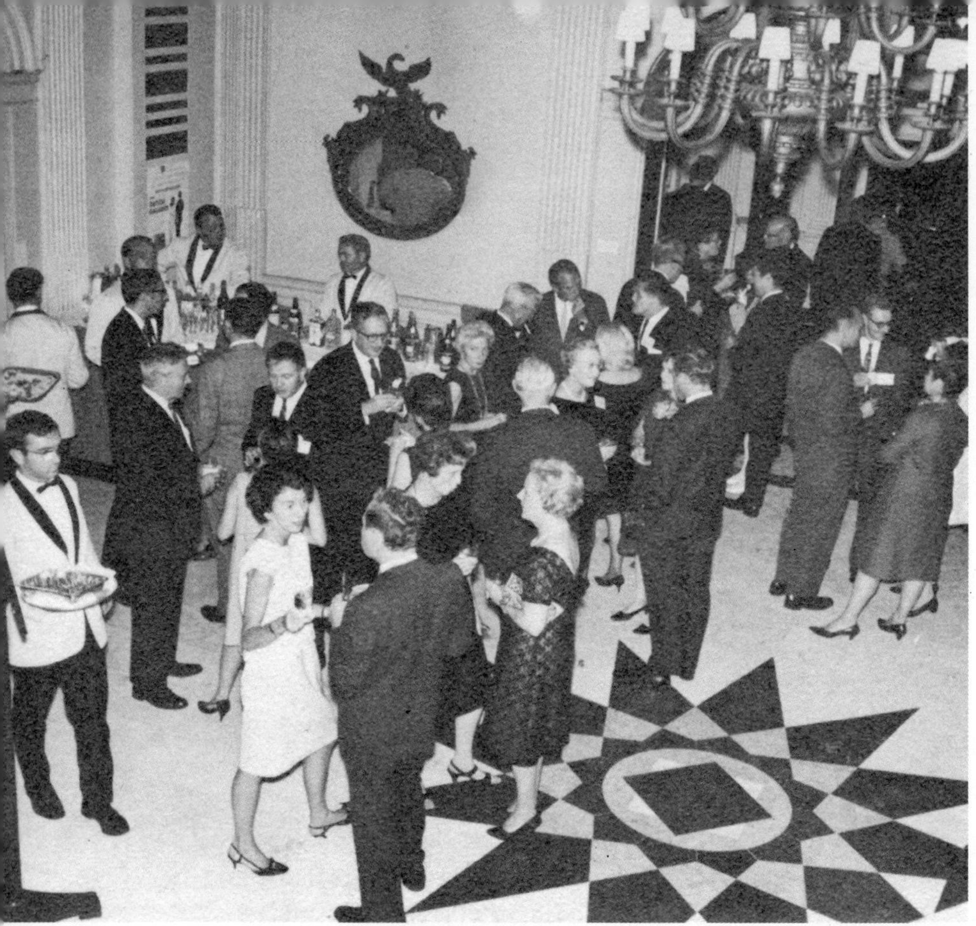

Some of the grandness of the Museum of the City of New York is on display as seminar participants mingle over cocktails in the entrance hall at the end of the first day. (Photo by Werner J. Kuhn.)

Can I say one thing? I'm here, certainly not with any intention of giving definitive answers about anything. I agree with Marshall McLuhan that the most efficient way I can act is to probe into things; to challenge assumptions, to try to come to some conclusions as to whether a particular technique is good, and if it isn't good, throw it out. If it is good, keep it. If we find something that isn't good, what is a good alternative? I want to find out by probing.

[The meeting was adjourned at 4:00 PM.]

The Multi-Media Orientation Gallery

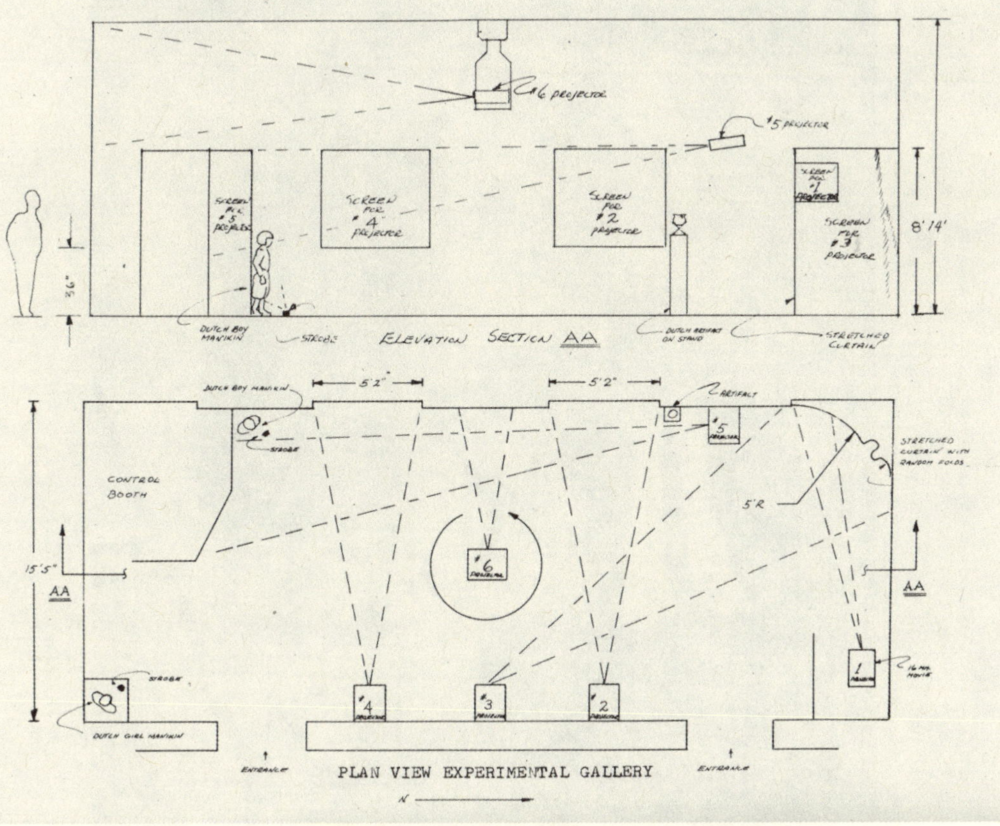

Diagram of an Experimental Gallery, mounted for the seminar by Harley Parker and referencing the Museum's Dutch Gallery. Parker hoped to make museums aware that they were actually in the business of training perception and challenging cultural assumptions. (Courtesy of the Parker Estate.)

Designed by Harley Parker as a multi-media orientation to the permanent Dutch Gallery of the Museum of the City of New York, the whole area was painted black with a few panels of ochre for contrast. The sight-and-sound sequence was controlled by a programmer which automatically turned on and off the various projectors and tape recordings. The sequence lasted about sixteen and a half minutes.

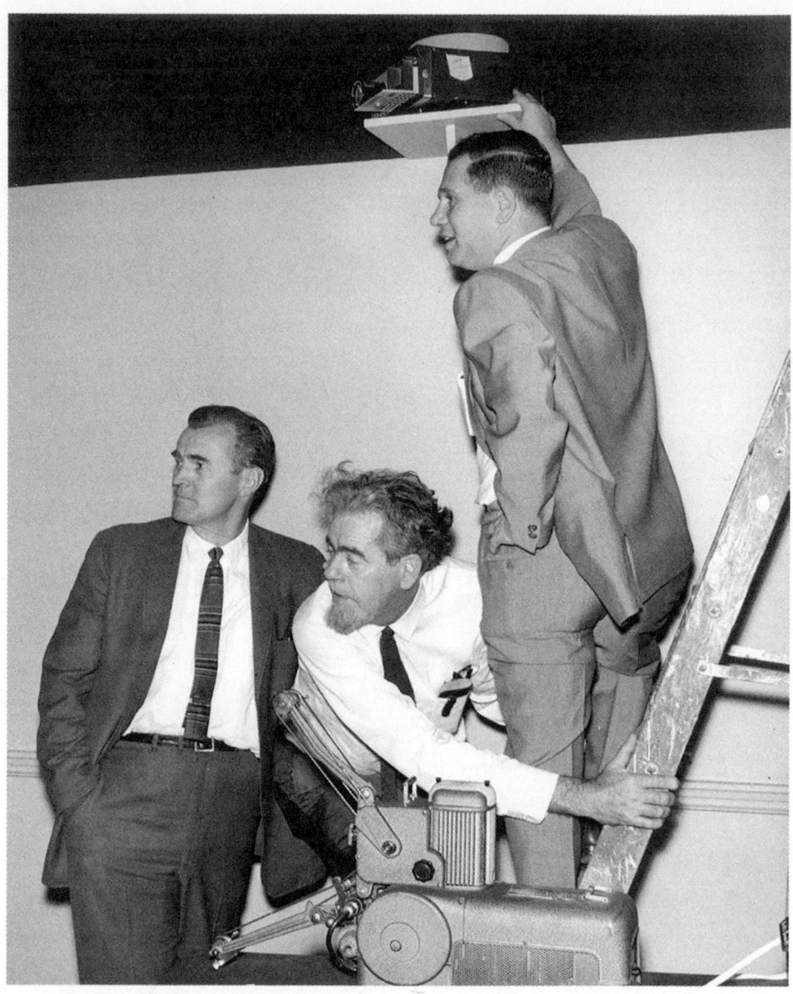

Harley Parker (centre) and Gerard M. Simon (right), install special equipment
in the experimental gallery, while Director Ralph R. Miller observes. Parker
had vast experience with the practical issues related to mounting museum
exhibitions due to his work as a designer at the Royal Ontario Museum.
(Photo by Werner J. Kuhn.)

The material included colour slides of Dutch scenes, with some models of New Amsterdam from the permanent Dutch Gallery, along with scenes of New York as it looks today; a movie[175] in black and white showing New York street scenes, featuring children at play; sound tapes which contrasted seventeenth-century Dutch music with the sounds of contemporary New York; strobe-lit mannequins of a Dutch boy and girl; and a few artifacts.

The projectors (except for #6 on the plan) were mounted eight feet above the floor. Numbers, 2, 4, 5, and 6 were Kodak Carousel fixed-focus projectors with zoom lenses. Number 3 was a Kodak Carousel self-focusing projector.[176] Number 6, hung from the ceiling, rotated clockwise a full 360 degrees. The elevation diagram shows #6 pointing south. A white curtain stretched vertically on a concave form was intentionally disturbed for half its length by making random folds, and served as a screen for slide projector #3, as well as for the 16-mm movie projector (#1), which overcast on part of the slides.

Tuesday Morning, October 10, 1967

[The Tuesday morning session of the seminar convened at ten o'clock
at the Museum of the City of New York, Dr. McLuhan and Mr.
Parker, Moderators.]

MR. PARKER: We only had a week to do this, and we have attempted,
here, to provide a kind of orientation to the New Amsterdam[177]
Gallery by using slides and film, sounds of various kinds.

We haven't been able to use such things as we ordinarily use,
such as smell and movement, perhaps a revolving platform. We
haven't had that kind of money or time. So we have thrown this
thing together with beeswax and chewing gum.

What I have done is to juxtapose a number of Dutch slides,
some showing the gallery as it exists, others with views of Holland,
various paintings, and artifacts. We have contrasted this with the
current New York scene. I got a Tony Schwartz[178] film with sound,
called *My Own Yard to Play In*[179] which is concerned with the children in New York streets, playing with all kinds of makeshift this
and that. I know that real children's games don't change much; so
if you want to extrapolate the children you see on the streets of
New York into New Amsterdam, I think you can do it that way.

We have Dutch music. We have also another soundtrack—I have
forgotten the title of it, but it's the sounds of contemporary New
York.

You may find, as I do myself, that, as an introduction to the
Dutch Gallery, it's probably a little overloaded with contemporary
New York. The reason for this is that it's much easier to get slides
of contemporary New York than it is of New Amsterdam. However,
we could have investigated the other museums for photo coverage
of models, *etcetera*. I hope you enjoy this as an experience, and just
look upon it totally in the sense that it's intended. Although we
have tried to create some kind of unity, don't look at it from that
point of view. We considered various possibilities. And the possibilities are unlimited. But the budget for this show was $500, and
one week of blood, sweat, and tears. If you find your head in the

way of the projector—the beams aren't very high—I wish you
would try to create a pattern.

[Participants visit the experimental gallery.]

Discussion

MR. PARKER: If any of you have questions, I would be delighted to
answer any I can. Or anything about yesterday's tour of the
American Museum of Natural History, outside of the fact that it
made McLuhan collapse.

QUESTION: Perhaps you're doing an injustice to the Museum without
considering any objectives it might have.

MR. PARKER: I'm not being facetious. Of course.

QUESTION: I doubt that this was the case, but it occurred to me that
perhaps their objective was not the normal museum's objective. In
other words, they were striving to do something technical rather
than being a museum, per se.

MR. PARKER: I don't know. But it seems to me that the Museum of
Natural History is a great public museum. It is not even in the
category of a university museum. I think one could excuse this
kind of thing much more easily in a university museum. But a
great public museum must appeal to a great public.

I still think I'm right, that it would be a very unusual person
who would go to the trouble to read, particularly where there is the
psychological pressure of a vast building, all of which they want
to see.

QUESTION: Would you say this is particularly true of the casual
visitor, the individual or the public, and it would be applicable?

MR. PARKER: That's right. I wonder what proportion, generally, of
museum visitors in a large museum centre are tourists and
compared to the visitors who are students? I would think it's probably about eight to twenty.

QUESTION: I think the mixed media demonstration upstairs was
extremely exciting, and very wonderful and educational. I think
it's supposed to get people interested to start with, but since the

museum has the principal function of dealing with artifacts, I was
wondering why you didn't spotlight the artifacts?

MR. PARKER: I did. The only thing I can say to you is, I am sorry I
only had a week and $500. Every time I bought a strobe light for
$60, I had to search my soul. There were many things I could have
done with another three weeks and another $500.

QUESTION: I missed it. I guess because the drama seemed to be on
film.

MR. PARKER: I tried to argue for twelve people at a time in there, but
obviously that would take five trips, and Mr. Miller suggested that
it would leave you people sitting around doing nothing. I would like,
during the cocktail hours, to run it again for anyone who wants to
go in and see it, possibly under a little better circumstances, with a
control of, say, ten people.

QUESTION: Some of us haven't yet gotten upstairs. Let's cut back to
this matter of yesterday and the Museum over there, and the
matter of audience.

We have touched on this several times, but to me it's a very
important point, and it's almost impossible to generalize about it,
because each audience to each museum changes constantly.

MR. PARKER: This is true.

QUESTION: And in terms of audience, consider the matter of a group
of specialists coming into the American Museum of Natural History
and looking around. This certainly wasn't devised for the specialist.
It was devised for what they probably considered to be their major
audience. And in terms of success, does it work with them?

MR. PARKER: Categorically, I would say no.

QUESTION: I would be tempted to deny this. Museum habits have
changed. I suspect that here, in New York City, what you get is not
just one visit to a museum. People are realizing that they can't see
a museum of that size in one visit. They come back again and
again, and many of us in this business are doing exactly that,
working on the principle that we will get our audiences back.

MR. PARKER: I'm primarily interested in the young, and within two
blocks of the Royal Ontario Museum, which is, after all, a pretty
great museum, there is Yorkdale Village,[180] which has perhaps

three thousand hippies and their friends. I have never seen a
hippie go inside the Royal Ontario Museum.

QUESTION: I was there for three days and I saw a number of hippies
go in.

MR. PARKER: Maybe I stay too much in my office, but I really haven't
seen them going in. There may have been something special going
on which appealed to them, for example, the period costume show.
We had a show called *Modesty to Mod*.[181] We had paper dresses
and all kinds of things. So it may have been that this particular
exhibition would draw a few of that crowd.

But I'm particularly interested in getting them in. I'm quite sure
I can get them into a sound-and-light show. It doesn't have to be an
Electric Circus.[182] I wouldn't even mind putting on a discothèque,
but I think this, too, can be sharpened.

QUESTION: Aren't you trying to frighten your audience too much?

MR. PARKER: I am not. I have spoken to several people who were at
the Electric Circus last night and said they enjoyed it.

QUESTION: Up to a point. I was one of those people.

MR. PARKER: How long were you there?

QUESTION: An hour and three-quarters.

MR. PARKER: The kind of light shows I am postulating for galleries
are fifteen minutes long, and I don't think anybody is going to get
bored. I really do believe we have to move into new technology in
order to stop this business of hoisting people out of modern society
and suddenly placing them back in, for instance, seventeenth-
century New Amsterdam. From the viewpoint of the pictures and
artifacts we have, it looks pretty quiet.

QUESTION: What about the observers of that? Aren't we falling into
a trap in trying to do this kind of thing? Couldn't it be argued that
people will need relief from this sort of thing that you have described?
This Electric Circus, with its continuous performance—

MR. PARKER: I know there is no aftermath. What I'm suggesting is a
fifteen-minute orientation centre. When they go through that, they
get some idea of the abrasiveness of what New Amsterdam was as
opposed to what New York has become. Then they are able to enter
even the Dutch Gallery with a little more feeling for humanity and

for the living qualities of these artifacts. But I still believe that it's impossible for someone of our society to be suddenly slapped with the Naskapi Indians.[183] They take a look around and all they see is some snowshoes and a little bark hut.

QUESTION: You're just saying something we have known for a long time, when you speak of orientation and approach and statement of what we're going to do. "First, I'm going to tell them what I'm going to tell them, and then I tell them what I told them."

MR. PARKER: But I think that's a very old, literate action. I don't think it's applicable to the twentieth century, especially not to the twentieth-century youngster.

QUESTION: Even if it works?

MR. PARKER: I don't think that it works. One of the things that's bothering schools is not that they have dropouts, but that too many of the dropouts are intelligent.

QUESTION: I have heard the question asked here, that if we dramatize and emphasize certain things, aren't we presenting a point of view? Aren't we doing something which is not the function of the museum, to present everything and let the viewers draw their own conclusions?

MR. PARKER: I certainly don't believe I'm presenting a point of view. I don't think there is any point of view in that light-and-sound show upstairs. It's multi-faceted sound, sight, modern New York against New Amsterdam, modern chairs, old chairs—

QUESTION: You did say you were emphasizing the quietness of New Amsterdam against the noise and bustle of New York.

MR. PARKER: That's what occurs to me. If you hire a designer you're going to get a point of view, because the designer designs within the perimeter of his own experience. That's automatic.

Well, you say you don't like this particular designer's sensibilities, and you can hire another. But I think a good designer does try to remain as catholic as possible, to encompass as many points of view as possible, and he is certainly subject to curatorial appraisals, etc.

But I have heard some comments. I remember once, up in our Far Eastern Gallery,[184] which is extremely rich archaeologically,

there was a piece of bronze labelled "Bronze Bridle."[185] So I watched
a number of people who glanced at these things. First of all, I
discovered that the children didn't know what a bridle was. So the
label was totally and completely meaningless.

I think that in the gallery here it would be quite possible to
provide an orientation centre of light and sound which gives visitors something of the flavour.

This thing could have set into it, for instance, a voice making
comments, here and there, about whatever it might be. In New
Amsterdam they did or did not do such-and-such. Everything could
be quickly interspersed in between. Perhaps that would be something. It may be academic.

QUESTION: Would this centre of light and sound be apart from the
exhibition itself?

MR. PARKER: Yes. It would be something you pass through as you
are going in. I think we can cut it down quite considerably. I would
like to see this one compressed into about ten minutes instead of
what I think is now sixteen and a half. So I would cut six and a half
minutes off that to advantage. I think I could also install speakers,
or cut into the Dutch Museum with contemporary New York
sounds, or other sounds.

QUESTION: I like the flexibility of your media in this introductory
area. It could even be tailored to certain groups.

You might answer the question, "Is the museum expressing
too strong an opinion?" If differing opinions could be expressed,
or neutral opinions—it's a wide, flexible medium, introducing the
gallery, that perhaps can't change too frequently. I think the two
work hand in hand.

MR. PARKER: I would say this: it's certainly true, you do get repeat
visitors, and a gallery doesn't change that often. However, I would
like to avoid certain attitudes towards galleries which I have heard
expressed. A friend of mine came down and told me that he had
been asked to design a temporary gallery. It won't last more than
ten years.

QUESTION: Would you see a relationship between what you have
been talking about, the preliminary orientation to a gallery, and

the new exhibition we saw yesterday, "The World Beneath our Feet"?[186] Some of us were talking about how we would apply the orientation idea to a gallery of that type.

MR. PARKER: The way I answer that always is this: I learned this lesson a long time ago when I was a young and very brash book designer. The chief editor handed me a book, and I told him I wouldn't do it that way, and he said, "How do you know?"

I don't know what I would do until I got my feet wet. If anybody is going to offer me three weeks' salary, I would go down and investigate it. I think it would be presumptuous of me to approach another man's design and say that I would do it differently, because I don't know how differently until I go into the matter.

I don't think my function here is to give advice to various people who have asked me, "What we want are definitive answers. How do you do it?" I can't tell you.

The old museum-like people don't come in limited editions. What I can only hope to do—and I trust we will succeed—is to raise in your mind the possibility that some of the assumptions under which you work should be challenged. You go back, and you begin to think about it and say to yourself, "Maybe there is a different way. Maybe we should look at this from another point of view instead of following what we have done before."

I recognize in some cases the limitations of staff and money almost preclude any changes.

QUESTION: I would like to try once more to get clear what doesn't really stay clear for me: your feeling about the linear story exhibit. It seems to me that what we saw upstairs is an excellent and important way of supplementing that other type of exhibit, but it seems to me that every now and then you have been saying that the other kind of exhibit is really not achieving very much, and that it should be dropped or abolished or replaced. I can't seem to accept that.

It seems to me that the two aren't equivalent at all, and what is accomplished by the Dutch exhibit at the museum here is quite different from what you were approaching.

MR. PARKER: Absolutely!

QUESTION: Are you saying that the story line, linear exhibit should be dropped?

MR. PARKER: Yes.

QUESTION: It seems to me here we're presented with a theory about how people know, how people understand. I admit I'm a nineteenth-century person, but it seems to me that there are many ways of understanding, and that the storybook way is going to have to remain one of the ways to learn a subject.

MR. PARKER: I would refer you to much of the best contemporary literature, which has dropped story line. It's still a book but not a story line.

I would also like to point out to you that we're in no danger of losing all kinds of linear expositions throughout the country for a long time. What I'm trying to say is, please let's start looking after our youngsters who don't think in that way. Even those of them who are square are having some of this multi-dimensionality, simultaneity of insights all bearing down on them at once.

The man who lives in an oral world, that is, where the primary method of communication is by mouth to ear, lives at the centre of a sphere where communication comes into him simultaneously from all sides, banging at him; whereas the man who lives in the world of the eye is living in the world of one-at-a-time. The business of logical, connected space is inherent in the mechanism of the eye. You have to turn, look.

The ear is a simultaneous instrument from all sides. Tactility is much the same. It's disconnected space. I told you yesterday that to the blind all things are sudden. Unconnected, here-to-here. But visually, I can connect, I can see the relationship from this to this.

I believe with Dr. McLuhan that we're moving into a world of simultaneity. As somebody said yesterday, there is a possibility we're raising a little tribe of Eskimos. I believe this is true. And this is not based on any mere theorizing. I have brought up three children,[187] seen two of them through the teenage stage, and I have a seventeen-year-old daughter[188] whom I am watching now.

I really do believe this, that our whole method of receptivity has been changing. I think one of the reasons for the dropout of

so many intelligent children is the kind of schizophrenic situation
that is set up between the world outside and world of the school,
which has a nineteenth-century basis, and hasn't taken advantage of the new electronic media. I have worked in Metropolitan
Television[189] education, and I found the school system trying to
prove that television doesn't do as good a job as the book did.

QUESTION: Could we take one scene, let's say the story of New
Amsterdam, which would seem to have a certain continuity and a
certain development? Couldn't your experience of simultaneity
convey an idea of development?

MR. PARKER: There is a very good book by Henri Poulet[190] called
On Human Time, in which he pointed out to the media men that
time wasn't on a line, time was a multi-layer thing. Many times
co-existing simultaneously. In other words, it's related to our
sound appreciation, rather than to our visual appreciation.

Is it necessary, though, that history has to be taught in a chronological manner? Or is that not assumption based on literacy, on
an attitude of mind which is created by the literate stance? I believe,
as I told you, in pattern recognition, except for historians. Historians
may have to treat their subject in a chronological way, but I find
they come through the other way. They finally come to a pattern.

That's the way I had to learn art history. I did it by little snip-
pets and bits and pieces, and finally, after a number of years, it
began to coalesce into some kind of a pattern. This was good for
me, because I was interested in it. My daughter didn't want to
become an art historian, but I would like her to have a general
knowledge of what our history is about. This, I think, can be done
by this technique.

QUESTION: The audio-visual installation that we have just seen is
meant as an imaginative substitution of the gallery itself. This
doesn't mean to say that one can't use a linear element in audio-
visual presentation.

For example, somehow, to superimpose sound where someone
read that letter which a seller sent to the Dutch West Indies
Company,[191] recounting the purchase of Manhattan Island.

MR. PARKER: Yes. I saw a movie the other night, where it was all
   juxtaposed, abrupt. After fifteen minutes of that I was bored to
   tears. On the basis that a scream sounds loudest in a quiet room,
   some linear juxtaposition would have been more meaningful.
QUESTION: I found the saturation of imagination after a point,
   before the linear image.
MR. PARKER: I told you I wanted to compress it. I felt that the voice
   carried the linear element.
QUESTION: One of those elements could have been the capture of
   historic information.
MR. PARKER: Yes.

[Dr. McLuhan arrives and joins the discussion.]

MR. MILLER: Ladies and Gentlemen: We're ready to go, officially. Dr.
   McLuhan has seen the experimental gallery with the last group,
   and we're ready for anything that transpires: questions, answers,
   or whatnot.
       You might all be interested to know that we went up in three
   different sections. The first section that went up, as those in it will
   recall, were rather carefully indoctrinated by Harley Parker as to
   what the gallery was about, and how it had been constructed and
   how it had evolved. The second and third groups weren't given any
   pre-indoctrination, so there have been some interesting observations as to the group behaviour pattern in relation one to the other.
   But apart from that, I leave the meeting up to you.
DR. McLUHAN: I can only apologize for having faded from the scene
   yesterday, but I'm glad to be back.
QUESTION: Before we start, having been a member of the third
   group, I should like to know the problem that was presented to the
   designer, which he solved in the way that we have just seen.
MR. PARKER: The problem wasn't presented to me. I formulated it
   myself.
       What I did was try to provide some sort of orientation to the
   New Amsterdam Gallery. One of the salient factors of contemporary art is transparency,[192] so I thought I would use the quality of

transparency by juxtaposing the contemporary New York scene to the photographs of artifacts, actual artifacts, and photographs of models of New Amsterdam.

DR. McLUHAN: As a successor to lucidity, "transparency" is a rather confusing term. It's the exact opposite. One image overlying another image is a transparency, and this is what you get in any newspaper or magazine, or any of the twentieth-century formats, and in this show. I found most of the transparencies very witty, very amusing.

MR. PARKER: In terms of their juxtapositions?

DR. McLUHAN: Yes, but we live surrounded by these overlays and transparencies in every aspect of our daily lives, and it cannot be just accepted passively. You have to make some sort of response to it, and the best one is euphoria and amusement.

    We live very much in an "entertainment world." Show business[193] is the main business of mankind from now on.

MR. PARKER: I would suggest that museums are in show business, too.

QUESTION: One point I think was not clear: whether the orientation as we saw it would merely precede the existing exhibit that we saw yesterday, or whether it would supplant the first part.

MR. PARKER: It would simply precede. It would be something into which you went first. I would like to shorten it, somehow. But it would be a ten-minute prelude to the gallery.

MR. FREDERICK RATH (Vice-President, New York State Historical Association):[194] In terms of any particular audience?

MR. PARKER: No, I don't think so. I find that the things that intrigue children almost automatically intrigue adults, because usually adults know even less about the subject than the child.

QUESTION: Have any children seen this?

MR. PARKER: Not so far. We're trying to make arrangements.

MR. MILLER: We're making arrangements. That will happen tomorrow, at both grade-school and college levels.

MR. PARKER: We have college-level students coming in from Fordham.

QUESTION: Why the inclusion of artifacts?

MR. PARKER: Why not? They're part of a gallery. They add a three-dimensional quality to something which is essentially photographic.

DR. McLUHAN: The man-made environment is artifacts, is works of art.

MR. PARKER: It's a touchstone to reality, different from the vicarious experience of the film.

DR. McLUHAN: One of the things that Wright Miller[195] mentioned about Russia in his book is the almost total absence of a man-made environment in the overall. He feels this has a profound effect on the make-up of the Russians.

But we live in a complete surround of made-made environment. One question that was put to me yesterday was a good indication. I was asked whether, by visual bias, I meant sensory bias. It never occurred to me that it could mean anything else. It has nothing to do with any mental bias. Every culture has a sensory bias. Every artifact is an instant indication of the sensory bias of the culture. You can read it like a book or a language. But we haven't spent much time teaching people how to read the sensory languages of cultures. In any museum you have an incredible richness of artifacts that are clues to the sensory bias and preferences of a whole people.

MR. PARKER: The study of the history of art is based mostly on style, without any understanding that the style is dictated by the sensory bias. This is a thing behind the stylistic quality in an art form.

DR. McLUHAN: In the seventeenth century the phrase came up, "Style is the man."[196] It's like saying "Style is it."

There's a wonderful line in Eliot,[197] "I bring the horoscope myself. One must be so careful these days." You see, the sensory bias is foreignness and flow. In other words, the English used linear in the antique sense, to keep the mob back. It's a class strategy. It's not for the purpose of stressing ideas.

MR. PARKER: It eliminates the whole richness of the Cockney[198] and Lancashire[199] man.

MR. G. CARROLL LINDSAY (Director, New York State Museum Services):[200] This is beside the point. The idea of multiple projections like the motion picture is one that intrigued me. We plan to do something of this sort on a sophisticated scale.[201] Even before we begin to get to the problem of devising the presentation, we are faced with one of the great problems represented by world fairs and Expo: the length of time it takes a given group to see a display of this kind. If anyone comes up with an idea on how to run the public through a presentation without great waiting lines—

MR. PARKER: Duplicate it four times. Put four groups in simultaneously.

MR. LINDSAY: The cost is a problem, too.

MR. PARKER: Mind you, I think that it can be limited to about ten minutes. If you have a sufficiently big room you can get sixty people in. Then you're going to have 360 people in an hour which isn't bad.

MR. LINDSAY: In a small museum it's not bad; for a large metropolitan museum, when you're dealing with three thousand an hour—

MR. PARKER: I wouldn't suggest one orientation centre for the entire Museum of Natural History. I would suggest multi-orientation centres for the various kinds of disciplines involved.

MISS FISHER: There were a number of repeat shots. Technically, could it be set up like film loops, just to keep on going?

MR. PARKER: Certainly. You can project stills on a film and get many more. It's a matter of pulsing them.

MISS FISHER: You also wouldn't have a story line, there.

MR. PARKER: You don't have a story line there. I think the story line is completely irrelevant in this form of presentation.

DR. McLUHAN: When you have multi-screen projection.

QUESTION: Is that necessarily true? Didn't Eames[202] use this same technique for supporting a story line in New York[203] and Seattle?[204] He definitely used this technique in a manner far more complex than your experiment, but specifically to support a story line.

DR. McLUHAN: That's the great mistake they made at the World's Fair. It puts the audience in a passive state of relationship.

QUESTION: On the contrary, they were in a continual state of action. You can't fall asleep with it.

DR. McLUHAN: You can't have a story line and multi-screen simultaneously.

QUESTION: Let's assume it has been done. We'll debate over whether
it's been successful.

DR. McLUHAN: There is no story line in your newspaper, there's a
date line.

QUESTION: You only see one part of it at a time. With this multi-
vision technique, the whole intention is to see a dozen.

DR. McLUHAN: No, you see the whole front page at once. There is no
story line possible. The editorial page is a story line. To reduce all
those individual stories to one story line would be perspective;
that is, an editorial. You can't put it on Page One.

MR. PARKER: Let's accept the fact that it was done. I would say it's
about as appropriate as putting films on television. It's a wrong use
of the medium, because inherent in multi-screen, multi-media
projection, there is the possibility of the richness which comes
from simultaneity, and to limit this seems wrong to me.

MISS FISHER: To explain to the average citizens the concept of the
computer with that kind of technique and the story line—it seems
as if there were no other way to do it, to get the general public to
understand and have some respect and feeling for what is involved
with a computer. But to abstractly give an impression—

MR. PARKER: It's not being done abstractly.

MISS FISHER: I thought it was quite abstract.

MR. PARKER: I think the improvement of all the senses coming to life
is no abstraction. Taking one sense and using that in the linear
form, that's an abstraction.

MISS FISHER: Are we talking about abstracts and abstractions?

MR. PARKER: I would say that the most abstract art that has ever
been revealed is the art of the Renaissance, because it abstracts
one sense at the expense of all the other senses.

QUESTION: I'm not sure whether you gentlemen saw the IBM Pavilion
at the World's Fair,[205] but you have seen *Labyrinth*[206] at Expo. It
seems to me there was a very sophisticated but nevertheless real
story line in *Labyrinth*.

DR. McLUHAN: You name it; what was it?

QUESTION: I got the impression that *Labyrinth* was designed to
represent the classical Labyrinth, with the visitor acting the part

of the hero, and our purpose in going through it was to find the enemy at the end. And it turns out that the last film was about old age.

DR. McLUHAN: You mean you were matching *Labyrinth* against an old myth? Because the story line in the Minotaur myth[207] is that of human cognition, leading to the confrontation of human identity, which is the monster. This is what *Labyrinth* was. It simulated the act of cognition. It has nothing to do with any story whatever.

QUESTION: Nothing to do with the Greek myth, but a story line— What is an act of cognition?

DR. McLUHAN: The act of cognition was total involvement, and it has no literary meaning whatever. It has no story line because by definition story line is visual continuity. We really ought to make that point. You can't have the story line without continuity and connectedness. A story line means continuity.

When you're using many senses, or any other sense than the visual, there is no continuity. You can't have a story line in music. It's impossible. The ear doesn't permit a line.

QUESTION: Explain to me again what you understand is the purpose of the Labyrinth, actually.

DR. McLUHAN: It's this dramatization of the act of cognition.

QUESTION: That's not a story line?

DR. McLUHAN: No, indeed not. You might as well say a drama is a story line.

QUESTION: I think it was one of the most marvelous story lines I have ever been exposed to.

DR. McLUHAN: You have classified it as a story line, which gives you satisfaction.

MISS FISHER: As you went into *Labyrinth*, I thought it was explained that there was some; this is what you're going to see.

DR. McLUHAN: That there was some correlation with the old Greek story?

MISS FISHER: Something we were expected to follow out of it.

QUESTION: There was a message.

MISS FISHER: What is the difference between a message and a story line?

QUESTION: They are identical to me.

DR. McLUHAN: This is an example of complete misunderstanding, not partial.

MR. PARKER: You jump into the water. That's a message, but it isn't a story line.

DR. McLUHAN: What you people are trying to interpret is having an idea. We're trying to train your perceptions. We have no "idea." We're trying to alter your perception of life without any "idea."

You will find the story line starts only in places that are highly visual, and that oral cultures don't use story lines. A myth doesn't move on one level, it moves on many levels at once and you can't have a story line on many levels.

MR. PARKER: Ted Carpenter says, if a native tells a story, he's just as likely to start at the end or the middle. He might start at the beginning and then go to the end and then give you the middle.

QUESTION: Would you believe, I have always thought that was a story line? I have never thought there was necessarily a beginning or an end, and I have the feeling that you gentlemen are applying this sort of a definition to "story line" where some of us might have felt that it wasn't necessarily a limiting factor.

MRS. GASTEYER: Is this because the eye retains what the ear doesn't?

QUESTION: A lecture is essentially built around a story line. Most lectures.

MR. PARKER: Not necessarily.

DR. McLUHAN: Because they are based on the written word.

QUESTION: Many of us have seen many lectures which are illustrated with multi-screen presentations, and all kinds of media mix, and they all happen simultaneously.

DR. McLUHAN: Yes, you have multi-story lines. You have many story lines going at once.

MR. PARKER: I have a little trick I do in public presentations. I take two sets of slides and I stand up there and I idly shuffle them and handle them to eliminate any possibility of connectedness.

QUESTION: Why?

MR. PARKER: Because I believe the total experience is more valid
than a lineal and sequential development.

QUESTION: Do you then present them in silence?

MR. PARKER: No, I may have a tape recorder going, or I may talk.

QUESTION: Why do you have to talk at all?

MR. PARKER: Sometimes slides don't stand by themselves.

QUESTION: That's the point. Wouldn't it have been better to have
some sort of a logical message?

DR. McLUHAN: The word is out. Logical. You might as well say
rational. Both of them are synonyms for visuality only. Logic and
rationality are visual.

QUESTION: To a blind man there is none.

DR. McLUHAN: Unless he had learned to see before he went blind.

MR. PARKER: Or if he reads Braille.[208]

DR. McLUHAN: The English language has a built-in quality that is
not characteristic of Chinese. We vest our language with this visuality, at the expense of all the other senses.

QUESTION: Do you gentlemen feel that you could have involvement
or commitment without confusion?

MR. PARKER: Have you ever read *The Rational Man*?[209]

QUESTION: May I speak on organization again? One could go into a
kitchen and put all the ingredients of a cake out on the table. This
in itself is not satisfying to me. Much more is gained when you
make the cake and enjoy it.

I see these multi-experiences upstairs as unsatisfying. They do
not put anything together in a form that gives me satisfaction.

MR. PARKER: At one point people can say that what you're doing is
imposing a point of view and then somebody else comes along and
says you're not imposing a point of view, and I wish you would.

DR. McLUHAN: The "point of view" is logic.

MR. ELLIN: This orientation gallery follows, I think, the broadest
definition of the story line in the Hollywood sense, and there is a
purpose in putting together the sound and vision presentation. To
say that we don't use a story line in an installation such as we have
just seen doesn't imply that we don't have a message to impart in

that show, and there is a kind of logic in it. There is point of view
that we seek to project.

I don't agree with my colleague that the Eames sight-and-sound
show had a story line. But he did seek to project the visual and
aural image of America in much the same way as the senses might
find it in perambulating from New York to Seattle.

Selection is necessary when you orchestrate or produce a
show of that sort. The absence of story line doesn't mean that
the human mind exercises no logic or choice in the selection of
images. Obviously, you do. You don't go into a slide file and pull
things out helter-skelter and say that this is the sequence in which
we will deal with these images and the sound.

You do think and feel, but that's not a story line. It's a process of
selection. I think this distinction should be kept clear.

MR. PARKER: As a matter of fact, it's much broader than just dealing
with film in terms of presentation. I believe that in exhibition techniques we should begin to exploit much more the business of
bringing together what the literary mind would call a rational
juxtaposition, but which to the ordinary human being means that
these objects strike sparks off each other.

So I can't see any real problem in presenting an Aztec[210] piece
alongside a Chinese piece if they strike sparks off each other and
illuminate the situation for the viewer.

MR. ELLIN: There is a logic and thinking and selection process in
putting this together, but the overall message that will result is
certainly not a story line.

MR. GOLDSTONE: In all this discussion of contrasting multi-sensory
impacts as opposed to intellectual, linear, visual, logical presentation, I'm very much surprised that there has been no mention of
emotional involvement in communication. As I look back at the
experience at Expo, the half-dozen exhibits there, whether they
were intellectual or multi-sensory,[211] that really cut deep in the
matter of communication were ones in which, to me, there was an
emotional involvement. And I'm sure that everybody has a different
emotional involvement with other things. Non-intellectual technique seems to be much less important than the end result you

really want to communicate to people. I made a list of exhibits that did have emotional involvement at Expo, and I wonder if you would like to comment? It's very difficult to do in a museum, to get people emotionally involved.

MR. PARKER: I would say that we merely missed the adjective. We have taken it for granted that the very word "involvement" implies "emotional."

DR. McLUHAN: Always. And the experience of detachment, when it was new in the age of print, was an emotion, an emotional thing— very exciting, absolutely unknown to any previous age.

That's why Plato urged that anybody coming to his university[212] should study Euclid.[213] Euclid was the Greeks' first experience of detachment, the man who invented visual space, making detachment possible. This is very exciting, and the very idea of detachment is emotional. We also think of it as the antithesis of emotion. But now detachment is absolutely *verboten*, and only involvement is possible in our electronic age.

QUESTION: I saw the exhibition before the orientation gallery, and was already familiar with the material. Why wouldn't it be just as effective at the end of the exhibition?

MR. PARKER: I believe not, because I'm aware of the emotional stance which is created by our world outside. You walk in off the street, and you have been involved in the subways, etc., and this creates an emotional stance which I think is inimical to an appreciation of a thing as remote as seventeenth-century New Amsterdam.

QUESTION: But you can draw it in through the film.

MR. PARKER: This is why it comes first. I change the emotional stance by using transparencies, overlay. I believe that creativity occurs only at the point of abrasion.

DR. McLUHAN: Consciousness is created by abrasion. If you want to hypnotize anybody you stress one sense only. Concentration on any one sense will hypnotize anybody so that they lose consciousness. Consciousness itself is an interphase of the senses. That's what the word means.

QUESTION: What do you propose be done with all the art history
departments in all the colleges?

MR. PARKER: Don't tempt me!

DR. McLUHAN: I think that they have a lot of exciting times ahead of
them. Pure discovery is opening up.

QUESTION: This is what I was driving at. If we are familiar with
some of the very effective artifacts, it has some meaning when we
see them on the slides. Because I knew and had seen them.

MR. PARKER: Yes, you're suggesting—There is no question about
that, this adds a new dimension to the artifact.

I know very well, for instance, from lecturing, if you want to
make a work of art out of a piece of advertising, blow it up ten feet
high on a screen. People suddenly look at it as a work of art, while
if it's in the magazine it's simply another ad. So it's placing the
object in an unusual circumstance that makes it art.

DR. McLUHAN: When one environment goes around another, the old
one becomes art. When you put any object inside another environment, it becomes a work of art. When it goes into a museum, it
becomes a work of art. After all, there are objects of everyday use
that are now in the museum, and when they're in the museum they
become works of art.

QUESTION: This is not true at all. If you take just any table and put it
in a museum, this does not make a work of art of it, unless it's a
well-constructed table in the first place.

DR. McLUHAN: Oh, no. Even if it's a very badly constructed table.

QUESTION: Art to me has to have a certain degree of quality.

QUESTION: How about a broken bust with no nose and no ears?

QUESTION: I don't think putting it in a museum makes it a work of
art. It's a classification.

QUESTION: You have just shown us a great deal of organized chaos.

DR. McLUHAN: Leave off "organized."

QUESTION: I understand why you wanted to do it. I think that to
introduce a period covering several centuries of the development
of New York, you have to do it in a form such as you used.

I was really more concerned with trying to stand in an area
which was uncomfortable, to see a multitude of images placed

with some degree—and here you're going to quarrel with me—
some degree of relationship between them, which would introduce
me to the exhibit I was about to enter.

I was more conscious, as a museum man, of the technical problems which I could see accompanying this type of presentation.
Unfortunately, this kept my consciousness and my degree of
involvement at a certain distance from the show itself, because all
I could see were the problems I would have in my own museum,
keeping all of these different machines working in the way in
which you designed them.

I was also concerned with the exhaustion I could see around
me—and I'm quite sure, unless it were shortened, it would not
come across as an effective introduction.

MR. PARKER: This is a point of view. Do you think a work of art
exists unequivocally?

QUESTION: No.

MR. PARKER: In other words, it depends upon the response of
people. If I put this in a museum, people will think, "There is a
table in the museum. It's a work of art."

QUESTION: That's their error.

MR. PARKER: It may be an error, but I'm talking about people's
responses. Where do you draw the line between a piece of art and
non-art? If a person looks at this table and finds it beautiful, to
him it's a work of art.

QUESTION: Whether it's in a museum or not. Whether it's inside
something else or not. Up to now it could only be a work of art if it
were inside something.

DR. McLUHAN: I was only pointing out the principle that any object
that goes inside a new situation becomes a work of art. It's the
interplay of environment that creates the art. No object, as such, is
a work of art, unless it has an environment.

QUESTION: I think the work of art is a form of communication. If
you want to look at the bowl of fruit, go look. But if you look at the
painting of it, you're looking at what someone is saying to you:
"Look, I saw this and I want you to see it."

DR. McLUHAN: That's why the artist is hated. He's the enemy. He's always telling people to go look, and this they would rather not do.

MR. PARKER: I think a work of art is a process, not a product. If a person can look at the bowl of fruit creatively, then he has created a work of art. It's the process of creativity which is important, not the product.

QUESTION: I think there is one thing to be said here. Yesterday Dr. McLuhan used what I think is an accepted Greek or eighteenth-century dictionary definition of museums. I think that we're all aware of the fact that in the last sixty-seven years this definition has been changed by the dictionary three times. We're all aware of the fact that many museums in the United States fall into the early twentieth-century definition, "a collection of curios."

There is now a new definition of "preservation" and "conservation," and just recently they have added "education" in the new dictionary. Many museums fall into the "curio" definition, but I think that many museums are coming to realize that they don't have to be curio keepers.

DR. McLUHAN: I had forgotten about the word "curio"[214] as a nineteenth-century term, but they used it as a means of specifying what a work of art was. Curios, curiosity is, by definition, something which attracts a great deal of attention.

QUESTION: It was used, certainly, in America. A prime example is George Washington's[215] towel. It was a poor towel when it was originally put in the museum, and I hope, for Heaven's sake, it will soon be gone. But it makes a great exhibit for the sole reason that it was George Washington's.

QUESTION: Such artifacts have enormous emotional attraction. For example, that pair of children's shoes from Auschwitz[216] in Expo. There's nothing but a pair of shoes there, but there is terrific impact in the way it's shown.

MR. PARKER: Incidentally, the Czechoslovakian Pavilion just won a prize for the best use of film in Expo. There is no story line. Father O'Brien[217] said he heard a man say in great indignation, "That isn't religion, that's life."

DR. McLUHAN: And there is no better name for anarchy and chaos.

QUESTION: In the light of your comments contrasting flat screen
and television, would you feel that the involvement could be
increased by projecting these illustrations through television?

MR. PARKER: I would think there would be an easier way, just put
them in low definition.

QUESTION: But you're saying the television viewer becomes the
screen.

MR. PARKER: If you put film into low definition, there is a tremendous tendency for the person to be the screen because of the
enormous sense of involvement.

MR. DUNN: Is there any relationship between the chaotic browsing
of most museum visitors as they jump from gallery to gallery, and
the collection of slides that you have presented to us?

MR. PARKER: I would think this is true, because what I'm trying to
do is to create what is actually realistic in view of people's habits.
We don't live a linear, sequential life. We're constantly being
bombarded. And in that sense, "chaos" very nearly approaches the
normal human sensibility.

MR. DUNN: I think this is very important, because most visitors don't
follow the story line. They jump around the gallery and come back
from one thing to another.

QUESTION: This is one of the things I was driving at when I talked
about the objects: that people, seeing these on the screen, are
unfamiliar with them and the objects speak very gently. If they see
the screen first, they may not relate the object to the picture; if
they saw the film afterwards, they would immediately recognize
the object.

MR. PARKER: I think that could possibly have been alleviated by a
feed-in of somewhat witty commentary for relief. I stress the word
"witty," because I don't want to be flatfooted and pedestrian, and
some wit could help. I'm most concerned about the fact that we
have to have a bridge between contemporary life and that gallery.

QUESTION: But would this destroy the effect, if it gets too witty?
Somebody selected those fine examples, and if the visitors pass
them by, they are lost. Again, if people see you have selected them
to reproduce on the wall, they may go back and take another look.

MR. PARKER: I will try it. It gets away from being an orientation gallery, it becomes a supplement.

QUESTION: That was the intention.

MR. PARKER: No, I wanted it as supplement too, but as an orientation gallery.

QUESTION: Would you let us have your views on the difference between teaching and learning? Here, with a group of museum directors, all the emphasis I have seen is on how to dish it out.

What I'm interested in is this: after a multi-sensory exposure, what does the person come away with? How does he make that part of his experience productive in his own life, unless it can be organized in some way to form what we have always considered an inner intellectual product?

DR. McLUHAN: The necessary ingredient is surprise, and this is wit, too. The children today are turned on. That means they're looking at a new world, and they have this thrilling sense of being involved in a new kind of world. They're turned on in a way that no teacher has ever discovered how to do.

And the environment itself has become a teaching machine.[218] The schoolroom is not that turned on nor that thrilling; this is a simple matter of observation. You don't have to guess about this, but it should be possible, and it is the sort of thing I work at: to try to find out the reasons why this happens. I know it is happening, I feel it happening, I see it happening, I want to find out why. Instead of telling people that it is happening, it's more desirable to find out why.

I think most artists are absolutely aghast at the world they live in, and they just wonder how is it possible for the world to be like that. And they never stop until they have shaped a pattern that explains why. They are incredulous. They simply say, "It couldn't be. Nothing could be that amazing."

How do you get the children to a point where they are absolutely amazed at the world they live in? We're seeing it happen to our children. It never happened in any recent period in human history, as far as I know, but these children are turned on, and it gives them a sense of power. That's one of the most noxious and

nauseating things about the teenagers—power. They feel that they
can do anything, so they do.

What you're really saying is: How can we arrange a museum
or an art gallery so it gives people that sensation of power, of
tremendous new discovery, of insight and perception? I think it is
possible. That's what Harley was trying to do with his juxtaposition, trying to rub one thing against the other to release the sense
of discovery.

For example, the sounds of the city environment are incredibly
beautiful at times. Tony Schwartz is the great discoverer of this
fact with his tape recorder. But to discover the city as a work of art
takes quite a lot of imagination, because we're overwhelmed for
the most part with just music. The artist simply refuses to be overwhelmed by his environment. He's so excited that he finds some
means of making other people see it. When surrounded with a
very oppressive thing, most people would rather turn it off. So the
artist is the enemy, because he's always wanting to turn it on and
say, "Look, listen to that!"

And that's why the art of any period is always very challenging
to that period when it's new.

MR. PARKER: This is why a designer in a museum is sort of *persona
non grata*.[219]

QUESTION: You would like to make us all artists?

DR. McLUHAN: Yes, nothing less.

MR. PARKER: One thing I would like to stress about museum presentation: there seems to be a tendency to feel that if the presentation
is in good taste, if the exposition lies within a surround of good
taste, the museum is fulfilling its function.

Not long after I was in my first museum job, about one month, I
quipped that good taste is the first refuge of the witless.

DR. McLUHAN: And the frightened.

MR. PARKER: Don't move for good taste. Move to communicate. Let
the aesthetic look after itself.

You set out to communicate. If you communicate well, you
can take it for granted that what you have done will gradually

degenerate into good taste, ten years from now, and everybody will be doing it without any meaning.

DR. McLUHAN: *Vogue*[220] magazine, or *McCall's*,[221] or any of the fashion magazines, exist to comfort and allay anxiety. Most people in any class of society live in a state of perpetual anxiety. And they feel much better when surrounded by good taste. The artist is always experimenting. He doesn't want any aspirin whatever to be dished out.

MR. PARKER: *Apropos*, people react to products they already own, to confirm their opinion that they have been very judicious in buying a particular piece of equipment.

DR. McLUHAN: The advertising men discovered this and they still don't know what to make of it, to judge by their surveys. In the newspaper, real news is bad news. Advertising is good news. It takes an awful lot of bad news to sell good news.

But art is bad news to most people. They don't want to hear about the horrible things going on in the world, Giacometti-style.[222] It's really news. "Art is news that stays news."[223] That's a phrase of Ezra Pound's.[224] It's a discovery that will always be a discovery.

I think it's possible to exhibit artifacts from other cultures as pure discoveries on the part of those cultures. Breakthroughs. Every artifact was once a breakthrough, whether it's an axe or a fire engine. And to enable people now to see them as breakthroughs is surely the goal of any exhibitor. That's the way to teach the history of any art or literature or painting, as a history of break-throughs in human perception, new dimensions.

I think many of you have read Hall's[225] *Hidden Dimensions*,[226] which simply refers to the fact that much of what is completely hidden is that which ordinarily surrounds us, with which we live day by day. We deliberately refuse to perceive this, in order to feel more comfortable.

He has fascinating illustrations of this principle. One that first comes to mind is the Arab world, where he discovered that good taste in personal relations is a distance of eight inches. Unless you can smell the other person every moment you see him and speak to him, he considers you hostile. Good taste there means smelling the person you speak to at all times, not just looking at him and not just handling him, but smelling.

I'm not sure this is characteristic of other cultures in that area, but Hall has done a lot of research on the matter. He calls it "the hidden dimension" and I think there is a distance which is ideal for every artifact and view. There is a distance that will reveal it, that will turn you on and make you feel that this is an exciting break-through. This distance is not the same for any two people or any two artifacts. But it is possible to discover it by experiment.

That's what Harley was trying to do in that show, he was trying to discover the distance that should obtain between experiences, in order to turn them on and make them exciting.

MR. PARKER: I would like to point out that the crowd pattern is rather interesting. Mr. Miller has pointed out that certain observations were made. One of them was that, in my initial briefing, I asked people to stand against the wall, and they did.

One of the reasons is that the room was so narrow it was impossible to project on all four surfaces. If the room had been wider I would certainly have projected on that fourth wall, and the group of people would have stood in the middle.

It's interesting that in the other groups, which were not briefed, they also stood against the wall, and the reason was that the projection was on two walls. This is not good, but the physical plant as such dictated it.

MRS. CONGER: When I bring a class of schoolchildren tomorrow,[227] you suggested that there should be only ten. I was wondering whether you meant just for physical comfort? Actually, they would be fourth graders, nine-year-olds, and we would have little mats. Would it be absolutely necessary to have only ten?

MR. PARKER: If you sat them on the floor, you could hold fifteen fairly comfortably. The seating, of course, ideally would have been quite a bit higher, too, and the room larger.

QUESTION: Are you planning to expose teenagers to this as well?

MR. PARKER: Rather late teenagers. We're bringing them in from Fordham.[228]

QUESTION: It would be interesting if you brought a few students from one of the disadvantaged schools to see how they respond to this.

MR. PARKER: I think all that would be extremely interesting. We would be getting something back which would serve a very great purpose in terms of later shows. This depends on whether or not we can keep it up. We have some very expensive equipment tied up upstairs. It's a matter of economics.

MR. SWINNEY: How will response to this be measured?

MR. PARKER: I wouldn't say I would measure it. I would be extremely interested in the response of children on tape; just the verbal response.

MR. SWINNEY: You would merely interpret the words which children utter?

DR. McLUHAN: But you would also get a tonality that is helpful with a verbal phrasing.

MR. PARKER: One of the most beautiful remarks I ever heard about anything I designed occurred when I took a group of schoolchildren through the gallery in Toronto. A boy asked me, "Did you design that?" and I said, "Yes," and he said, "Wow!"

MR. SWINNEY: What did you read from this response?

MR. PARKER: We tried an experiment,[229] in which we had two sensory chambers in front of two classrooms in new rooms, one in an upper middle-class school and one in a disadvantaged school. The pupils couldn't enter the classroom without going through these chambers, where they had tactile things and smells and sounds; and for something to taste, we put in two little pouches, one containing some cut carrots and the other candy, with a sign that said, "Take One."

When the students from the middle-class school went through, there was no response, they just walked right through and sat down, and the teacher asked them, "Didn't you notice anything as you came into the room?" And they answered, "Yes." And she said,

"Why did you think we did this?" The answer was, "We thought you were trying to confuse us, and when we got to the carrots and candy, we would pick the wrong one and pick the candy."

When we asked the students in the disadvantaged school—first of all, they nearly blew the roof off the tape recorder. They were screaming. We asked them what they thought, and they were wild about it. We asked them, "Did you notice anything at the end of the room?" And we asked them, "Did you taste those two things?" And one of the kids said, "I tasted everything."

MR. SWINNEY: Because the upper-class Newburgh[230] children didn't say anything, do you assume there was no response?

MR. PARKER: There was a response, but it was as if they were being tested. It was obvious that the middle-class students, with their visual background, tried to find a line and a climax, and they thought candy was the climax because they are conditioned to school, and the question was, "Will they pick the candy or the carrot?" Whereas Dr. McLuhan says students from a disadvantaged school were much more tribal in nature.

QUESTION: There was a response to it which the tape recorder didn't measure.

MR. PARKER: Right.

QUESTION: I have one question that has concerned me through the last twenty-five minutes of your discussion. In accepting the presentation upstairs without making any sort of judgment, I found—even with my preconditioning in history—that I had very little involvement with the seventeenth-century artifacts, photographs, or slides, in comparison to the degree that I could enjoy or be involved in the contemporary ones. Would this be possibly a mistake on the part of the presentation, or was there intentionally less weight on the historical side?

MR. PARKER: When I took the first group up, I explained that. Actually, it's much easier, if you have only a week, to find background on contemporary New York than on New Amsterdam. If I had another week I could research various museums in this area, and probably come up with a better balance. It wasn't a mistake, it was expediency.

QUESTION: There is another technical point. If you could have the
time to get better slides of New York, would you have avoided the
stereotyped views, which turned me off a bit?

MR. PARKER: Yes, we were forced to go to a commercial enterprise
and buy slides.

MR. RATH: I would like to branch off to discuss what has to do with
learning and several other things. My question has to do with the
limitations of the museum in terms of space and the capacity to
take people at certain hours. It has to do with the responsibility of
museums to key into the formal educational system in some way, so
that the materials of the past—and I am talking as a historian—can
be made available in better form to those who are trying to teach in
schools. In the schools we have, for example, chemistry and physics
laboratories. Why can't we have history laboratories and workshops?

This is the line of reasoning that has guided us in trying to set
up in Cooperstown[231] during the last three years, a course for
highly directed teachers who, in turn (based on that principle of
the 1950s, when Sputnik[232] came along and we got excited about
the scientists) would train other groups in regional centres. We
have taken these people and we have worked with them to help
them to understand the materials of history and their use. Has this
validity in your terms?

DR. McLUHAN: Yes. I mentioned yesterday that there is this huge
area of history that no historian has ever looked at: war as education.[233] Why not let the kids loose on it?

If they know that the historian has never wised up to this
aspect of war, they know they are the first in. They have it all to
themselves for the first time. I think teams of children—not individuals, teams of children—could be released into the history of
war as a brand-new, untouched territory, in which they would have
to discover, for example, what the Gauls[234] learned from Caesar.[235]

QUESTION: This is the method we're using, the induction method. It's
interdiscipline as well. It calls on geography and sociology, all of
these things. I refer again to this matter of the responsibility of the
museum to reach outside of itself.

[The meeting adjourned for luncheon, 12:30 PM.]

Tuesday Afternoon, October 10, 1967

MR. MILLER: This is our last session of the seminar, and I have some
announcements that I would like to make.

[Announcements made off the record.]

DR. McLUHAN: During the break, as always happens, unexpected
points emerged.

We were standing in front of the case with the old fire engine,
and somebody asked, "In what sense would you say that this
object has made a new environment here for itself?" I suddenly
realized that, just like the comment about visual bias, which
turned out to mean, not a mental, but a sensory bias, totally
unconscious—so here too what I had taken for granted had been
misunderstood. I meant to say that these objects created their own
space in their initial impact, when they were new. Like the Model
T, like the railway, like any other form, they create their own space.

I grew up close to a fire station, when there were no trucks,
just the horses. And a more exciting place for kids to grow up was
unimaginable. We knew all the firemen and all their horses, and
we knew all their problems, and we used to slide up and down that
pole from the second floor. It was a great spot.

But the fire engine creates a space that permits people to live
in congregated togetherness. Without the fire engine the space
between houses would have to be fantastic. The whole city space
is altered by the existence of the fire engine. In the same way, the
Model T created road systems, as the railway did, and created
totally different relationships between people at play and at work.

In a museum, that fire engine doesn't create any new space at
all; it's put in an old space, but a space that is new for it. It never
could have existed in a glass case at any other time. It's a new
situation for the fire engine as an artifact to be in a case, or in an
exhibition hall, and that turns it into a work of art.

The fire engine in its natural habitat is not a work of art. In a museum it becomes a work of art, because it's not a natural environment for it.

This reminded me of Sigfried Giedion,[236] whose work I have followed since 1939. He was in St. Louis[237] then, giving the lectures that were published as *Space, Time and Architecture.* I became acquainted with him and have known him ever since.

Giedion's whole approach to art and technology is environment. He called the environment non-museum history, because people are always unaware of it. Now the study of environments as a new perception and new teleology is his theme; so the secret of Giedion is indispensable in the context of here and now. His whole approach to the study of changing styles in art and architecture is something I have taken for granted since '39, when I first met him. It was all new to me then.

So perhaps I have taken too much for granted. This Giedion approach (like Hall's educational approach,[238] which we mentioned earlier, to the hidden dimensions of experience) is one that seems to me indicated for our time.

And now, there were some other basic facets that popped up during cocktails. Would somebody please remind me of one or two before I stop?

QUESTION: The research on the involvement of a person.

DR McLUHAN: Oh, yes. We have done an experiment in Toronto over the past four or five years under an IBM grant, and we call it a study of sensory quotient or sensory profile of individuals and groups.

We work on the IBM personnel, who are wrappers, systems engineers, etc., in order to discover a sensory profile. We used various forms of experience, various kinds of objects were felt, handled, heard, seen, and they had patterns; each of these situations was patterned. The whole idea of measuring was based on how long it took them to spot the patterning, triangular, rectangular, circular, anything. The timing was done by computer, and naturally those who had aptitude or special preference in this or that area tended to be a little faster in recognizing that form. And so from these tests, over the years, we have been able to build up a sensory profile of these occupational groups.[239]

The report hasn't been published, but it is finished.[240] It's amazing to see the sensory quotient of individual members of this firm. All of them tend to have a high IQ and considerable educational background, because it is a highly demanding kind of occupational world. But there is very little correlation between IQ and sensory quotient. SQ and IQ just don't correlate.

We found, for example, that the sensory profiles of a secretary and systems engineer are almost identical, and when you think of this, it doesn't seem so odd: a secretary is also a systems engineer. A secretary has to play the whole field of a great variety of factors simultaneously.

I don't know of any other experiment like this anywhere. I wish there had been hundreds of others. Has anybody ever heard of a similar effort to discover sensory profile or quotient?

QUESTION: The English parlour game of taking twenty objects, passing them around the room and at the end of the game finding out who can remember all twenty objects.

DR. McLUHAN: I have heard of that game, but I haven't heard of it in relation to this. But at the Expo they had this sensory sort of— Some of you may have had this experience: they give you various olfactory, thermal tests, but they never asked which one you preferred.

QUESTION: What was the influence of age on this profile? Because what you have been suggesting to us is an all-encompassing sensory perception of what we're doing.

DR. McLUHAN: The profile, the age groups, tended to be pretty homogeneous.

QUESTION: How could you resist the temptation to go and get some kids and see what their profiles were?

DR. McLUHAN: That's actually going on now. The same materials are being used outside IBM with different age groups. This sort of knowledge of sensory preference revealed instantly a profile curve, so that you could pretty well tell which kinds of people would excel in which kinds of areas, and which kinds of activities.

You could tell which would be natural airmen or natural literary types or natural architects.

QUESTION: That's aptitude testing.

DR. McLUHAN: Highly visual.

MR. PARKER: He is suggesting that it's a kind of aptitude test.

DR. McLUHAN: I thought you said architect. These aptitudes are implied in any profile, and this is something we all use as a rule of thumb in our dealings with people anywhere; but nobody has ever tried to give it a precise measurement. I'm pretty sure that it can have considerable use.

It will also enable you to spot where learning disabilities would lurk in quite intelligent individuals. Most IQ tests are visual as such. Nearly all the items in an intelligence test are visual. And so it doesn't help to reveal learning disabilities. Some senses, the senses that impede learning, are often tactile or auditory and not in any way related to vision. On the other hand, there are a great many learning difficulties closely related to vision.

QUESTION: I'm not familiar with the test. Could you tell us just what is measured?

DR. McLUHAN: Active and passive touch, hearing and seeing.

QUESTION: Could you be a little bit more specific? The person came in front of an object—

DR. McLUHAN: No, they handled objects with different designs on them or in them, but they weren't allowed to see them, so they had to discover by active or passive touch whether these things were triangular or rectangular, etc. The time of recognition was checked, how long it took them to recognize the form.

MISS FISHER: Did you say some preference came into that?

DR. McLUHAN: Oh, sure, because some people can recognize in an instant.

QUESTION: What kinds of objects did you have?

DR. McLUHAN: In size, these were small things, mostly an inch square or so. They were just large enough to be handled or touched.

Then there was the hearing test which was rather complicated, because to get space into hearing for testing is not easy. The visual test wasn't so difficult. But it wasn't a simple one. It was based on different textures. Lighting on different textures. Again, this was to reveal pattern.

As I say, this will all be written and published in the immediate future. It has never been done by anybody before as far as I know, so it's a little difficult to explain in brief.

MR. PARKER: You were mentioning this morning that any artifact exists as a sensory index, so an extrapolation might be very interesting. To take the work of an artist, find out what the sensory profile of an individual is, and correlate it to the work of art; it will help us to arrive at some kind of insight into the way to read artifacts. Obviously, a man whose orientation is most highly tactile is going to produce objects which express that.

DR. McLUHAN: Let's say that the Japanese world is fascinated with the intervals between objects and with textures. This is extreme preference for the tactile. So Japanese flower arrangement is entirely devoted to the theme of finding the right space between objects.

But this is true of the whole tactile world that is under our noses. The whole young crowd on our own doorsteps is devoted to textures. Their clothing interests aren't based on appearance but textures. The teenagers today look horrible, they don't care about photogenic qualities in clothing; they care very much about the active and passive tactile qualities of clothing and shoes.

MR. ELLIN: But they don't think they look horrible.

DR. McLUHAN: They don't care about their looks. They want the feeling of involvement.

MR. ELLIN: But the textures in clothing that are being used are age-old, so therefore the miniskirt and microskirt—

DR. McLUHAN: I'm thinking of the colours and the clothing textures. They prefer leather, heavy surfaces.

MR. ELLIN: People preferred leather before.

DR. McLUHAN: No, not in highly upper-class circles.

MR. ELLIN: Oh, yes, the hunting jacket, for instance.

DR. McLUHAN: But that's not for daily dress.

MR. ELLIN: But it was preferred.

DR. McLUHAN: That's a hunting uniform. Paul Bunyan,[241] Daniel Boone,[242] they have a costume. This isn't daily dress. You're not getting a costume confused with daily dress?

MR. GEORGE BOWDITCH (Adirondack Museum):[243] Isn't daily dress a costume?

DR. McLUHAN: No, because it's supposed to be invisible.

MR. FREDERICK M. LEHMAN (Wantagh Historical Museum):[244] I think colour and styles are different.

Let's keep our eye on the thing and let's not worry about the words we're using.

QUESTION: I would like to ask one other question, going back to environment. You used the example of a fire engine, which gave rise to congested living. Wasn't it congested living that gave rise to the fire engine?

DR. McLUHAN: Yes, and with the coming of the motorized fire department, congestion became much greater. Now it's the actual vehicle that causes the congestion, but originally it was the congestion that was caused by reason of quick access.

QUESTION: Then it was congestion that created the fire engine.

DR. McLUHAN: No, exactly the opposite. You couldn't put houses close together until you had motorized fire equipment.

MR. BOWDITCH: My comment was that the fire engine was something that arose out of an environment. But that the fire engine didn't create the environment of congested living.

DR. McLUHAN: But I disagree flatly. Did I hear someone use the phrase, "The Fire of London, 1666"?[245] Because that was one of the most notorious examples of the lack of fire engines.

MR. BOWDITCH: But the congestion existed before the fire engine.

DR. McLUHAN: I see what you mean. It was the fact that the housing materials were inflammable, then. It wasn't just congestion, it was the fact that they used wood, very inflammable materials, for housing.

Gradually, that was dispensed with. They began to use brick. England avoided wood buildings from a quite early period. But in 1666, London was all wood.

QUESTION: We weren't fighting the fire, but the fact that the congestion existed first.

DR. McLUHAN: You're using a term that we read in our daily papers.
It's not a term ever used in the past. Not for cities. The slum conditions in the past were never referred to as congestion. That's a
recent term. So we're talking about different cultural conditions,
altogether. Congestion as created by vehicles is a very different
thing from the slum, which is not created by vehicles but by
human laziness and willingness to stay close together for many
years, like *La bohème*,[246] like artists, bohemians. Artists' slums get
crowded together because they like to talk to each other. It has
nothing to do with poverty in our present sense of the word.

MR. PARKER: They also like the richness of the environment. They
don't like the antisepsis, the barbered lawns of suburbia.

DR. McLUHAN: They don't like an abysmal environment. They like
an involving, much mixed, sensuous environment, like a pub.
There's nothing in North America like a pub, because the British
Cockney or the British lower class are much more sensuous than
people in this country. The pub is a very rich, tactile, olfactory,
auditory environment. Like the Beatles.[247]

MR. PARKER: Are they olfactory?

DR. McLUHAN: But the North American pub or tavern is, by comparison, a very hygienic and visual spot. It's rectangular. It has
vertical walls. These are features that any pub would carefully
avoid in favour of low beams and uneven walls.

When you saw the picture yesterday of Prince Charles entering
Cambridge,[248] I hope you noticed that countenance. You can't
produce a countenance like that from a visual environment. It's
monstrous. No visual, self-respecting people would put up with
such features. This is part of a British aristocratic, Cockney, world
(the two are often close together), in which characters produce the
most incredible fungi as features. You can see it in a film here in
New York called *Dream Street*.[249]

But this kind of tolerance of the monstrous is natural in
Cockney and aristocratic environments alike, because they don't

live by appearance. The world of appearance is for a much lower middle-class society.

QUESTION: I think you don't know Boston or the South.

DR. McLUHAN: All right, it's full of old-country Cockney slum types, and Irishmen, etc. Who's the Englishman who rents his castle, the Duke of Bedford?[250]

MR. PARKER: He's written a book recently[251] in which he describes how to prepare a jacket properly for wearing. You buy a very expensive jacket, you put stones in each pocket, and then hang it on the line during a rain, and then you put it on. The pockets hang properly.

MISS FISHER: How about the uniform of the City,[252] a very tightly furled umbrella?

DR. McLUHAN: It is carried by a strictly middle-class person who lives by visual values.

MR. PARKER: That's strictly a uniform, too, isn't it?

QUESTION: I'm convinced that I didn't understand the definition of story line, but I would like to go back to something we were discussing this morning. I wonder how it is that you have ascertained that the method of exhibiting and orienting which was shown this morning communicates to the child, who, as you say, is television-educated? But how is it the child, who you say is used to sitting no more than eight inches from the television screen, can comprehend and meaningfully relate to the images all around which are, as a matter of fact, rather hard to relate to, because they move so quickly? On what grounds have you decided that this is a meaningful way to communicate to children and/or adults?

MR. PARKER: The quality of television is much the same as the quality of the newspaper, capable of very sudden movements from one point to another point. The quality of television is that you're able to change rapidly from one image to another. You can be in Vietnam and almost at the same moment in downtown New York or other points.

QUESTION: That's a news program. How about the *Lucy* show?[253]

DR. McLUHAN: That's like the stockbroker with the umbrella; it is a carryover from the past. We live in visual comfort, and naturally people will turn to these forms of entertainment.

QUESTION: So from this you selected the next points of departure?

DR. McLUHAN: Television doesn't need a story line because it doesn't have any time sequence. The movie tends to retain a story line because of its time sequence. There is no time sequence in a newspaper or telegraph; so there is no story in them.

QUESTION: What was that again?

DR. McLUHAN: Television doesn't need a time sequence. The images don't have to be related in time any more than they do in the newspaper.

QUESTION: But they follow in time.

DR. McLUHAN: No. They can if you're imposing another medium on television. If you're imposing a movie.

QUESTION: If you're looking over a duration of time—

DR. McLUHAN: The commercial follows the *Perry Mason* show,[254] but you don't connect them.

MISS FISHER: Suppose we took something like your *Medium is the Massage*[255] produced for television and projected that in a movie theatre.

DR. McLUHAN: The movie theatre is the massage. Being inside is getting the full treatment.

MISS FISHER: There seemed to be an indication that there is something coming out differently.

DR. McLUHAN: When you get massaged you do come out quite different.

MISS FISHER: That was a fabulous television program, and I think that it would be fabulous—

MR. PARKER: It may be fabulous but it would be totally different. The high-definition image masseur of the film is going to change the message.

MISS FISHER: Speaking of definition, what is high definition and low definition?

MR. PARKER: It's very simple. Just compare the television screen, a low definition, to photography, which is high. You feed in imaginatively in order to complete the experience.

DR. McLUHAN: We have been waiting for somebody to arrive, and that's Miss Román.[256] She's doing an anthropology degree, and

she's interested in all aspects of the TV industry, including the star
system.

The star system in your world is free, a prize exhibit, the expensive object. I suggest it's finished, that the environment is going to
take the place of the object.

MR. PARKER: What implications does that have on the Leonardo da
Vinci we bought recently? That's a star system. The idea of this
session is that we get some feedback from the floor.

MRS. MARY BLACK[257] (Director, Museum of American Folk Arts):[258] I
would be glad to start. My opinion is that you two gentlemen have
changed enormously in two days, and I have been trying to figure
out why you're here and why I'm here, and I think I've come to the
conclusion that it is to get us off our duffs and talking back to you,
is that correct?

DR. McLUHAN: Right.

MRS. BLACK: I didn't see the performance of this morning. I think,
Mr. Parker, that you're a very brave and gallant man to present
what you have presented to us with so little money and so little
time. It's awful, but it's a pattern that perhaps we can fill out, and I
think this is the purpose.

I think we all know more than we say in our museums, and I
think that's why you're here, to jog us into saying more; is that
correct?

MR. PARKER: Correct, too.

DR. McLUHAN: There's a phrase of James Joyce, "Who gave you that
numb?"[259] Every name is a numb because it ends tension. When
you have labelled something, perception flickers out. You have
classified it and that's the end of perception.

You can start thinking about it if you like, but you stop
perceiving. The artist is never content with labels or names or
categories. He's always insisting on sticking a pin right into you.

MR. PARKER: This is actually *apropos* of my proposal to build a gallery
with no labels, and get some feedback and then label it properly,
and get some other feedback. I know what the difference is.

MR. DUNN: How does your gallery without labels differ in essence
from the small, historical museum in the very small village in

Western New York with, not a random, but a very carefully
selected accumulation of artifacts relating to this town, often
without labels, not because they don't want them but because they
don't know how to write them, with the articles often in their
environment?

MR. PARKER: I already said I didn't know which was the better one.
What I would like to have from such a museum is the feedback.

MR. DUNN: The feedback is that this is good, and what we as high-
priced professionals are doing to the museums is bad. In other
words, when we go to one of the small-town museums and say,
"You're doing the wrong thing," and say, "You're not saying
anything with these articles, you're simply exposing them to the
local townspeople, you're not doing a full job," then the local
townspeople say back to us, "We like it that way."

MISS FISHER: Have either of you ever come across the museum in
Edinburgh called the Museum of Childhood?[260] I discovered it
there. It has the most enchanting labels. These are witty in a low-
toned way, not coy. It is a kind of label that asks the questions.
These are toys and clothing of childhood, but their labelling
system is something that seemed particularly good. In discussions
of the museum we always hassle over the question of labels, how
much to give. But these are very leading and humorous.

MR. PARKER: It may be good to adopt the attitude that, unless a
person is prepared to ask a question, don't give him an answer.

MR. ELLIN: Are you prepared for some more feedback?

DR. McLUHAN: Has anyone ever studied why children prefer
cartoons to pictures? The cartoon has very low quality and very
little information, whereas the picture is loaded with information.
Children don't like that.

MR. PARKER: Of course, it most closely approaches the child's
recognition.

DR. RICHARD B.K. McLANATHAN[261] (Museum Consultant, Writer):
What is the relation between the information and understanding?

DR. McLUHAN: At the moment of information overload, pattern
recognition tends to occur. As long as the information is strictly in

a reasonable quantity, nobody ever sees the pattern. But give it the overload treatment and the pattern suddenly stands out.

DR. FLEMING: In your film experience upstairs I kept asking myself, what would a person get out of the images of the portraits, the paintings, if he could not identify them? I couldn't identify a great many of them. They were coming too rapidly.

But what is the understanding, what is the value, of the image if you can't identify it?

MR. PARKER: The quality and flavour of the time we're trying to present, not specific data about it. It doesn't matter whether Rembrandt painted it or Vermeer, the quality of the thing comes through—of the time, the age.

DR. FLEMING: What do you mean by the time? Do you mean the age?

MR. PARKER: Yes.

DR. FLEMING: But suppose the person doesn't even know the age? You had pictures from various ages.

MR. PARKER: I agree, except there is a big span between today's New York and the Dutch.

DR. FLEMING: I'm not sure a person, one who belonged to the seventeenth century—

MR. PARKER: Does it matter that it was that particular time? Does it matter? What matters is the quality and flavour of the age, not whether it's the seventeenth century, but rather just the age.

DR. FLEMING: But what if you don't know the age?

MR. PARKER: You will find that out.

DR. FLEMING: If somebody didn't tell you what the age was, you would miss the whole point.

DR. McLUHAN: That's an interesting remark, but I think it's one that needs much thought. Chronology—we value chronology. In the present age you can have access to all the ages that ever were, at any instant you want. You don't have to wait for chronology anymore, and that goes for the future as well as the past.

The programming of environments on the moon or elsewhere can be done here. You can have the experience of what the moon travellers will feel like in a few years. You can have it here, now;

but I don't think it's likely to reveal anything that we don't already know.

The history of utopias is a fascinating study because men in utopias always thought they were projecting ideal images of some age to come, whereas they were in fact taking detailed pictures of the days just behind them.

That's just as true of George Orwell[262] as it is of *Bonanza*[263] or Plato's *Republic*.[264] They are all rearview mirrors of the preceding age.

That's what we're doing now, today. Is not a museum an image of the preceding age, not the present? It's a utopian image of a preceding age, not our time at all.

MR. ELLIN: There is a level of response that I had hoped to find here, and I'm somewhat disappointed that we haven't talked more about it.

I think we, as the audience, are here to investigate new ways of approaching our own communications role. In order to do this, it's totally important that we begin to recognize the fact that the museum is a particular medium of communication, with highly specialized attributes. We should begin to think about what these attributes are, and take some cognizance of the fact that we have a power to use this medium in its own special way for its own special attributes and purposes.

DR. McLUHAN: It's a prepared environment; prepared for special effects.

MR. ELLIN: It's also an inherited environment, in that those of us sitting here—to a large extent—have up to this point not shaped its attributes. We find ourselves the custodians of environment which is highly architectural, which has a very unusual dimension in that the time and flow of people through its interior spaces is an important part of the environment. Its subject matter consists of other environments which it houses.

It is a far more complex medium in my opinion than film or television or books or other things we can point to, and I think it's terribly important that we address ourselves to analyzing what this animal is, what kind of an environment it is, and how we, as custodians, can begin to manipulate it to the end that we seek.

DR. McLUHAN: How much do you think of it as a teaching machine, programmed?

MR. ELLIN: My own personal view is that it is an environment, a medium, which is meant to be highly programmed, and I think that we haven't programmed at all. But in the coming years we will be called upon more and more to program it, and I'm not speaking about ten years hence, I'm talking about this year, next week, tomorrow. I think we must begin to think about how to program this environment and to what end.

Isn't this the sort of thing we should be talking about at this point?

MR. PARKER: Along these lines, I think of the fact that your audience is part of your environment, and so little is known about your audience. It strikes me that we should shift our attention. We have had a great deal of scholarly research done upon the collections. Let's do some of that research upon our audience.

MR. ELLIN: Day before yesterday was Sunday, and I took advantage of the time to work on my car in front of the museum because we have a nice shop, and while I was underneath my car, a few feet from the door of the museum, on a Sunday afternoon, I learned more about my audience than I have in six months, because I was a tape recorder, and I was hearing what was said as people entered and left.

I think one of the first steps is to begin to understand our audience. Television is a powerful medium, because it has devoted a great deal of attention to how to make it with the audience. Whether it's doing it the right way is another matter.

We seem to think very little about our audiences. I doubt if there is anybody in this room who has any real understanding of how people move through museum space. We talked about this before, and you said something that I thought was very interesting. When you do an installation, before you start, you walk through an empty gallery for a day and begin to get some feel of how a person would move through this architectural space, what his natural resting points might be.

DR. McLUHAN: What is your concept of the happening[265] in relation to museums? Are museums happenings in the new sense of the word?

MR. ELLIN: I think this is what is going to happen to museums: they are going to be happenings. They are going to be more and more in-capsule environments, as a happening is, and less and less an archive or storehouse of artifacts.

MR. PARKER: Of course, a happening is not a spectator sport and it's highly programmed.

MR. ELLIN: No, it is a participating event, and that's why I say that museums have to be highly programmed in order to make it with the audiences we will be addressing ourselves to. I would like to have some response.

MR. RATH: I wonder why Mr. Ellin thinks that the audience is not responsive? He's with the Guggenheim Museum, which has been taking in hundreds of thousands of people who are evidently responsive.

MR. ELLIN: I have an uneasy feeling that that's not necessarily true, and I have occasion, almost daily, to look at the people who come off the chute at the bottom, and I think I know what fungus looks like, whether it's Prince Charles or an enlightened face. One gets to know or identify the species that one works with, and I have an uneasy feeling that we get through in a very meagre and unsatis-factory way.

MR. RATH: You should be concerned, but isn't this a matter of performing some act of stimulation so people will conceivably come back to you, or go to some other museum and make valid comparisons?

MR. ELLIN: But the act of stimulation is not performed anymore, in my opinion, simply by installing objects in some linear matrix for people to encounter in a very unimaginative architectural itinerary.

MR. RATH: I can agree with that.

MR. ELLIN: I think we have to begin worrying about this and concern ourselves with how to remedy the situation. We're dealing with an audience that has, in our sense of the word, a much reduced span of attention. So much exciting visual material is competing for their attention that they simply don't get turned on in the museum anymore.

QUESTION: How do you deal with the fact of the Wyeth show[266] and its incredible popularity?

MR. ELLIN: I don't measure response by the box office. I think the number of people who go to any exhibition is not a fair indication of what has gotten through. It's much more an index of how successfully the exhibition has been promulgated as a news phenomenon.

I don't think it's a reliable index. I think a sampling of the people who walk through a successful exhibition would, surprisingly, show no greater impact than an exhibition which has drawn a few hundred people.

I think we're too smug in accepting attendance as an index of success in our work.

QUESTION: Why is it any less reliable than pulling facts out of the air?

MR. ELLIN: I suggest we begin to interphase with the human being when his response is fresh, that we begin to make studies and surveys and integrate people with the data, and try to measure how we're reaching them, if at all.

MR. KINGMAN: Have you a measure, in your large attendance, of those who have come for sightseeing and those repeaters who come for seeing what you're specifically offering?

MR. ELLIN: We don't have a measure.

MR. KINGMAN: But this is an exciting showplace. Do people come who have never been to the Guggenheim before, or because of the show you have on there?

MR. ELLIN: I suspect—and I hesitate for obvious reasons to try and verify it—but I suspect that a large part of our attendance, and the attendance of any museum which is a landmark—and there are others in the city which are—is due simply to the fact that we're on a standard sightseeing itinerary, a stop on a route; and regardless of what we have, a certain predictable and large portion of our attendance would simply continue.

I think if we followed Allen Cambro's suggestion of making an environmental sculpture out of the Guggenheim, we would have an acceptable box office.

MR. RATH: I remember Oliver Wendell Holmes[267] saying that the best test of the truth is the open market, and I would suggest that perhaps the best test of the museum is the open market. We have lived through some fabulous years, when museum attendance, for some sociological reason that we ought to understand because we have been in business for many years, has accelerated. In this matter of knowing your audience, we have stated the fact that no two audiences are exactly the same. There are no valid things that you can say about the ROM that will apply to my situation in Cooperstown,[268] New York, that I would think worth a damn, because that's not the audience that I have.

But we know something about our audience, if only because we have been in the business for a long time, and we sense this thing. We work with that audience.

MR. ELLIN: Do you really think there are different audiences depending upon geographic location?

QUESTION: But also subject matter. Why don't you differentiate between the kinds of museums? Isn't that infinitely important?

DR. McLANATHAN: Could you be a little more explicit in connection with what you mean by orientation?

DR. McLUHAN: When we use the phrase, "we who are in this business"—the one thing that is almost inevitable for anybody in "this business," whether it's the museum industry, the knowledge industry, or the hardware industry, is that he does not know its boundaries or environment, because he is too close to it. People in a business can't possibly perceive it.

MR. RATH: This leads to the Duncan Cameron theme[269]—your Canadian friend who has been making some surveys up there. We talked at great length with Duncan, and I couldn't disagree with him more. If Duncan is right, and if you're right, then I have wasted thirty years in this business. If I don't know something about my business at this point, I ought to quit.

MR. SWINNEY: Is that your recommendation?

DR. McLUHAN: Peter Drucker,[270] the management consultant, has spent his whole life invading other people's business to reveal to them how little they know about it. They pay him very fancy prices for that.

MR. RATH: I have some experience of this, and damn it, I'm finished telling the expert what to tell me, because I have to give him the basic information on which he makes his judgment.

DR. McLUHAN: So you talk to Peter Drucker. I don't think he's quite like ordinary psychiatrists, but I was telling someone about the Negro fellow who was apprehended outside a house with a sofa on his head. When questioned, he said, "I ain't a looter. I'm a psychiatrist and I'm making a house call."[271]

Here is our movie star, Miss Román. She's the anthropologist working in the star system, and provides a very pleasant occasion for a change.

Miss Román, this group has expected you—they're curators and museum directors and art gallery directors—and I had sort of promised them that you would have a few words to say about the star system, because naturally, these people are very much interested in major exhibits and objects of major attention, and what changes are taking place in the public taste in this matter. So, since we're almost ready to disband, does anything come to mind in this area concerning the present state of the star system in the different parts of the world?

MISS LETÍCIA ROMÁN: I think the star system in America, as far as your concept of star is concerned, has pretty well left the actor and entered other fields, such as television. My feeling is, a product is a real star, and the actors very much the public.

The product is the link between actors and public. They both use Dash[272]—and the image that the Hollywood star used to have, today it is the product that has that image. Television stars cannot betray you by changing their image, as Ingrid Bergman did years ago when she ran away with Rosselini,[273] and everybody felt very betrayed.

The product can. We expect a certain quality. *Chrysler* shows[274] are always one-hour, strong, dramatic. Actually, they're almost the same words that Chrysler itself uses to advertise the car. This, in other parts of the world, is not true. As a matter of fact, exactly the opposite happened in Italy, where the star, the local star, the vehicles of the local star, were always very close to reality, so the public couldn't escape seeing Italian films. You will all remember *Rome, Open City*.[275] There was little one could escape from.

The American star and the vehicle with American stars made in Italy offered escape; but local films never did. It's only now, with the advent of television, that there is an escape possibility.

Advertising is the most popular thing in Italian television. We have a half-hour program called *Caraselli*,[276] and men come home from the office to watch it. I think they like it because it has that escape valve which our products usually do not have. They can start from a plateau which is common, but they can enter and exit from a world which is completely special.

DR. McLUHAN: I think your comment that the audience has become the star is of great relevance to this.

MISS ROMÁN: I think a funny thing has happened. When I watch television I feel that the way the product is talked about—Let's put it this way. Let's look at television plots. They are not 1967 plots. There is no suspense value. They are almost all out of studio archives, and we can look at them for ten minutes and we know what is going to happen. Even our favourites aren't too special-looking.

I should think that the only thing that is really 1967, if not 1968, is the commercial, and it's closer to us because the advertising sort of takes the trouble to find out how we dress and how we talk and what we want to see and what we bring. And this famous image that it does create extends throughout the whole show. Take cigarettes, for example. Cigarettes will not sponsor serious shows anymore. They have entered the family circle. They sponsor soap operas. Actually, lighthearted comedies, to sort of counteract the guilt that is connected with smoking.

I think if one can equate the star method that was used in Hollywood from 1920 on, one can find a pretty good parallel with the Madison Avenue technique of publicizing products—whereas television stars have no publicity whatsoever, or very little. They are subservient to the products.

They create a nice pause between commercials. I'm not crazy about commercials. That's what I think is happening. It's not true of Germany or many other areas.

DR. McLUHAN: Are there people here, for example, who would like to comment on any of these observations, or would, perhaps, a comparison of museum audiences in Germany, France, and Italy be enlightening? Would there be motives for going to a museum in Germany quite different from those for going to a similar museum here?

I was amazed at the recent German documentary CBS had two or three weeks ago, on which they just casually mentioned that eighty percent of all German schoolchildren now leave school at fourteen. They go to trade schools and vocational schools at fourteen. The show associated this fact with the great German uneasiness because of lack of image or identity. They can no longer relate themselves to a Hitler image or to that period, and they haven't found a new image. This creates terrible unhappiness inside, and guilt feelings.

Perhaps this is not an ideal time to bring it up, but the Minotaur story[277] has something to do with it. The quest for identity is always associated with violence, and that applies to group identity as well as private. Perhaps museums don't offer enough violence as a means of discovering their purposes or who they are. What are we here for?

The John Waynes[278] represent very old-fashioned, nineteenth-century violence as a means of acquiring private identity. But the twentieth century is not so much interested in private identity as in corporate image.

What Miss Román just said about the fact that the Hollywood star has yielded to the audience as a star is very interesting. I

never thought of that. I never thought of the audience as part of
the new star system. But the statisticians are very busy building
up the image of the object as star—just what we were talking
about a minute ago.

The audience is the new star, and the desire is to be associated
with the right audience, especially in subject.

MR. RATH: That's no different from Valentino.[279]

DR. McLUHAN: He wasn't an audience.

MR. RATH: But his audience, at that time, was the star. What's
different today from the star system of years past—just plucking
Valentino out of the air as an example?

MISS ROMÁN: We have to discuss what really goes into the making
of a star. What is the prerequisite for a star to become a star? The
star has to have a plateau, a common denominator, from which we
can start our trip into specialness, with which everybody can identify. He has to have some sort of common place in which one can
put the feet down.

For instance, Valentino was extremely beautiful, but he had
some very common features. He was a man's man; every man
could see himself without too much trouble, and then he could
vicariously enter the world of extreme beauty.

Or Cagney[280] or John Wayne, they all had what was common
to all Americans. They represented what everybody had done,
a little. This was very necessary for stardom: a sort of area-of-X
factor that is extremely special, almost superhuman, where one
can enter and exist. To me, the actor has to be like a fixed star. He
has to hold his image almost immobile. He can't change at any
time. He must stay there for people to come in and out of; to wear
at will. Today we don't do that.

QUESTION: How about Cary Grant?[281]

MISS ROMÁN: Oh, yes, we still carry on. At least I do; I don't know
about you.

But let's take television, Barbara Parkins,[282] or any other beautiful television actress. She's in a normal situation. She says normal
lines; she always looks like the girl you have just left. You don't
want to enter the skin of her boyfriend to make love to her; you

just ring the doorbell of your own girlfriend. This trip isn't necessary, and it was very necessary before.

I remember the fans, also, who asked magazines to shoot
layouts of their favourite stars having lunch with another favourite
star. It's a sort of motorized desire to want to enter a person for a
very brief moment, and act through that person. That's what made
the Hollywood star.

I wonder if any one of you wants to enter the skin of Lorne Green[283]
and make love? You don't even think about him. He's right there.
He's a friend of yours. He comes right at you; he invades you with
light. Whereas in movies you stay in the fetal position, in the dark,
looking at a projected image.

MR. STUART SILVER (Metropolitan Museum of Art):[284] I would like to
know if I'm drawing the wrong inference. It seems to me that the
purpose of this whole interview is that a parallel or an example is
being implied: that the star system of the movies is a thing of the
past, and the parallel to us is that the star system of objects to be
viewed in a museum is also a thing of the past; whereas in the
product system, which television has produced, if I understand the
comment you made, the viewer is the screen and the product is
important.

This also relates to Mr. Parker's experiment this morning.

DR. McLUHAN: The environment is not so readily inclined to become
a star as the product in the environment.

MR. SILVER: Mr. Parker, would you say that, within the limitations,
technical, financial, etc., of the work that you did upstairs, it represents a fair example demonstrating some of your hypotheses and
theories?

MR. PARKER: No. I have already said that I have thought of it purely
as an introduction to an almost unlimited area for exploitation.

MR. SILVER: As long as people think in nineteenth-century terms
and like to have strictures put down to which they can come back,
it seems to me that you may have caused a little more harm than
good by showing something that you felt doesn't represent...

QUESTION: This is why I asked if we might have a little exposition
on your part, of what you mean by the orientation process, what

your purpose is, because I think we all have something in common, and I would be interested to know what your ideas are.

MR. PARKER: I believe simply that if you take a person of the twentieth century, living in New York, he has certain attitudes towards space, and certain other attitudes towards time. He has a general orientation to the world in which he lives which can act as a barrier to an understanding of an alien culture. The purpose of an orientation gallery is to provide an interim period in order to let him adopt a stance which is a little more congenial to appreciation of the gallery.

QUESTION: How does this work? Is it by being bombarded by many images?

MR. PARKER: Yes, I think so, because in exposure I believe the approach is much closer to the way people actually live. I would regard multi-media shows as being very highly realistic in a sense that they tend to correspond to the general orchestration of sensibilities.

QUESTION: But you're saying you're preparing them for an appreciation of another world of a very different pattern.

MR. PARKER: That's right. I'm bringing into their consciousness the fact that this is the way they think, because if you're totally unaware of the way you move through your world, it's going to be very difficult to come into a different world. I'm trying to bring into consciousness the way we orchestrate our sensibilities, and I'm also trying to reach a *rapprochement* with the audience of today.

QUESTION: Suppose you get together with your audience of today, what does this do to introduce your audience of today to the world of yesterday?

MR. PARKER: Let's say they are unconscious of the fact that this is the way they use their sensibilities, and if it is raised into consciousness, it is then possible to use it as a method of insight.

QUESTION: How about the idea of decompression?

DR. MARTIN: I still don't get the connection between heightening aspects of today's world, and contributing to the understanding of yesterday's.

MR. PARKER: By heightening consciousness you heighten perception.

MR. RATH: May I offer something that perhaps can help Dick[285] and
    me understand this? One of the best museum exhibits I have ever
    seen consists of five objects on a bench. On that bench there is an
    early nineteenth-century truncheon, a wooden planter, a partly
    carved out log with a chisel, and a hammer. There are the five
    objects.

    Again and again a relationship is established between the
    finished object and the unfinished log, and we have watched again
    and again a father pick up the chisel and hit it with the hammer
    and say to his son, "See, this is how it's done." Would you substitute
    this for a multi-media presentation of the same thing?
MR. PARKER: I don't know. I haven't seen the particular display, and I
    don't know what I would do until I went to work on it.
MR. DUNN: Another example of the same thing, and perhaps the
    most unsuccessful, is an exhibit on gambling. The purpose of the
    exhibit was to teach visitors to the museum in Wisconsin that
    gambling was a lost cause.

    So we recreated Las Vegas very effectively, complete with
    confiscated slot machines, a roulette wheel, marked decks, dice
    tables, etc. We found that the graduate students who had come
    from a very sheltered environment, where these machines weren't
    permitted, were lining up to get into the gallery, and when you
    walked into the gallery it was really because at every machine
    there was a graduate student. They didn't bother to read the labels,
    which were trying to prove to them that it did not pay.

    And the real consolation was that one of them stole the deck of
    marked cards to use in the fraternity house. The moral is that an
    exhibit need not be successful to be effective.
DR. McLUHAN: I should have thought that was enormously successful.
MR. DUNN: I didn't prove the point that I started out to prove, that
    gambling would tend to lose money.
MR. MILLER: Unless there is a tremendous desire to go on with some
    terribly weighty facts, I think we will declare this session closed,
    and also our seminar, with the exception of the banquet this
    evening. We look forward to seeing you all at seven o'clock.

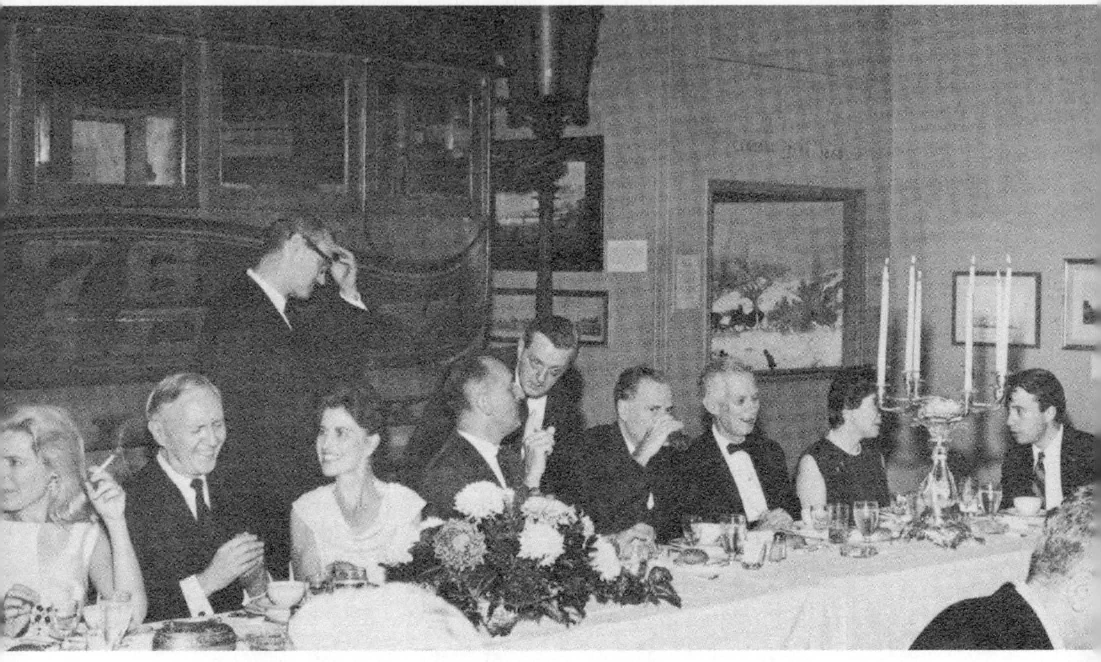

The speakers' table at the banquet, which was also held in the museum. From left to right: Mrs. Vivian G. Cahan, second wife of Dr. William Cahan; Professor Jacques Barzun; Mrs. Corinne Lewis McLuhan (1912–2008); President Louis S. Auchincloss; Marshall McLuhan (drinking); August Heckscher; Mrs. Ralph Miller; John Hightower; and in the immediate foreground, Harmon Goldstone. (Photo by Werner J. Kuhn.)

Tuesday Evening, October 10, 1967

[The program at the Tuesday evening banquet commenced at 8:30 PM, with introductory remarks by Mr. Louis S. Auchincloss, President of the Museum of the City of New York.]

MR. LOUIS S. AUCHINCLOSS: Ladies and Gentlemen: On behalf of the Director and Staff of the Museum of the City of New York, I'm happy to welcome you all here tonight at this concluding ceremony of our two-day seminar. Because we have four distinguished speakers tonight, your director and three leaders of the seminar, I shall make what I have to say very brief.

When Ralph Miller first took me about the museum as a blushing new trustee, to instruct me in the nature of my fiduciary duties, he gave me a helpful tour on the future techniques of museum display. I was dazzled at the prospect of how much could be done with varied lighting, with soundtracks, with pieces of cardboard, with crayons, with paintbrushes, and even, amid other accessories, here and there an artifact tastefully displayed.

I began to understand that the pictured history of New York, which was our ambition, could be more a question of museum presentation than of what that museum owned. What will we do with our collection, demanded I, in my naïveté? I was promptly hushed by our nervous and cautious director.

I have since discovered that we don't, after all, have to dispense with our collection, and I find myself converted by what has already been accomplished. That, of course, is the real function of a museum trustee, to be impressed by his director and by his staff. [Applause.]

I sometimes think that the ideal trustee is one who has inherited the idea of a museum display as that of a wall entirely covered with paintings, not a single inch of plaster showing, as in the Pitti Palace.[286] Such a trustee is bound to gape most satisfactorily before the advances discussed in the last forty-eight hours, and yet there may be noted a curious link between the most old-fashioned and the newest.

When I was looking at the remarkable assemblage of the pictures
that Mr. Parker has put together, as I saw children playing in our
streets in Harlem beside the sombre countenances of Erasmus[287]
and Charles V[288] in full colour, as I saw a Jackson Pollock[289] flit
over my head across the ceiling, and Pennsylvania Station[290] in all
its old glory start up before me, I was actually and a bit appeal-
ingly reminded of the variegated splendours of the Pitti Palace.
[Applause.]

Perhaps there was futurity in that ancient scheme, more than
we ever knew. I should like to make known to you, in case they are
not already known, the ladies and gentlemen sitting on the dais.

I shall not ask them to stand, nor shall I ask you to applaud.
I simply want to satisfy the natural curiosity of every guest here
tonight.

[Introductions were made.]

I now wish to introduce our Director, Mr. Ralph Miller.

MR. MILLER: Ladies and Gentlemen, we are delighted to have had
you as a part of this seminar that is now drawing to a close, regret-
fully, in some minds, happily, perhaps, in others. The point of view
is extremely important and has been for the past two days.

However, my task now is very brief, and I only wish to thank
the New York State Council on the Arts who are represented this
evening by John Hightower, the Executive Director, for having
the foresight and perhaps the courage to fund this seminar from
its inception. We are very grateful. We feel that somehow the
museum profession has been changed ever so slightly. How we
work this out in the years and months to come is something,
perhaps, that we all individually will be more concerned with.

I give you a very cordial welcome this evening, and on to our
next speaker. Thank you.

[Applause.]

MR. PARKER: I was just given a cigar which I didn't have an opportunity to smoke. I'm going to use a little joke which I have used before,
and if any of you have heard it, please forgive me.

It is incumbent upon anybody who faces an audience to start
out with a joke. I don't really know why, but I think that it's
designed to place the listeners at their ease. And I don't have a
joke, but I have an experience.

These jokes that we give out when we begin to talk don't bear
any relationship to what we're going to say. This is automatic. This is
not a joke, this is actually an experience: there is in Houston, Texas,
a sign in a drugstore window that says, "We dispense with accuracy."

I don't know about your political affiliations, but I picked a little
news up today, a little item that says, "World educators face challenge year."[291] It says that President Johnson[292] has challenged
world educators to use modern communications to extend learning.
I don't know whether that's the kiss of death or not. However, I
have come down here to New York from Toronto, and I have had
certain experiences which I would like to comment on, quite briefly.

One of the things I would like to say to you is that I have
encountered, in the Museum of the City of New York, one of the
few museums that I feel is really concerned with moving into the
twentieth century. [Applause.] I have found here a desire to take
this stance. Now, we all know that it is a very difficult thing to do,
to know how to move into the twentieth century. Mere desire is
something I don't encounter very often.

I have been asked to talk about what has happened over these
days. About our symposium here (at least I'm talking for myself) I
would say this: I don't know that I am right, but I know that I am
thinking.

Several things have happened in conversation outside of the
seminar, actually, and one of the things is this: people have come
to me and said, "Okay, do you expect me in my museum to keep
seven tape recorders, three projectors and two movie cameras
going simultaneously with the staff I have?" I don't expect that at
all. I think, in a way, technology is irrelevant. What I'm asking for
is an attitude, not the technology.

You may or may not have the facilities to use the technology, but inherent in the technology is an attitude of mind, because the technology is conditioning the audience. This is the thing I ask you to be aware of. I think this is the thing we have been talking about constantly.

I have said there is nothing the matter with being concerned about objects, their conservation, their preservation. But please understand that I think in our time the shift in audience sensibility has been of a kind which the world has never before encountered.

So my plea really is to ask you to pay a bit more attention to the audience, in order that we may really communicate. The Director of the Metropolitan Museum[293] approached me at the end of this last session and said, "I would like to ask a question. Is it that we are purely concerned with communicating to twelve-year-olds, or is there something behind this?" Then he said, "Is it that if we manage to communicate to the twelve-year-olds now, we're going to be in a better position to be able to communicate to the forty-year-olds later?"

And I said, "Yes, this is exactly the point."

At the age of twelve you can condition them, you can make them aware of their environment, you can make them aware of the input that is actually happening to them, and at this point I would be confident that you will have an audience when my son, who is now twenty-three, is forty.

I think that there is a tremendous need to extrapolate many of the things which were said in the course of the seminar into the museum world. I leave this to you. To extrapolate from the generalizations about the whole world we live in and from the specific comments on the world we live in, and to take these into the museum world.

I have been approached by people who said, "Look, what we really want to know is how to do it." I say no, because human beings don't come in groups, really, any more than museums do. Each museum is a different thing. People have come to me and said, "Okay, there is a case you say is bad. What would you do about it?" And my answer is, I think I said, "If you're prepared to pay me three weeks' salary I will come down and make a survey of it, and at the end of three weeks, I may have some insight." Somebody said to me this morning would I eliminate this or that. I don't know. I might do exactly the same thing.

All I trust and hope is that this seminar has been of a kind where you will go back to your area of endeavour and question your assumptions. If the ones you find are valid, hold them. But I think it's possible, if you begin to question some of the assumptions on which you work, that you might find it a little better to do a somewhat different thing. This is all I hope for. If we have aroused this kind of attitude, then I think we have been eminently successful.

I think that during the course of the seminar it came out—at least I stated it, and I'm sure that Dr. McLuhan agrees with me— that one of the great functions of art is the illumination of the environment, because if you can perceive environments then you do have a possibility of controlling them. Therefore, the onus, once more, lies upon you, to perceive your environment.

The point came up today with a bit of acrimony. Someone said, "I have been working in the museum world for thirty years, and if I don't know anything about it I should quit." And somebody said to him, "Is that an offer?" or a proposition, or some such thing. However, to stop being facetious, I would say that it's very true, as a psychologist has said, that the greatest discoveries have been made by one man invading another man's environment. So I arrive here from Toronto, invading your environment, and I can only hope that possibly I can make some discoveries which will help. I live in that hope.

And now to finish this off, I trust that you generally have found this seminar as profitable as I have. I have made many friends here, I think. Many more friends, I believe, than I have made enemies. And so I would hope to keep in touch, right across the board, with all the people who have been here, and see if we can't help each other in terms of moving the museums into the twentieth century, because I myself am absolutely convinced that, unless you make some positive move in the next ten years or fifteen years, the

museum world will become less and less a potent force. We have
to move into the contemporary world, and of outstanding importance to this is the necessity of research projects in understanding
our audience. And I think I will just leave it right there. Thank you
very much. [Applause.]

DR. McLUHAN: Mr. Harley Parker reminded me of an incident. Two
Navajo Indians were conducting a little chat across the big valley
by smoke signal. And in the middle of that chat the AEC[294]
released an atom bomb charge. When the big mushroom had
cleared off, one of them sent up a little smoke signal saying, "Gee, I
wish I had said that."

I wish I had said what Harley just said, and what he just said
I'm very happy to endorse. I have never been with a more exciting
group before. It is perhaps a little too exciting, in the sense that it
demands too much participation, but anyway, it has been a great
experience, and I wish to thank all of you for permitting me to
share it. Thank you.

[Applause.]

MR. AUCHINCLOSS: Now I introduce our principal speaker of this
evening, Mr. Jacques Barzun. The title of his speech will be
"Museum Piece 1967." [Applause.]

PROFESSOR JACQUES BARZUN: Mr. Auchincloss, Mr. Miller,
distinguished guests from the far North, ladies and gentlemen:
I have adopted a form of title[295] used by some of our artists—
you know the style: Predicament No. 3, Imposition 1942—in order
that what I have to say shall remain free from any suggestions of
an overarching thesis. I do want to marshal some facts in a certain
order, and I can't help having opinions about those facts, but the
collection is for you to look at from any point of view, whether in
bits or as a whole, and in any case not as a doctrine to espouse or
oppose.

That is another way of saying that I feel myself to be speaking
within the family. You have been discoursing for two days as a
study group—and I do not want you to turn suddenly into a part

of the general public. To that end I have refrained from supplying an advance text for newspaper notice. I would rather not be summarized or classified, and if I am to be misunderstood, let it be by you who have heard me through. For I am concerned with questions that press hard on me, and that I can only hope you will find relevant to your work. I need not add that I am not connected with museums except as a visitor, nor am I an expert in or on communication. I have kept myself ignorant of Information Theory[296] by dint of great effort and pertinacity. I am only a student of history, including the history of our own times, insofar as it can be known. This makes me a superfluous sub-Socrates[297] in a world teeming with essential experts. In a word, I can only raise questions, point to facts (or what I take to be facts), and do one of the things which no expert will risk: that is, try to think of as many different outer connections with as many kinds of feelings and ideas as possible about any one subject. So you may shortly think that I am wandering when I shall be only wondering, perhaps to some purpose.

Here let me interpose one small item of logistics: when I was bidden to discuss this general subject and told I could devote some forty-five or fifty minutes to it, I did not know that we should be starting so late, so I want to say that I shall not be hurt if any of you want to leave in the middle of my remarks. Indeed, I shall be sympathetic.

We start, naturally, with the fundamental museum question: How to interest people, especially the young, in what the museum collects? Collecting for public show presupposes a good reason which is shared, or can be shared, by rational beings. The child who accumulates bottle tops, or the eccentric who saves up orange peels has no problem. But the librarian and the museum director must ask themselves why they are there, sitting on a heap of things. The answer is, broadly: to convey, preferably in some organized form, knowledge with pleasure—aesthetic pleasure sometimes, and the simple pleasure of knowledge at other times. In either case, the work is infected with pedagogical intent. I say "infected" because I believe it is a peculiar mark of our age, and particularly of our country, to charge nearly every enterprise with educational zeal. Having lost religion as a means of saving our neighbour, we have substituted art and knowledge as supreme goods which we want everyone to possess willy-nilly; so we take steps to thrust these goods upon all the helpless and captive, as well as on the natural seekers. We should always be conscious, for reasons soon to appear, that thrusting art and knowledge on the unwary is an invasion of privacy, perhaps justified, but an invasion nonetheless—as great as that of thrusting religion, a practice we have outlawed. And we should also remember that the special sign of the pedagogical intent is the use of contrivance—the school, the museum, the lecture.

Well, the twentieth century is committed to education, and that effort is often the chief cause of our unhappiness and despair, for education is the worst game of chance ever invented. But like the missionary among the cannibals, we're too far engaged to back out: the pot is boiling. The best we can do is consider how to fit the teaching to the taught, and to consider (as you have been doing for two days) what unavoidable contrivances are suited to our innumerable and extravagant purposes.

It is such reflections as these that bring us to examine the power of words and sight and books, the worth of projections, diagrams, pictures, and objects, and the force of spoken harangues, now so easily taped and piped into the ear. In using these means, we immediately become aware of *radical* differences among groups, ages, numbers, temperaments. For in our educational drive, as soon as we give up self-selection in favour of universal appeal and indoctrination, we run into the solid barrier of human diversity and must multiply our contrivances. We quickly discover that you cannot talk to two hundred people the way you do to twenty or to two. We learn that some persons rely on verbal memory, others on visual or muscular. We discover that the requisite organ for cultivating art in the modern museum is the calf of the leg. Hence the needful physical education, we must give thought to the working of the senses and the mind. Is it true that there is no solid or pleasurable learning without questions or dialogue?

Is the transparent fallacy about one picture being worth a thousand words itself a factor in closing the mind—just as the mere sight of numbers on a page freezes the blood in four out of five? We must, in other words, investigate the penetrative power of the contrivances that we use, and this not only in order to pierce the individual skull, but also in the effort to traverse the layers of society as a whole.

At this point, an illustration of each kind may be in order. Our kind hosts, Mr. Auchincloss and Mr. Miller, will, I trust, forgive me if I take my first instance from this museum, and indeed from its most recent, splendid panorama of life in Dutch New York.

The exhibition begins with words, by way of furnishing historical background: it does seem reasonable to account for the presence of a sensible people like the Dutch on this particular island. The first words tell us that the capture of Constantinople by the Turks in 1453 forced Christendom to turn westward for trade routes to the Indies, and thereby make voyages that led to the discovery of America. Now it so happens that this event, caused by Christopher Columbus, was conclusively disproved in a book by the late Professor Lybyer,[298] published, not last week, not last year, but in 1913.

You understand that if blame is to be thought of at all, it must rest on the whole of our culture, which allows an important discovery or conclusion to remain undisseminated for over half a century. The museum director, the educated man, entitled to find either in his own schooling or in the common reference books, the sifted knowledge and general truths that he may need. I have taken a typical, not an exceptional, instance. Educated people carry in their heads thousands of items of knowledge that are items of carefully instilled misinformation. I conclude that our apparatus of scholarship is grossly deficient. We have books in abundance, but we have not begun to learn their proper use.

Let us now turn to a device of an apparently greater penetrative power, the picture. The example that suggests itself irresistibly is of course the *Mona Lisa*.[299] Its cosmic dissemination was proved with great *éclat* when it came to this country a while ago, though I heard of some who were disappointed not to find Leonard da Vinci[300] nearby to autograph a copy. Well, what of the *Mona Lisa*? On a calendar, she has the requisite come-hither look, but by modern standards she's overdressed, and repetition in many sizes and colour has made her dull. Her effect is that of a trademark, and the upshot that should bother us is the phenomenon I have observed a number of times in front of the original. The honest man who has never seen the actual work, but is all too familiar with the face, goes through a dismal time of teetering: do I admire it or not? If I do, is it because I am supposed to admire? I do not, is it because I am reacting against conventional admiration? The most perceptive end up by asking themselves: do I actually see it when I look at it, or am I peering through a fog of reproduction?

Granted that the *Mona Lisa* is an unusual case, it is nonetheless indicative of what unlimited means of reproduction tend to produce. The *Sunflowers* of Van Gogh,[301] the Fifth Symphony of Beethoven,[302] to say nothing of gobbets [303] of Shakespeare,[304] are in the category of the *Mona Lisa*, and our proud machinery is catching up to do the same to anything that enough experts declare to be transcendently good and great.

Let me put the same facts more generally in historical terms. The warm, liberal mind of the nineteenth century entertained a generous belief that, thanks to cheap books and free schools, everyone would be well educated; that, thanks to lithography[305] and photoengraving,[306] everybody would soon become an amateur of art—all in parallel with the free newspaper press, which would make everyone a good citizen—a whole world of democrats and aesthetes at small expense. We now know better. A measure of our disappointment may be found in the one domain of simple literacy, when we number the so-called functional illiterates by the tens of millions, and when the children of the well-to-do suffer from reading difficulties and carry mental "blocks" with them to the day of happy release as high school dropouts. But that sad debacle, though related to our concern, is for the moment a byproduct. What is central is the obvious effect of the sum of demands on the modern senses, mind, and memory.

We speak of media as if their proliferation through technology meant simply more channels for a reasonably constant quantity of stuff. That is not so: the media themselves continually break up the product and give it out again manifold, in bits and pieces. It is a prime case of division that turns out to be multiplication.

The several media, moreover, distort in various ways—as when a novel becomes a film and then the film is televised, additional fragments, multiplied scraps, that find their terminus in our human sensoriums. Nothing in evolution or physical training has prepared us for this overload of stimuli so we meet it through the natural protective devices of the body, unconsciousness or narcosis. Mentally and nervously we "faint" without knowing it a hundred times a day, or we sink for a stretch into a waking coma.

At the risk of making my point by causing just such a syncope[307] in yourselves, let me simply enumerate what it is we undergo—the equivalent of so many physical blows, though we cover up the reality by dozens of abstract terms, such as "art exhibits," "public-affairs broadcasts," "educational television," "continuing education," "film retrospective," not to mention "valuable two-day symposium followed by a remarkable lecture."

[Applause.]

All these conceal innumerable strokes of the hammer on nerve ends, ears, and eyes that already receive unsolicited advertising, unauthorized jargons, and ephemeral knowledge, such as: radio, news on the hour, desolating or seductive weather forecasts, exhortations and indignations from all articulate acquaintance, entertainment enlivened by warnings as to teeth and hair, and steady reminders of taxes, diseases, and insurable risks—the whole of this mental whirl being bounded by danger to the body from machines, under the *obbligato* of fused noises that declare their presence.

Never mind whether it is good or bad, remedial or not. It is the barrage of mingled tedium and clangor that pounds and pulpifies our senses before we even begin to take in an object or idea that

we desire, attend to what is soberly proposed to us in hopes of our
desire. The commonest such object, of course, is something said or
written, and thus by an identical excess Word and Machine noise
have come to produce the same intolerable irritation. Against the
Word, the senses close up and the mind quietly hibernates. We
are all sick of print, of reports, memos, and agendas; of junk mail,
newspapers, newsletters, and magazines; of reprints in pamphlets
miscalled the "literature" of innumerable agencies. This glut of
paper and the cellulose mush of the prose induce a paralysis of
the visualizing function—whence the popularity of rapid reading.
What they teach is the new art of letting the eye brush harmlessly
over the page. We long simply to feel and taste—why not get rid
of the book? An inventor called on me with a machine that would
enable the user to turn a printed roll past a little window and
thereby absorb *The Brothers Karamazov*[308] in fifty-four minutes.
When you know the anguish of perusing that work, you can think
of the reading machine as just the painkiller we all need.

As for talk, I need not elaborate. Hemingway's request, "Will
you please, please, please, please, please, please stop talking,"[309]
has fallen on deaf ears, quite logically: deaf ears are the last resort
of silence, since even in the desert (as we know) there is a voice
clamouring.

But if the Word, which was in the beginning, has now come to
an end, what have we substituted for pleasure and wisdom? The
obvious answer is: the vision, arts, and music, more particularly
visual and musical patterns—not pictures with moral or intellectual overtones, not music with dramatic structure and climaxes.
The symphonies of Beethoven are too connotative, too graphic to
give us what we want, which is to be let alone, to be insulated and
to mull. The painting, sculpture, and architecture we prefer also
refrain from giving too clear a direction to our thoughts. Their
virtue is to be non-coercive. If you think this generality over-
looks the shocks administered by modern art, consider that such a
shock is always momentary and inconsequential. It is amusing and
not coercive. I invite your attention to the remarkable fact that
in our day the highest merit—in public life, society, and art—is to

amuse: "furniture for fun," and buildings for laughs; and by framing
the familiar can, Campbell's soup[310] becomes the cream of the jest.

While we thus take our visual experience as raw as possible,
we are disposed by our spatial mobility to enjoy most what we
can come upon unexpectedly, from all sides and at any time.
This defines the happening. We praise and mock up the three-
dimensional. In the same way, we relish film and tape because we
like—the freedom they give us in relation to themselves: they are
dead things that we can interrupt and abandon, flouting beginning, middle, and end. By tuning in and out we feel a little less
enslaved. We no longer care whether this liberty amounts to
liberties taken with masterpieces built for a different mode of
perception. What could we change, even if we did care? So we step
into the bar or the taxicab and readily endure the closing chords of
the piece as a sufficient whiff of high art. We believe we can recap-
ture the whole whenever we like, though we should know that
this is an illusion. For the fragmentation that we condone is not
reversible. The senses and the memory are delicate organs from
which we can erase little, or nothing. But no matter, the breakup
of high art has an important role to play in our cultural revolution. It is by pulverizing the former kind of artistic experience that
we are getting rid of the Renaissance outlook and all its work. It
is by the exposure to simple shape and pattern and the practice of
tuning in and out that we discard consecutiveness—or at least the
consecutiveness of intellect. Together these new habits change the
character of Attention, making it lively in response to every fresh
pulse or start, meditative in response to what is gently uniform,
and dull or absent in response to anything discursive. In such ways
the sensibility of man is renewed and refreshed. The best icono-
clasm has always been indifference and incomprehension, total
blindness to what earlier men perceived and cherished. These are
the coming circumstances of our culture, and as foreshadowings
of the *tabula rasa*, they augur extremely well for the rebirth of art
and thought that lies ahead.

But what is good for the soul doesn't necessarily bake bread,
and in the decline of Attention and the phobia against words,

we are left with the workaday problems that we class under
the heading of Communication. The paradox here is one of the
choicest in the history of man. From the original three ways of
transmitting notions—the spoken word, the drawn image, and the
bodily gesture, each requiring a living soul—we have passed in
a short time to dozens, if not hundreds, of machine devices that
extend, record, duplicate, and transform for later recovery the
notional elements in our common life. If we were a grateful people,
Baron Muenchausen[311] should have his statue for inventing the
frozen words that thawed out in the spring: he was our forerunner.
Yet—here is the best paradox—by virtues of these very devices,
their multiplicity and their aggressiveness, the beneficiaries find
that they have lost the thread. Communication halts. There is a
buzzing in their ears, and each man carried a private Bedlam[312] in
his head.

The obvious countermeasure, which is repetition, only aggra-
vates the disease. Those who can no longer catch anything on
a first hearing soon have to hear everything ten times before it
penetrates, and they end up impervious while the repetition goes
on. Nor are the secondary results satisfactory. Public education
stalls and social fabric disintegrates to an accompaniment of the
spiritual malaise that is bound to come with isolation in the midst
of Babel.[313] The rising pitch of every shrill claim on attention;
fraudulent attempts at concentrating interest on a few ideas, a few
names, a few works; the equally false colouring lavishly applied to
suggest variety and to make the over-familiar look original—all
these emergency measures only increase disaffection, breed panic,
and incite the young to secede.

Only slight relief is felt when the pounding temporarily stops.
Rather, the drilled sensorium aches with a sense of vacuum as
disturbing as the failure of a scheduled explosion. So the pupil
turns on the squawking radio to do his homework, parties get restless at general conversation and break it up into cacophonous
tête-à-têtes, and loud humming machines are marketed to protect
urban sleep. At this point of common anesthesia, the bold and
inventive propose a radical remedy; and it is here—in case you

have been wondering—that our concern with the modern sensibility turns particular and practical. For all these indescribable experiences of chaos and fury, all these longings for sensation and silence are democratically distributed among those with whom we deal from day to day, and it follows that any hope we entertain of reaching that drunken mind in our neighbour, our pupil, our colleague—let alone controlling the staggers in ourselves—must depend on some action appropriate to the predicament.

The remedy I refer to is familiar. It is based on the principle of like cures like. According to it, our flaps and flits would decrease, and communication would resume, if we only gave up the direct effort and, instead of resisting the inevitable bombardment of stimuli, exploited it for the supersaturation of our senses—and not one sense at a time, but all together. Give up trying to sort out a single line of meaning from the confusing concomitants. Give in, rather, to a calculated assault on all the doors of perception. Forgetting the linear and the flat, plunge into the actual thickness of the four dimensions. Light, shapes, colours, sounds, touches, and smells are to be our simultaneous instructors, converging on the expanded psyche, filling the gaps in our attention, reproducing without effort from us the totality of experience—that "booming, buzzing confusion" that William James[314] imagined to be the baby's accurate awareness of the world. This proposed remedy has quickly become a program and also a pastime, and since a crusade benefits from having an enemy to put down, books and the art of linear print have become the *infâme*[315] that we are to crush.

If I were a cyclical historian,[316] I should rejoice in this turn of the wheel of culture. For the artifice of communication through all available channels of sense is not wholly new in Western civilization. The ancients used trees, stones, weapons, fires, and monuments to fix in the mind great events or oaths taken or truths learned. By strong association the right feelings were aroused that spurred the mind. And the need for such messages in concrete form long survived the abstraction in written word. Even more elaborate was the *multi-media educational centre* known as the medieval cathedral, where music, painting, and sculpture pillars, vaults, and pulsing bells; light effects, recitation, and relics, play-acting, and miracles besieged the believer. So when Victor Hugo in Notre-Dame[317] contrasts the printed book with the cathedral and says that the one will kill the other, he may have prophesied an endless duel with alternating victims.

But I am not a cyclical historian: I am rather a broken-spiral historian,[318] and I read the story differently. The turns of history are irregular and the apparent samenesses betoken only delays and analogies. For hundreds of reasons, the cathedral is only *analogous* to the proposed kaleidoscope based on technology. It is a strange linear delay that brings us, in 1967, to ponder the merits of simultaneous sensations for expressing and conveying the contents of the modem mind.

It was in the Cubist[319] decade, between 1905 and 1914, that what we take as our transformation of sensibility was first observed and even given embodiment. I have a particular reason for knowing this, because I was born and reared as it were inside the volcano. More than that, the very terms now in opposition—linear versus simultaneous—were first used with their modem connotations by my father,[320] who was one of the theorists of that aesthetic revolution. In a book written in 1911 and published the following year, he has these words:

> The psychological repercussions of our modern times require the abandonment of the single poetic line as a means of expression…The commercial categories…of poetry, music, painting, and sculpture are but the several facets of a single human expression, which must be reunited to constitute what alone deserves to be called art…The work of art will thus be musical through rhythm, sound, and voices; plastic through form and structure; pictorial through sight and participating action; and poetic through inspiration and total expression….Only the polyphony of the simultaneous voices of the world can give direct expression to the realities of our new century.[321]

And in a second study, published the next year, occurs the magic word linear, used in our modern sense, together with our familiar onslaught on print. He wrote: "Today, on the threshold of the year 1913, the living reality of poetry, which is the human voice, is dying under the excesses of a detestable medium— drowned in ink, suffocated by paper, and buried under books."[322] That same autumn the tidings were brought to America by Ezra Pound who wrote that although these notions of H.M. Barzun's might "seem at first better fitted for comic than for serious expression," he was "not sure that he has not hit upon the true medium for democratic expression, the fitting method of synthesis."[323]

Now the point of harking back to these beginnings of theory, soon tested in practice, is that the Cubist movement in art and literature aimed not solely at innovation in the arts; it aimed at reconstructing, re-educating, if you will, the emotions and spirit of man. In all art, and especially at the outset of new art, there is an adaptive function, a desire to mediate between the nascent forms of life and the conventional mind. "Look!" says the poet or painter. "If you want to be in tune with all that is, take in what I project, and you will find yourself made over. Your eye will be clearer, you will feel stronger, restored to unity, possibly happier." Cubist painters and poets and musicians of simultaneity were seeking to refashion the Western mind for the booming, buzzing confusion which we now know and of which they heard only the first rumblings. They broke up the linear and the monotone with their cubes, collages, colour organ, atonality, sculpture in motion, and the explosion of syllables, syntax, and typography on the page.

Whether their handiwork pleases us still is another question, which is here irrelevant. The point is that they routed in everybody that came after them the expectation of regularity and discursiveness. We are where they predicted. But with our added perspective of nearly six decades, we are able to make at least one new observation: it is one thing to revitalize the soul and harmonize the feelings by a fresh experience of life through art; it is a different thing to give instruction or publish information by the same means to a clamorous democracy. We rightly say that art communicates; but we use that word in another sense when we say that the propositions of Euclid[324] and the articles of the United States Constitution[325] communicate. In one's submission to a work of art, as in passing through life, no one is bound to notice and retain all that is there to be seen and felt. Indeed, the chances are that neither art nor life offers a fixed sum of items to take up. There is neither a minimum nor a maximum, which is why we feel that art and life are inexhaustible. But the geometry and the law (which I use here just to represent the apparatus of our practical life) are finite, therefore definite, therefore to be understood in some measurable way, minimum or maximum. And so it is with anything that we make into a formal subject of teaching, as against an occasion of spiritual or emotional uplift. Thus a drama of many simultaneous voices, with colour, motion, light projections, percussion noises, and even the burning of incense could produce in an audience a splendid and highly unified impression. But it is doubtful whether the simultaneous reading aloud of different axioms, propositions, and dates, no matter how artfully orchestrated, would ever teach the calculus or the history of art. We are thus driven to distinguish between *communion* and *communication*, the one a group experience, educative and invigorating, in the way of synthesis; the other, an individual experience— even when had in the presence of others—and concentrated upon analysis.

With this distinction between communion and communication, we are nearly at the end of our road, or rather, we stand at the edge of the cliff. For suddenly we see what it means to be leaving behind us the past millennium of the Renaissance period. It means much more than a change of style, or (as we say) of orientation, much more than the replacement of a few tastes and habits to give zest and seasoning to the rest. Rather, it is a change of state, as of solid to liquid: the stuff is unrecognizable and shows different properties. To specify: the past five hundred years have carried abstraction to excess: now we will only feel. We have been deadened by verbal discourse: now we will only gaze and dream, uncoerced. We loathe machinery in all its forms, the literal machines and also the intellectual, social, and religious machinery of civilization: now we will put our faith in non-coercive art, the bath of sensation, and in communion through spontaneous group happenings, from art to drugs and lovemaking. In short, we will rub out the individual in the collective, and attain an exhilarating sense of freedom by simplification. In a word, we will recover the bliss of the early Christians.

Unfortunately, we do not approach this land of promise with clean hands. We are not simple peasant folk. Most of the means for making this new world depend on a continuance of the old. To create that immediacy of the real that we seek, we need all the resources of technology—the lights, the tapes, the power lines— all the gadgets. But if both communion and communication call for so much contrivance, where is the new simplicity? The best drugs come from horribly bourgeois laboratories, and those cheap and convenient clothes of the dropout from society are the outcome of mass production, which will not last very long in the hands of machine-haters. Nor is it probable that easy mobility and freedom from soul-destroying toil will survive the dissolution of the social system.

Such likelihoods are enough to show the inner contradictions in the cultural revolution of the twentieth century, at least in its present stage. One part pulls towards the ever more complex and sophisticated, the other towards the simplified and primitive, though both claim their inspiration from the intolerableness of the linear life, established systems, and abstract intelligence. It may well be that the work of both parties has but one end, which is the elimination of everything we know as art, society, and liberal mores. But it is clear that the two types of destroyers cannot both command the future. Which will conquer—or deserve to conquer? This uncertainty is what puts a burden of choice on anyone living now whose responsibility it is to teach, or in some kindred way to carry on tradition. Does he, in the first place, choose communion or communication? And if in order to be up to date, in the swim, a good rear-guard pioneer, he espouses the gospel of communion, does he go the way of simplicity or of technology?

I wish that, like a tipster, I could throw out a hint about the outcome of the struggle; but I am a mere historian, not a prophet, and I can come to a close, but not to a conclusion. In closing, then, all I can offer are two or three questions with which to surround a cluster of topics so far unexamined.

To you, who direct repositories of tradition, the first question must be how far you are bound to teach, how far you can afford simply to show and present. Teaching music is a relatively recent affair, and it may contribute needlessly to the overdose of information and suasion. Imagine a return to original purposes: a library with only books in it—no posters, exhibits, advertising, or lectures; a museum with only pictures and carvings (no quartets)—how restful! Let me quickly add that this is not a recommendation: it is a question.

Next, I wonder whether the garnering of impressions, the bath of suggestion and sensation that we go in for, is not a mere transitional stage in the refreshment that we are after? A sensation does not physiologically end in itself. It looks for something to do—if only to make us jump with joy—and in those with the right gift it sparks what we call creation. When we speak of the creative imagination, we know the power of shaping sensations into some form and meaning, the two fused into a single object of future contemplation. To have this power of imagination and to prevent it from generating meanings-in-form is extremely difficult, which is why the artists of today who have taken a vow against meaning suffer the pains of miscarriage. Or again to put it as a question for study, is not our instinctive decision to dwell in the senses alone anything more than a purge? Through our electronic sounds, for instance, we break down tonal clichés; but the imagination of structures will spring out of these new sounds. In poetry, ambiguity is an escape from platitude. But the time comes when we want to be at one with the poet and his dominant emotion, and ambiguity won't do. Is it right, then, to discredit as a matter of principle the idea of meaning, which includes the significance that soon clings to form?

I might phrase the question still more simply: how soon will we get sick and tired of the "interesting experiment" which hinges on some little play of sensation?

Another consideration: the young are today more numerous and more precocious than ever before, and hence more likely to outlive both their particular education and their various ways of getting rid of it. Faith and fashion were never more restless than now, which is what makes calamity of so long life. This suggests the need for the young to be armed against the boredom and futility to come. If that is true, how can we ask them to make the heavy investment of study and effort, when the company is declared bankrupt every six months? [Applause.] Yet they cannot avoid loss if they are only sensitive, uncoerced by reason, dependent on communion, cut off from communication. For it is sad but true that communication occurs only through the means we now distrust and reject: words written and spoken. And exact communication is at best difficult. We tend nowadays to believe that it occurs between a transmitter and a receiving set, and we try to make the transmitter stronger and stronger. Nothing can be falser than this image. Perception, the receiving set, needs an activity in the recipient, and that activity can begin only after the mind at work has accumulated an apperceptive mass—facts, ideas, images cognate with the subject. Any theory that concentrates on the transmitting, the giving out, and goes after the passive, casual, vagrant mind is bound to fail.

There is worse. We rely for the giving out on more and more machinery, and we forget more and more that the machine is a liar. We keep saying that thanks to television, millions can see Shakespeare or Bob, instead of a few hundred sitting in a theatre. But what the millions see is only a poor simulacrum. It is *not* Shakespeare but Punch and Judy;[326] it is not Bob Hope but an absurd homunculus,[327] strange in colour, moving in a cage, and making harsh noises only faintly reminiscent of the human voice. Where is the immediacy of the real? And the machine lies in still subtler ways when it professes to ascertain our opinions and feelings, and thereby direct our future.

Precisely because good communication must include some sensory communion, the machine is not enough, any more than communion alone is enough. For communication coerces; teaching coerces; learning is self-coercion; therefore all theories of communication by non-coercive means—based moreover on humouring the native ignorance or acquired laziness of the passive subject—will defeat communication. All right, you may say. Suppose it's so: why bother? Well, unless mankind scatters into the desert as hermits having given up society, the thin black line of communication will have to be kept intact. Its maintenance, so far as I can see, is prerequisite to most other goods, including the communion of art, love, freedom, and religion. It may be, indeed, that we shall pass through an age of anti-intellectual, wholly pictorial, and sensorial experience. But if we do, it will not be an era of peace and harmony. Mankind is too diverse and impulsive for automatic order to establish itself; even if by the grimmest sensitivity training we approach mutual mind-reading, all the greater will be the mutual horror and indignation.

So before the keepers of tradition jump on the bandwagon in a rush to give up words, print, the *Bill of Rights*,[328] the *Book of Etiquette*,[329] and linear equations, let them use the artist's power of imagining the result. And in deciding what that result will be, let them act impartially and not as threatened property-owners. They have a real choice, for man's articulate speech and the art of writing will not be lost, even in eclipse. Nothing is permanent, not even destruction. The alphabet, we must remember, was invented by illiterates.

[Standing ovation.]

Notes

1.   In a then-unpublished manuscript Parker explains "why the word 'linear' is used to describe visual organization. The sense of sight is the only sense we have which gives the feeling that all spaces are connected, uniform, static." Parker, *The Culture Box*, 39.

2.   Anthony (Tony) Schwartz (1923–2008) was an American sound archivist, sound designer, media theorist, and creator of advertising. McLuhan worked closely with Schwartz during the year he spent at Fordham University in New York (1967–68).

3.   Established in 1869, the American Museum of Natural History is located in Manhattan's Upper West Side.

4.   James Arthur Oliver (1914–1981) served as Director of the American Museum of Natural History from 1959 to 1969, emphasizing during his tenure the need for biological conservation.

5.   Louis S. Auchincloss (1917–2010): American lawyer, novelist, historian, and essayist. In his capacity as President and Chairman of the MCNY, he came up with the funding for the seminar's closing banquet.

6.   Carlin Evans Gasteyer (1917–2003) was Assistant Director of the MCNY and later became Vice-Director for Administration for the Brooklyn Museum. She was closely involved in the planning for the museum seminar and coordinated the visit of youth and children to the prototype gallery. (Laurence Maloy to Carlin Gasteyer and Ralph Miller, April 19, 1967. MCNY Archives.)

7.   Laurence Maloy (1936–2005): Arts Administrator for the American Arts Council. He served as a consultant for the MCNY and was closely involved in the planning for the museum seminar. (Laurence Maloy to Carlin Gasteyer and Ralph Miller, April 19, 1967. Museum of the History of New York Archives.)

8.   Elizabeth M. Conger (b. 1940): Director of Education at MCNY.

9.   In order to make the text of the report more accessible, it has been thoroughly annotated. To this end, information about historical figures has been provided, and texts of McLuhan and Parker dealing with issues similar to those discussed in the report have been referenced. It should be noted that the vast majority of scholarship on McLuhan cites only two of his texts, namely *Gutenberg Galaxy* and *Understanding Media*. What is particularly noteworthy about the seminar report is that its main points of reference are not only writings from the journal *Explorations*, but a cluster of post-*Understanding Media* texts (1966–72) that are informed by emergent lines of argument not found in his two major monographs. In line with the dialogical character of *Explorations*, McLuhan (echoed by Parker) sought to attack text-based linearity, ensuring that the seminar was grounded in oral dialogue and was performative in nature. (It is instructive that a pre-seminar tape recording, rather than a written text, was circulated to participants). And while the printed version of the seminar made certain concessions to print, its conversational character was retained as far as possible. The original subject index has been removed from the current version.

10.   The Centre began operations in 1963. The 1965 draft Constitution for the Centre stated that it had been "established to advance the understanding of the origins and effects of technology" to "investigation into the psychic and social consequences of technologies."

11.   Born: July 21, 1911; BA in 1933 and MA in 1934 from Manitoba; (second) BA in 1936 and PHD in 1943 from Cambridge.

12.   Wisconsin: 1936–37; St. Louis: 1936–39 and 1940–44; Assumption College, now University of Windsor: 1944–46. The course at Fordham, "Understanding Media," was taught by McLuhan and Parker during the 1967–68 academic year.

13.   Now the Lakehead, Ontario. Parker was born on April 13, 1915 and died on March 3, 1992.

14.   Now OCAD (Ontario College of Art and Design) University.

15.   Founded in 1933 by John Andrew Rice as a private liberal-arts college in Black Mountain, North Carolina, it espoused John Dewey's educational philosophy emphasizing holistic learning and the study of art.

16.   Best known for his work as an abstract painter and a theorist, Joseph Albers (1888–1976) worked in several artistic fields and is considered to have been one of the most influential teachers of the visual arts in the twentieth century. He taught at the Bauhaus, Black Mountain College, and Yale University. He is the author of *Interaction of Color*, published in 1963. See Nagel, *Medieval Modern*.

17.   The Staatliches Bauhaus, commonly known as the Bauhaus, was a German arts school (operational from 1919 to 1933) in Weimar, Germany.

18.   The Royal Ontario Museum (ROM) is a museum of art, world culture, and natural history. Established in 1914 and located in Toronto, it is one of the largest museums in North America and the largest in Canada.

19.   The original seminar report identified female participants as either "Mrs." or "Miss." While such information is considered irrelevant or inappropriate by a contemporary reader, we have preserved it here for historical context.

20.   McLuhan included a section entitled "Touch as interval" in his book, *Culture Is Our Business*.

21.   Henry Spencer Moore (1898–1986): An English artist best known for his large-scale, monumental-figure bronze sculptures.

22.   He is likely referring to the National Museum of Man (the present Canadian Museum of History) in Ottawa.

23.   This point is elaborated on in "Our World 1967 Full Broadcast."

24.   McHale claimed that since items can be easily reproduced, museums could exhibit such reproduced material to the benefit of visitors. McHale, "Plastic Parthenon."

25.   The *1967 International and Universal Exposition*, a "Category One" world's fair held in Montreal from April 27 to October 29, 1967.

26.   While Manhattan is an island, the City of New York comprises five boroughs including the island of Manhattan.

27.   See note 18 in this section.

28. Social psychologist Omar Khayyam Moore (1920–2006) taught at Washington University, Northwestern University, Yale, Rutgers, and Pittsburgh. In addition to writing on a range of social issues, he was an inventor, most notably of the "talking typewriter" in the 1960s. This "talking typewriter" provided feedback to children, supposedly enhancing their ability to learn. This was an instance of a "responsive environment" that reacted to input from persons engaging with it. See "Education," *Time*; McLuhan, *Culture Is Our Business*, 116–17, 152, 168; McLuhan, *Counterblast*, 100–08.

29. The term "Eskimo" was still in common use at the time. Indigenous people found it offensive because it was imposed on them, preferring to use "Inuit" instead. Edmund Carpenter, however, continued to refer to them as "Eskimo" because he believed that the term "Inuit" lacked authenticity, arguing that it had emerged mostly for administrative reasons. Carpenter, "That Not-So-Silent Sea."

30. "Bucky Fuller" refers to Richard Buckminster Fuller (1895–1983), an American architect, systems theorist, writer, designer, inventor, and philosopher. He and McLuhan developed a close relationship and corresponded frequently. Fuller discovered that if a spherical structure was created from triangles, it would have unparalleled strength. He coined the term "geodesic dome" based on experiments undertaken at Black Mountain College in 1948 and 1949. He received a patent for it in 1954.

31. Edmund "Ted" Snow Carpenter (1922–2011): American anthropologist best known for his field work in the Arctic and in Papua New Guinea. He worked closely with McLuhan at the Centre for Culture and Technology at the University of Toronto, accompanied him to Fordham, and edited *Explorations*. Carpenter, "Eternal Life"; Carpenter et al., *Eskimo*; Carpenter, "Space Concepts."

32. Extra-Sensory Perception.

33. While working on a study of media for the National Association of Educational Broadcasters in 1959, McLuhan had come up with the idea of devising a test "to measure what he called the 'sensory typology' [referring to the] sensory balances or preferences of entire populations." To this end he believed that "educators, politicians, and others would have the most formidable tool yet known for shaping policy and altering human lives." Dr. Daniel Cappon was able to produce such a test using IBM personnel working through the company's office in Toronto. According to Marchand's biography of McLuhan, McLuhan and Cappon both claimed ownership of the test with the latter eventually prevailing. McLuhan decided "to have nothing more to do with it" as he considered it to be "ill-designed and ill-executed." Not surprisingly "the test sank into oblivion." Marchand, *Marshall McLuhan*, 160–64.

A somewhat different account emerges from a section of the McLuhan Papers in Ottawa. While at the Centre for Culture and Technology at the University of Toronto, McLuhan had supported the development of a Sensory Profile under the direction of Daniel Cappon with funding from IBM. He felt that the early results had been promising. However, during the year that he spent at Fordham (1967–68), some University of Toronto faculty members thought the results had dubious academic merit; a final report never materialized. After his return to Toronto the following year, McLuhan no longer showed any interest in the venture. Marshall McLuhan Fonds, Library and Archives Canada.

34. This refers to a girl in her late pre-teen or early teenage years who closely follows adolescent cultural trends.

35. The Ming Dynasty ruled from 1368 to 1644 after the collapse of the Mongol-led Yuan dynasty.

36. In European history, this period is viewed as a transitional one between the Middle Ages and Modernity covering the fifteenth and sixteenth centuries. It was marked by an attempt to revive and build on the accomplishments of classical antiquity. McLuhan, *Counterblast*, 32, 123.

37. Artistic style that emerged in Western Europe (particularly in Rome and Florence) during the early sixteenth century. It was characterized by heroic, centralized standards of composition and drawing.

38. Nightclub located at 19-25 St. Marks Place between Second and Third Avenues in New York City's East Village, in operation from 1967 to 1971.

39. Miller, *Russians as People*.

40. McLuhan, like many of his contemporaries, subscribed to a "Great Divide" view of history, with orally based societies being superseded by modern ones grounded in print. While he viewed the earlier societies as largely backwards, he nonetheless believed that the earlier period of orality had some virtue, reflected in his claim that orally based tribalism challenged the domination of print culture.

41. McLuhan had six children: Eric (d. 2018), Mary, Teresa, Stephanie, Elizabeth, and Michael.

42. Leighton, *My Name is Legion*.

43. Members of the American counterculture often espoused Hindu and Buddhist beliefs during the 1960s. It was their view that these were superior to American religions as they emphasized freedom, peace, mindfulness, and happiness. McLuhan and Parker, *Through the Vanishing Point*, 66.

44. Leonardo di ser Piero da Vinci (1452–1519): Italian polymath active in a range of artistic and scientific fields during the High Renaissance.

45. These sentiments reflect McLuhan's experience of Expo 67, and may have been fuelled by McLuhan's participation in a satellite TV broadcast of June 25, 1967, "Our World 1967 Full Broadcast," a historic television offering described as follows (Schlack, *50 Years On*):

> June 25, 1967 is a monumental date in the history of television, both for Europe and the world. The Eurovision program "Our World" was the first live international television production, and it was a two-hour broadcast, around the globe, between 9 PM and 11 PM CET on a warm Sunday evening, 47 years ago.

46. Presumably the nose cone of a rocket.

47. Darwinism, as espoused by the British scientist Charles Darwin (1809–1882) and his followers, was a theory of evolution that stressed development through a process whereby organisms have a greater ability to compete and survive through the natural selection of small, inherited variations.

48. Edmund Burke (1729–1797): Anglo-Irish statesman and thinker, widely considered to have been the founder of modern conservatism. McLuhan, *Counterblast*, 71.

49. The quote comes from Burke, "On Conciliation with America."

50. Friedrich Wilhelm Ostwald (1853–1932): Baltic German chemist and philosopher of colour.

51. Electrical telegraphs transmitted messages from a sender to a receiver via wires using symbolic codes. They were used from the 1840s until to the present, though currently only for very limited uses. McLuhan, *Culture Is Our Business*, 198, 325; McLuhan, *Counterblast*. 37, 94, 125–26.

52. Aristotle (384–322 BCE): Ancient Greek philosopher and thinker. McLuhan, *Counterblast*, 117.

53. This idea was later central to the tetrad, as expressed in M. McLuhan and E. McLuhan, *Laws of Media*.

54. This claim is elaborated in one of McLuhan's subsequent texts, *Culture Is Our Business*. One of the chapters of the book bears this title as well.

55. Paul Cézanne (1839–1906): French Post-Impressionist painter.

56. Georges Pierre Seurat (1859–1891): French painter who developed the pointilliste technique. Parker had pointed him out to McLuhan. Marchand, *Marshall McLuhan*, 143.

57. A nineteenth-century art movement emphasizing an accurate depiction of light in its changing qualities.

58. Contrasted light effect resulting from the falling of light and shadow unevenly. McLuhan, *Culture Is Our Business*, 332.

59. Seurat was interested in Egyptian art, which can be seen in the way he painted people in *A Sunday on La Grande Jatte* in profile. McLuhan and Parker, *Through the Vanishing Point*, 24–25, 59, 137, 139, 157, 160–61.

60. James Augustine Aloysius Joyce (1882–1941): Irish novelist, poet, and literary critic. His *Finnegans Wake* was a major point of reference for McLuhan. McLuhan and Parker, *Through the Vanishing Point*, 137, 219, 229, 245; McLuhan and Fiore, *Medium Is the Massage*; McLuhan and Gordon, *Relation of Environment*, 10; McLuhan, *Culture Is Our Business*, 164, 168, 172, 214, 260, 280, 282, 284, 300, 302; McLuhan, *Counterblast*, 59, 71, 81, 97, 113, 117.

61. McLuhan, *Counterblast*, 90. In a letter to Barbara Ward, he wrote, "Television does not present a visual image, but an X-ray icon which penetrates our entire organism. Joyce called it 'the charge of the light barricade—part of the Crimean war against mankind.'" McLuhan, "Marshall McLuhan to Barbara Ward."

62. Variable resistor that is used for controlling the electric current flow.

63. Abraham Kirshner (1917–2004): Montreal-based optometrist who developed a unique method for treating learning disabilities. These included such unconventional tools as trampolines, pinball, and electric trains to engage youngsters as part of a highly inventive program. "Obituary: Abraham Kirschner," *Globe and Mail.*

64. McLuhan worked with Hurst in studying the relationship between TV and dyslexia. "Veteran Pioneered Learning Techniques," *York Region.Com.*
McLuhan had received the backing from Hurst who had published a study on reading and visual achievement. Marchand, *Marshall McLuhan*, 164. For the original study, see Hurst, "Vision and Reading Achievement."

65. The ulna is a long bone found in the forearm that stretches from the elbow to the smallest finger.

66. Charles André Joseph Marie de Gaulle (1859–1969): French army officer and statesman who chaired the Provisional Government of the French Republic from 1944 to 1946. McLuhan, *Culture Is Our Business*, 82.

67. Georges André Malraux (1901–1976): French novelist and art theorist who served as both Minister of Information and of Cultural Affairs. Malraux's *Museum Without Walls*, described as "an imaginary museum constituted by the artbook," was an important point of reference for both McLuhan and Parker. Cavell, *Explorations of Carpenter*, 35.

68. Pierre-Auguste Renoir (1841–1919): French artist who was a leading painter in the development of the Impressionist style.

69. Joan Miró (1893–1983): Catalan artist whose work spanned painting, printmaking, sculpture, and murals.

70. Georges Henri Rouault (1871–1958): French painter, draughtsman, and print artist, whose work is often associated with Fauvism and Expressionism.

71. See note 24 in this section.

72. Nickname of Dame Lesley Lawson DBE (née Hornby; 1949–). English model and cultural icon. McLuhan had a fascination with her and what she represented. See McLuhan, *Culture Is Our Business*, 304; "McLuhan Will Study Twiggy," *New York Times.* McLuhan also appeared in a documentary titled, "Twiggy: Why?" which aired on ABC Television on June 23, 1967 at 8:00 PM.

73. Alberto Giacometti, (1901–1966): Swiss sculptor and painter.

74. Edgar Allen Poe (1809–1949): American writer, poet, editor, and literary critic. He was an important point of reference for McLuhan, whose story on the maelstrom was frequently cited by him. McLuhan, *Counterblast*, 4.

75. Formerly a colleague of McLuhan who spent the 1967–68 academic year with him at Fordham University, Carpenter at this time had been teaching at San Fernando Valley State College in Northridge, California. (See note 31 in this section.)

76. Kenneth E. Boulding (1910–1993): English-born American economist educator, peace activist, and interdisciplinary thinker.

77. See Parker, "New Hall of Fossil Invertebrates."

78. Margaret Parker.

79. Lake Champlain forms the boundary between Vermont and New York for most of its length, and lies in a broad valley between the Adirondack and Green Mountains.

80. Elsewhere, McLuhan wrote, "A joke really requires a hidden ground of grievance, for which the joke is only a figure sitting out front." McLuhan, "Man and Media," 278.

81. Stephen Valentine Patrick William Allen (1921–2000): American television personality, radio personality, musician, composer, actor, comedian, and writer.

82. McLuhan referred to this statement again in McLuhan, *Culture Is Our Business*, 288.

83. An interdisciplinary field of engineering and engineering management that focuses on how to design, integrate, and manage complex systems over their life cycles.

84. Likely the Canadian Museum of Nature, a natural history museum that was built in Ottawa between 1905 and 1911.

85. Theatrical term for the frame that separates the stage from the audience, creating a "fourth wall" illusion.

86. McLuhan and Parker, *Through the Vanishing Point*, 73, 77.

87. See "Our World 1967 Full Broadcast," 1:10, 1:24.

88. The Moscow Pavilion was designed as an exhibition pavilion for the Soviet Union at Expo 67. The team of architects designing it was led by Mikhail Posokhin. McLuhan, *Counterblast*, 56.

89. Gertrude Stein (1874–1946): American novelist, poet, playwright, and art collector who became known as a pioneering figure in Modernism.

90. Ernest Miller Hemingway (1899–1961): American novelist, short-story writer, and journalist. His novel, *A Farewell to Arms*, was first published in 1929 and was set during the Italian campaign of World War I. It follows ambulance driver Frederic Henry.

91. McLuhan, *Counterblast*, 63.

92. Gombrich, *Art and Illusion*; McLuhan and Parker, *Through the Vanishing Point*, 6, 9, 225, 239; McLuhan, *Culture Is Our Business*, 148, 119.

93. McLuhan described acoustic space as "spherical. It is without bounds or vanishing points...It is not a container. It is the space in which men live before the invention of writing—that translation of the acoustic into the visual." Theall, *The Virtual Marshall McLuhan*, 145 (quoting a letter from McLuhan to Wyndham Lewis, December, 1954). This notion was further elaborated in an article by D. Carleton Williams the following year; Williams, "Acoustic Space." The notion of acoustic space served McLuhan as the ground to the figure of lineality, which anchored his critique of conventional museums.

94. Fisher, "Children's Museums."

95. 1963 Italian comedy-drama film directed and co-written by Federico Fellini.

96. Roy Moyer (1921–2007): Art historian and arts administrator. McLuhan
     corresponded with Moyer in 1966.

97. Art history.

98. Donato di Niccolò di Betto Bardi (c. 1386–1466): Florentine sculptor of the
     Renaissance period.

99. A sculpting technique referring to an unfinished work.

100. Frédéric Auguste Bartholdi (1834–1904): French sculptor and painter.

101. Michelangelo di Lodovico Buonarroti Simoni (1475–1564): Italian sculptor, painter,
     architect, and poet of the High Renaissance.

102. Hieronymus Bosch (1450–1516): Dutch/Netherlandish painter frequently referred
     to by McLuhan and Parker, *Through the Vanishing Point*, 30, 77, 235.

103. Franz Kafka (1883–1924): German-speaking novelist and short-story writer based
     in Prague. McLuhan and Parker, *Through the Vanishing Point*, 77, 219.

104. Conger was responsible for the Museum's children's program.

105. Oscar-Claude Monet (1840–1926): French painter known as a founding figure of
     Impressionism.

106. See note 89 in this section.

107. Time period associated with the reign of Queen Elizabeth I (1558–1603),
     considered to have been a golden age in English history, the high point of the
     English Renaissance.

108. Joseph Addison, (1672–1719): English essayist, poet, playwright, and politician who
     was the co-founder of the influential magazine, *The Spectator*, a daily publication
     he co-founded with Richard Steele in England, lasting from 1711 to 1712.

109. Everything occurring at the same time. The term "all-at-onceness" was created by
     McLuhan to describe the extent to which the digital age has broken down barriers
     of language and distance, creating a sense of overall conformity. "Our World 1967
     Full Broadcast," Parts 1, 2.

110. Charles John Huffam Dickens (1812–1870): English writer and social critic.
     McLuhan and Parker, *Through the Vanishing Point*, 222; McLuhan, *Culture Is Our
     Business*, 150, 196, 224; McLuhan, *Counterblast*, 48.

111. More and Burnet, *Utopia*.

112. Plato (428/427 or 424/423–348/347 BCE): Ancient Greek philosopher. McLuhan,
     Counterblast, 81.

113. Socrates (c. 470–399 BCE): Ancient Greek philosopher. McLuhan, *Culture Is Our
     Business*, 244.

114. Everett Bernard Ellin (1928–2011): American museum official, art dealer, engineer,
     lawyer, talent agent, and founder of the Museum Computer Network. While Ellin
     is listed as an employee of the Guggenheim Museum, an art museum located on
     the upper east side of Manhattan, he had left this position earlier in the year to
     become a Division Director at the Museum of Modern Arts (MOMA). His main
     responsibility was to oversee the establishment of the Museum Computer

Network, a position funded by the Mellon Foundation. This shift in status might account for the assertiveness he displayed in the seminar.

115. Discussed in De Caro, "Moulding the Museum Medium."

116. Thomas Cook & Son travel agency, known for the hurried nature of its tours.

117. W. Stephen Thomas, a trained museum professional from Philadelphia's Academy of Natural Sciences, became the Rochester Museum's director in 1945. (The museum was established in 1912 as the Rochester Municipal Museum.) Under his leadership, the Museum saw the creation of state-of-the-art dioramas and growth of collections in history, technology, natural science, archaeology, and anthropology. Among the exhibits Thomas oversaw was a "pipe organ panorama" in the spring of 1955 that was visited by over ten thousand people. See Thomas, "Museum of Arts and Sciences," 174–76; Thomas, "How Do Museums Use the Mass Media," 123–31.

118. Its recent version involves a cruise of two-and-one-half hours around the island of Manhattan, allowing passengers to see many of the city's most notable landmarks.

119. This is currently known as the Manhattan-based Circle Line Sightseeing Cruises.

120. Eugene Kingman, (1909–1975): American cartographer, painter, muralist, teacher, and Director of the Joslyn Art Museum, Nebraska's principal fine-arts museum. It is located in Omaha and opened in 1931.

121. In a gallery of the Museum of the City of New York [this note appeared in the original seminar text].

122. *Alice's Adventures in Wonderland* (commonly *Alice in Wonderland*): 1865 English novel by Lewis Carroll. McLuhan and Parker, *Through the Vanishing Point*, 42–43, 140–41, 153; McLuhan, "Address at Vision 65," 206; McLuhan, *Culture Is Our Business*, 68–69, 234; McLuhan et al., *From Cliché to Archetype*, 140.

123. Macy's: Originally R.H. Macy & Co., an American department store chain founded in 1858 by Rowland Hussey Macy.

124. Charles Lutwidge Dodgson (a.k.a. Lewis Carroll; 1832–1898): English author, poet, and mathematician known mainly for his three "Alice" novels. He was an important point of reference for McLuhan and Parker. McLuhan, *Culture Is Our Business*, 192.

125. McLuhan and Parker, *Through the Vanishing Point*, 162–65. See also McLuhan and Gordon, *The Relation of Environment*, 15.

126. Carroll began planning a print edition of the Alice story in 1863. A diary entry for July 2 says that he received a specimen page of the print edition around that date.

127. John Tenniel (1820–1914): Principal political cartoonist for *Punch* magazine and the illustrator for Carroll's three "Alice" novels.

128. Later served as Assistant Director for Administration of the Brooklyn Museum.

129. Robert Torrens Hatt (1902–1989): Academic and zoologist with a long career in museum work, who served as Director of the Cranbrook Institute of Science (CIS), an internationally renowned centre for art, education, and science located in

Bloomfield Hills, Michigan. It was founded in 1904 by Detroit philanthropists George and Ellen Booth. Hatt retired in 1967.

130. Holman J. Swinney (1919–2006): Director of the Adirondack Museum and Director of the Margaret Woodbury Strong Museum in New York from 1972 until his retirement in 1982. The Adirondack Museum is now the Adirondack Experience, located in the hamlet of Blue Mountain Lake in Hamilton County, New York. It is dedicated to preserving the history of the Adirondacks.

131. See note 24 in this section.

132. Sir Arthur Evans declared the figurine to be a goddess and named her "Our Lady of the Sports," a title picked up by *Explorations* when she appeared on the cover of their June 1955 issue as "Mother Goddess, Our Lady of the Sports and Muse of Unofficial Poetry blessing the arena." https://www.rom.on.ca/en/blog/the-goddess-and-the-museum-whats-in-a-name.

133. Located in Centennial Park, Nashville, it is a full-scale replica of the original Parthenon in Athens. Designed by architect William Crawford Smith, it was built in 1897 as part of the Tennessee Centennial Exposition.

134. Empson, *Seven Types of Ambiguity*.

135. Frederick Dockstader (1919–1998): Noted authority on American Indian art, anthropologist, art professor, and museum director. Carpenter, as a member of the American Indian Museum's Board of Directors from 1973 to 1985, was confronted with a scandal arising from Dockstader's management practices. Cavell, *Explorations of Carpenter*, 199.

136. Now the National Museum of the American Indian, a branch of the Smithsonian Museum, Washington, DC. The collection was assembled largely by George Gustav Heye (1874–1957). Carpenter's last major publication examined "Heye and the complicated legacy of his collecting." See Cavell, *Explorations of Carpenter*, 197; in this book, Cavell discusses Carpenter's *Two Essays* in some detail (on pages 197–205).

137. See note 29 in this section.

138. A variety of materials was used to build traditional dwellings. Inuit lived inland as well. Beginning in the post-World War II period, the Canadian federal government provided assistance to explore the use of other building materials, such as cellulose. Debicka and Friedman, "From Policies to Building," 25–39.

139. McLuhan was poorly informed about North American Indigenous people, expressing views about them in line with the misconceptions of the day. He appeared to have relied on the writings of Edmund Carpenter for his reflections on the Inuit.

140. Martin was the first director of the Roberson Memorial. Roberson Memorial, Inc. was established in 1934 by Alonzo Roberson in Binghamton, New York, to create an "educational center…for the use and benefit of all people" (https://roberson.org/visit/our-history/). It opened to the public in 1954.

141. McLuhan believed an effort should be made to "blast those art galleries and museums which imprison and classify human spirit." McLuhan, *Counterblast*, 65.

142. Dr. Edward McClung ("Mac") Fleming (1909–1994) came to the Winterthur Museum in 1955 as head of the Education Division, a position he held until his retirement in 1974. Located in Winterthur, Delaware, this estate and museum has a rich collection of Americana.

143. Harmon Hendricks Goldstone (1911–2001) was named to the City Planning Commission in 1961. The City Planning Commission was created under the 1936 city charter and started functioning in 1938. Now the Department of City Planning (DCP), this department is responsible for setting the framework of the city's physical and socioeconomic planning. Goldstone also served as second chair of the New York City Landmarks Preservation Commission and had an instrumental role in the creation of the New York City Landmarks Law.

144. General Motors Company (GM): American automobile manufacturing company located in Detroit. McLuhan, *Counterblast*, 37.

145. Austronesian ethnic group native to the Indonesian island of Bali. This point is also made in McLuhan and Parker, *Through the Vanishing Point*, 6–7, 243; McLuhan and Gordon, *The Relation of Environment*, 7; McLuhan et al., *The Medium Is the Massage*, 137; McLuhan, *Culture Is Our Business*, 313.

146. See McLuhan and Nevitt, *Take Today*.

147. Dr. James Heslin (1916–1999) served as Director of the New York Historical Society, an American history museum and library in New York City, along Central Park West between 76th and 77th Streets, on the Upper West Side of Manhattan. The society was founded in 1804 as New York's first museum.

148. The earliest major book printed using mass-produced movable type in Europe. Preparation began soon after 1450; the first finished copies were available in 1454 or 1455. McLuhan, *Culture Is Our Business*, 126.

149. See *Art Treasures from Japan*.

150. Rembrandt Harmenszoon van Rijn (1606–1669): Painter, printer, draughtsman of the Dutch Golden Age. McLuhan and Parker, *Through the Vanishing Point*, 80.

151. Doménikos Theotokópoulos (1541–1614): Painter, sculptor, and architect of Greek origin who contributed to the Spanish Renaissance.

152. Established by Roscoe William Smith (1877–1976) in 1950. Dedicated to exploring and interpreting nineteenth-century rural life in the Hudson Valley.

153. *Titan: Story of Michelangelo* is a German documentary about Michelangelo. It won an Academy Award in 1951.

154. *Madonna della Pietà* (1498–99). Image of Jesus and Mary carved by Michelangelo.

155. Now the Anne and Bernard Spitzer Hall of Human Origins.

156. This exhibit was a version of *Transparent Woman*, which made its first appearance in the Cleveland Health Museum in 1950.

157. This was a "new hall [which drew upon] nine tenths of the world's species of animals to illustrate some universal biological themes." ("First floor, section 9," *General Guide to the Exhibits*, American Museum of Natural History.)

158. Kodak's pavilion had fifteen exhibit sections and two theatres. It sought to demonstrate the wealth of experience to be gained from photography.

159. Wayne State University (WSU), located in Detroit, is Michigan's third-largest university.

160. During the fall of 1967, McLuhan suffered frequent blackouts, which became more severe in late October. He was taken to the Columbia Presbyterian Medical Center for tests. A brain tumor the size of a tennis ball was discovered. Surgery began on the morning of November 25 and continued until the morning of the following day. Marchand, *Marshall McLuhan*, 201.

161. This is a replica of a scene, often in the form of a three-dimensional full-size or miniature model.

162. See Parr, "The Habitat Group"; Parr, "Habitat Group and Period Room 1."

163. Margaret Mead (1901–1978): American cultural anthropologist with whom McLuhan frequently corresponded.

164. Walter Scott Dunn Jr. (1928–?) at this time was Chief Curator of the Buffalo and Erie County Historical Society (founded in 1901, and now the Buffalo History Museum) in Buffalo, NY, and Director of the Des Moines Center of Science and Industry.

165. Collections of notable objects that became particularly popular in the sixteenth century.

166. See note 156 in this section.

167. Dr. Joseph Miles Chamberlain (1923–2011): Astronomer who at the time was Assistant Director of the American Museum of Natural History.

168. Parker discussed the "newseum" in a then-unpublished manuscript; see Parker, *The Culture Box*, 10–11 . There was no relationship between Parker's idea and the Newseum, an American museum in Washington, DC, dedicated to news and journalism that promoted free expression and the first amendment to the U.S. Constitution. Lauder, "Clash of Spaces."

169. The country's official name at the time was the Democratic Republic of the Congo.

170. Charles Ormond Eames (1907–1978): American designer, architect, and filmmaker. Some of the seminar participants were quite familiar with his film work at world's fairs. McLuhan had become conversant with Eames's media activities through Carpenter, who had been working with the filmmaker at San Fernando Valley State College (now California State University at Northridge). Carpenter noted in a memoir that when the American military bases closed, Eames acquired much of their film equipment, which he used to make highly regarded innovations, including the perfection of the multi-screen film. These were "experiments Hollywood lacked time and patience to attempt…. Several films took international awards." Carpenter recalls that McLuhan "followed this with great interest,

providing sharp insights." In effect by virtue of his friendship with Carpenter, McLuhan was able to vicariously experience what the latter described as "the first post-literate society" that was taking root in southern California. Carpenter, "That Not-So-Silent Sea," 252–53.

171. See note 2 in this section.

172. Czechoslovakia's pavilion, among the most popular at Expo 67, displayed the interplay between art, technology, and industry in an enchanting manner.

173. Produced by the National Film Board of Canada under the direction of filmmakers Roman Kroitor and Colin Low, the Labyrinth Pavilion (*Labyrinth/Labyrinthe*) was designed around the myth of the Minotaur. McLuhan and Parker, *Through the Vanishing Point*, 219.

     Jonathan Lovell and AnnMarie Brennan claim that *Labyrinth* can best be understood drawing on McLuhan's concepts of visual and acoustic space. Lovell and Brennan, "Labyrinth as Immersive Multimedia Environment."

174. There is no evidence that Fordham ever pursued this.

175. See note 179 in this section.

176. Slide projector that uses a rotary tray to project slide photographs.

177. New Amsterdam became a provincial extension of the Dutch Republic and was designated as the capital of the province in 1625.

178. See note 2 in this section.

179. A 1959 film by Phil Lerner—*My Own Yard to Play In*—about children playing in the streets of New York, featuring a soundtrack by Tony Schwartz.

180. This should have been referred to as "Yorkville."

181. Royal Ontario Museum's Centennial exhibition on Canadian clothing from 1780 to present (1967). Parker, who worked on this, likely painted the walls. Brett, "Modesty to Mod."

182. A nightclub located in New York's East Village, operating from 1967 to 1971. McLuhan, *Culture Is Our Business*, 88.

183. Naskapi nations of Quebec and Labrador; both groups speak the Naskapi language.

184. Formerly a gallery of the Royal Ontario Museum.

185. Possibly a bridle fitting. https://collections.rom.on.ca/objects/323672/bridle-fitting.

186. This exhibition (October 1, 1967–December 31, 1968) featured 250 minerals from the Museum's collection, arranged to demonstrate evolutionary sequence, and was curated by D.M. Vincent Manson, Assistant Curator of the Department of Mineralogy.

187. Parker had three children: Margaret, Eric, and Blake (d. 2007).

188. Parker's youngest child is his daughter Margaret.

189. Metropolitan Educational Association, formed in Toronto in 1959, whose objective was to use television broadcasting to serve the educational needs of the Toronto area.

190. Poulet, *Studies in Human Time*, 1956; McLuhan and Parker, *Through the Vanishing Point*, 9–10.

191. The Dutch West India Company was a chartered company of Dutch merchants as well as foreign investors, formally known as GWC (*Geoctrooieerde Westindische Compagnie*, of which a direct English translation would be "Chartered West India Company").

192. Quality of being able to see through (or partially see through) one or more layers in an artwork. Parker seems to have been using transparent overlays on film to create novel effects.

193. See McLuhan's commentary in "Our World 1967 Full Broadcast."

194. The New York State Historical Association is located in Cooperstown, NY and was founded in 1899 by New Yorkers who were interested in promoting greater knowledge of the early history of the state. In addition to serving as its Vice-President, Mr. Frederick Louis Rath Jr. (1913–2001) also taught museum management at the Cooperstown Graduate Program in History Museum Training.

195. See note 39 in this section.

196. Proverbial saying from the early twentieth century, meaning that one's chosen style reflects one's essential characteristics; earlier in Latin, and from the French naturalist Buffon (1707–88) in the form, "Style is the man himself."

197. Thomas Stearns Eliot OM (1888–1965): Poet, essayist, and playwright. McLuhan and Parker, *Through the Vanishing Point*, 83, 93, 101, 139, 73–74, 182–83, 235; McLuhan and Gordon, *The Relation of Environment*, 10; McLuhan, *Culture Is Our Business*, 44, 90, 110, 158, 160, 164, 270, 296, 326, 330; McLuhan, *Counterblast*, 50, 113.

198. The term "Cockney" has traditionally been used to describe a person from London's East End (usually working class or lower middle-class) who speaks with a distinct accent and dialect.

199. Historically the county of Lancashire includes Manchester and Liverpool, along with the Furness and Cartmel. It is known for its distinct vernacular speech (colloquially, Lanky).

200. G. Carroll Lindsay (1929–2013) was Director of the New York State Museum Services, established in 1836 as the New York State Geological and Natural History Survey and administered through the New York State Museum.

201. A version of the prototype gallery was curated as an exhibit in December, 1967.

202. See note 170 in this section.

203. The 1964–1965 New York World's Fair was held in Flushing Meadows-Corona Park, in Queens, New York. While its proponents described it as a "universal and international" exposition, the fair did not receive official support or approval from the Bureau of International Expositions. McLuhan was not enthusiastic about it, preferring Expo 67. Both McLuhan and Parker had been invited to a meeting at which planning for the Canadian Pavilion at Expo 67 was discussed. Leslie Brown

to McLuhan, November 26, 1964. Marshall McLuhan Fonds, Library and Archives Canada.

204. Also known as the Century 21 Exposition, it was held in 1962 and was attended by nearly ten million people.

205. Focusing on the influence of computers in contemporary life, the pavilion was designed by the Eames Office, which was responsible for the exhibitions, graphics, signage, and films.

206. In Greek mythology, the Labyrinth was an elaborate, confusing structure designed and built by the legendary artificer Daedalus for King Minos at the Knossos palace in Crete.

207. In Greek mythology, the Minotaur was a mythical creature, portrayed with the head and tail of a bull and the body of a man, and dwelt at the centre of the Labyrinth.

208. See also McLuhan, *Culture Is Our Business*, 116.

209. Veatch, *Rational Man*.

210. Mesoamerican culture that flourished in central Mexico in the Post-Classic period from 1300 to 1521.

211. See Gagnon, "The Christian Pavilion at Expo 67"; Gagnon and Johnstone, *In Search of Expo 67*.

212. The Academy, founded by Plato in c. 387 BCE in Athens, persisted throughout the Hellenistic period. It was destroyed by the Roman dictator Sulla in 86 BCE.

213. Euclid (fl. 300 BCE): Ancient Greek mathematician considered to have been the "father of geometry." McLuhan, *Culture Is Our Business*, 194n.

214. Something (such as a decorative object) considered novel, rare, or bizarre.

215. George Washington (1732–1799): American military officer who became the first president of the United States, serving from 1789 to 1797.

216. Auschwitz: Located in southern Poland, also known as Auschwitz-Birkenau, it opened in 1940 and was the largest of the Nazi concentration and death camps.

217. Reverend John (Jack) E. O'Brien (1924–2015): Professor emeritus and founder of Concordia University's Department of Communication Studies.

218. This claim is fully elaborated in McLuhan et al., *City as Classroom*.

219. Evidently, Parker did not get along with ROM director, Peter Swann. Genosko, "Where the Youth Aren't."

220. American monthly lifestyle and fashion magazine that began in 1892 as a weekly newspaper, eventually becoming a monthly magazine. McLuhan, *Counterblast*, 134.

221. Very popular monthly American women's magazine.

222. See note 73 in this section.

223. The quote was "Literature is news that STAYS news." Pound, *ABC of Reading*, Chapter 2.

224. Ezra Weston Loomis Pound (1885–1972): American poet and critic very much admired by McLuhan. McLuhan and Parker, *Through the Vanishing Point*, 270.

225. Edward Twitchell Hall, Jr. (1914–2009): American anthropologist and cross-cultural researcher whose work had an important influence on McLuhan. McLuhan and Parker, *Through the Vanishing Point*, 188n.

226. Hall, *Hidden Dimension*. McLuhan and Parker, *Through the Vanishing Point*, 3–4; McLuhan, *Culture Is Our Business*, 188.

227. Parker had previously noted that they were "college-level students." (See page 140 in the present volume.)

228. These may have been from the seminar course that McLuhan and Parker were teaching there.

229. This appears to have been conducted at Fordham.

230. City located sixty miles (ninety-seven km) north of New York City.

231. At the New York State Historical Association.

232. Sputnik I: First artificial Earth satellite, launched by the Soviet Union in 1957. McLuhan, *Culture Is Our Business*, 196, 330; McLuhan, *Counterblast*, 85, 143.

233. McLuhan and Fiore, *War and Peace*.

234. Group of Celtic peoples who lived in Europe from approximately 500 BCE to 500 CE.

235. Gaius Julius Caesar (100 BCE–44 BCE): Roman general and statesman.

236. Sigfried Giedion (1883–1968): Swiss historian of architecture who taught at the Massachusetts Institute of Technology and Harvard University.

237. McLuhan was teaching at the University of St. Louis at the time.

238. See note 225 in this section.

239. This was under the direction of Daniel Cappon (1921–2002), a psychiatrist and educator and a founding member of the McLuhan Institute at the University of Toronto. See note 33 in this section.

240. There is no evidence that the study was ever published.

241. Giant lumberjack in both American and Canadian folklore.

242. Daniel Boone (1734–1820): American pioneer and frontiersman.

243. Regional museum on a ridge overlooking Blue Mountain Lake in New York.

244. Located in a restored 1885 Victorian railroad station in Wantagh, Long Island, administered by the Wantagh Preservation Society.

245. Major conflagration that struck central London in 1666.

246. *La bohème*: Opera in four acts, composed by Giacomo Puccini between 1893 and 1895 to an Italian libretto by Luigi Illica and Giuseppe Giacosa.

247. McLuhan and Parker, *Through the Vanishing Point*, 258; McLuhan and Fiore, *The Medium Is the Massage*, 114; McLuhan, "Address at Vision 65," 29, 110, 132, 134, 158, 203, 252, 308.

248. Likely referring to Schmidt, "Cambridge Welcomes a Freshman."

249. 1921 American silent film directed by D.W. Griffith.

250. Likely John Ian Robert Russell, thirteenth Duke of Bedford (1917–2002), a writer and a British peer.

251. Likely Bedford, *Book of Snobs*.

252. "The City" is a term often used by New Yorkers to distinguish Manhattan from the
other boroughs.

253. *I Love Lucy*: American television sitcom carried on CBS from 1951 to 1957.

254. *Perry Mason*: American legal drama broadcast on CBS television from 1957 to
1966.

255. *Medium is the Massage*: In March, 1967 McLuhan explained his theory that "the
medium is the message" in the Season 4 premiere of *NBC Experiment in Television*,
an American experimental television show broadcast on NBC from 1967 to 1971.

256. Letícia Román (1941–2025): Italian-American actress, born Letizia Novarese, in
Rome.

257. Mrs. Mary Black (1922–1992): Formerly curator of painting, sculpture, and
decorative arts for the New York Historical Society in New York City.

258. The Museum's collection was launched in 1962 with the gift of a gate in the form
of an American flag, celebrating the nation's centennial. Its focus was on
eighteenth- and nineteenth-century vernacular arts from northeastern America.

259. "Can you nei do her, numb? asks Dolph, suspecting the answer know. Oikkont, ken
you, ninny? asks Kev, expecting the answer guess." Joyce, *Finnegans Wake*, Book 2,
Chapter 2.

260. Museum housing a collection of children's toys and playthings, situated on the
Royal Mile in Edinburgh. First opened to the public in 1955 and moved to its
present home in 1957.

261. Dr. Richard B.K. McLanathan (1916–1998): Art historian, administrator, and writer.
See "Oral History Interview with Richard McLanathan."

262. Pen name of Eric Arthur Blair (1903–1950), British novelist, poet, essayist,
journalist, and critic.

263. American Western television series carried on NBC from 1959 to 1973; McLuhan,
Culture Is Our Business, 168.

264. Authored by Plato around 375 BCE, a Socratic dialogue examining issues related
to justice.

265. An event or series of events designed to evoke a spontaneous reaction to sensory,
emotional, or spiritual stimuli.

266. Andrew Newell Wyeth (1917–2009): American visual artist known for his realist
paintings. His show opened at the Whitney Gallery, February, 1967.

267. Oliver Wendell Holmes Sr. (1809–1894): Boston-based physician, poet, and
polymath.

268. Mr. Rath was Vice-President of the New York State Historical Association, located
in Cooperstown.

269. Duncan Ferguson Cameron (1930–2006): Influential museum leader in both
Canada and the United States.

270. Peter Ferdinand Drucker (1909–2005): Austrian-American management
consultant, educator, and author whose thought influenced that of McLuhan.

McLuhan and Parker, *Through the Vanishing Point*, 242; McLuhan, *Culture Is Our Business*, 78.

271. This joke betrays McLuhan's insensitivity to racial issues and his lack of interest in the legacy of slavery. This is in line with his admiration of the life in the antebellum South. McLuhan, "The Southern Quality."

272. A brand of laundry detergent popular in the 1960s.

273. Ingrid Bergman (1915–1982): Swedish actress who starred in numerous European and American films, television movies, and plays. She became an important point of reference for McLuhan. She married Roberto Gastone Zeffiro Rossellini (1906–1977), Italian film director, producer, and screenwriter. McLuhan had addressed the relationship between Bergman and Rossellini in *The Mechanical Bride*.

274. Likely *Bob Hope Presents the Chrysler Theatre*, a Chrysler Corporation-sponsored series carried by from 1963 through 1967. Hosted by Bob Hope, (Leslie Townes "Bob" Hope, 1903–2003, a British-American comedian, vaudevillian, actor, and celebrity), it was in the variety-show tradition.

275. *Rome, Open City* (*Roma città aperta*, also *Open City*), directed by Rossellini, was a neo-realist Italian film released in 1945.

276. Italian television show broadcast on Radiotelevisione italiana from 1957 to 1977.

277. See note 207 in this section.

278. Screen name for Marion Robert Morrison (1907–1979), American film actor who starred primarily in westerns and action movies.

279. Professional name of Rodolfo Pietro Filiberto Raffaello Guglielmi di Valentina d'Antonguolla (1895–1926), Italian-born film actor from the silent-film era.

280. James Francis Cagney Jr. (1899–1986): American actor, dancer, and film director.

281. Cary Grant (born Archibald Alec Leach; 1904–1986): English-American actor who was one of Hollywood's most popular leading men from the 1930s until the mid-1960s.

282. Barbara Parkins (1942–): Canadian-American former actress, singer, dancer, and photographer.

283. Lorne Hyman Greene OC (1915–1987): Canadian actor, musician, singer, and radio personality, best known for his leading role in the TV series *Bonanza*.

284. Stuart Silver (1937–2021): Design director in the 1960s and 1970s of the Metropolitan Museum of Art, located in New York City and founded in 1870 with its mission to bring art and art education to the American people. He was known for his innovative use of theatrics for display.

285. Likely Richard McLanathan.

286. A vast palace in Florence built during the Renaissance.

287. Desiderius Erasmus Roterodamus (1466–1536): Dutch philosopher and theologian who made important contributions to the Northern Renaissance. McLuhan, *Counterblast*, 122, 133.

288. Charles V (1500–1558): Holder of numerous titles including Holy Roman Emperor, Archduke of Austria, King of Spain, Lord of the Netherlands, and Duke of Burgundy.

289. Paul Jackson Pollock (1912–1956): American painter who was a major figure in the abstract expressionist movement. He used the "drip technique" of pouring or splashing liquid household paint onto a horizontal surface.

290. Pennsylvania Station (1910–1963): Commonly known as Penn Station, a historic railroad station in New York City.

291. This was likely Farber, "School Aid Body."

292. Lyndon Baines Johnson (1908–1973): Thirty-sixth president of the United States from 1963 to 1969 who had previously been Vice-President and Senate leader. McLuhan, *Culture Is Our Business*, 272.

293. Thomas Pearsall Field Hoving (1931–2009): American museum executive and consultant who served as the director of the Metropolitan Museum of Art.

294. Atomic Energy Commission.

295. A revised version of the paper was subsequently published with the same title in Barzun, *A Jacques Barzun Reader*.

296. The scientific study of the quantification, storage, and transmission of information, with particular attention given to sender and receiver.

297. See note 113 in this section.

298. Lybyer, *Government of the Ottoman*.

299. Half-length portrait painting by Italian artist Leonardo da Vinci, considered to depict the Italian noblewoman Lisa del Giocondo. It was believed to have been painted between 1503 and 1506.

300. See note 44 in this section.

301. *Sunflowers* (*Tournesols*): Title of two series of still-life paintings (1887 and 1888) by Vincent Willem van Gogh (1853–1890), a Dutch painter who posthumously became an important figure in art history.

302. *Symphony No. 5 in C minor*, written between 1804 and 1808 by Ludwig van Beethoven (baptized December 17, 1770–died March 26, 1827), a German composer and pianist recognized as one of the most important figures in the history of Western music.

303. A small piece or lump of something, especially food.

304. William Shakespeare (baptized 1564–died 1616): English playwright, poet, and actor widely recognized as greatest writer in the English language. McLuhan and Parker, *Through the Vanishing Point*, 64, 74–75.

305. Printing from a stone or a metal plate with an etched smooth surface, invented in 1796 by the German author and actor Alois Senefelder.

306. Any of several processes for producing printing plates by photographic means.

307. Medical term for fainting or passing out.

308. Last novel by Russian author Fyodor Dostoevsky, originally published as a serial from January 1879 to November 1880.

309. This appeared in a short story by Hemingway entitled "Hills Like White Elephants," first published in 1927 in *Men Without Women*, Hemingway's second collection of short stories.

310. This is likely a reference to an artwork of Andy Warhol's, *Campbell's Soup Cans*, produced between November 1961 and March or April 1962.

311. Fictional character created by Rudolf Erich Raspe in his *Baron Muenchausen's Narrative of His Marvellous Travels and Campaigns in Russia*, published in 1785.

312. Hospital in London, "Saint Mary of Bethlehem," where the mentally ill were treated in the fifteenth century. The name of the hospital came to be pronounced "Bedlam" and the word increasingly denoted a chaotic state. McLuhan and Parker, *Through the Vanishing Point*, 235–36.

313. The biblical Tower of Babel myth and parable meant to explain why the world's peoples speak different languages.

314. William James (1842–1910): American philosopher, historian, and psychologist

315. A person who is a villain, scoundrel, snitch, rat, informant, or traitor.

316. He may have been referring to a model used by historians Arthur M. Schlesinger Sr. and Arthur M. Schlesinger Jr. They sought to explain fluctuations in American history as a cyclical fluctuation between liberalism and conservatism.

317. Victor-Marie Hugo (1802–1885), a French Romantic writer and politician, published the novel, *The Hunchback of Notre-Dame* (*Notre-Dame de Paris*), in 1831.

318. Seemingly a history combining teleology with disjunctures.

319. Brief avant-garde artistic movement (1907–1914) emphasizing multiple perspectives, geometric shapes, monochromism, and a flattened plane.

320. H.M. (Henri-Martin) Barzun (1881–1973): French experimental poet and artist who emigrated to the United States.

321. H.M. Barzun, *L'Ère du Drame*, Paris (*Figuière*), 1912, passim [this note appeared in the original seminar text].

322. *Poème et Drame*, Pais (*Figuière*) vol. iv, May 1913, p. 29 [this note appeared in the original seminar text].

323. *Poetry: a Magazine of Verse, Chicago*, October 1913, p.11 [this note appeared in the original seminar text].

324. See note 213 in this section.

325. Supreme law of the United States of America superseding the Articles of Confederation in 1789.

326. Traditional British puppet show based on the relationship between Mr. Punch and his wife Judy.

327. Representation of a small human being, originally in the form of small clay statues.

328. This comprises the first ten amendments to the United States Constitution.

329. Emily Post (1873–1960) was the American author and socialite who set the guidelines for good manners in her 1922 book, *Etiquette: The Blue Book of Social Usage*.

Bibliography

Albers, Joseph. *Interaction of Color*. Yale University Press, 1963.

Art Treasures from Japan: Exhibition, Los Angeles County Museum of Art, September 29, 1965–November 7, 1965, The Royal Ontario Museum, Toronto, April 24, 1966–June 5, 1966, and Other Institutions. Kodansha International, 1966.

Barzun, Jacques. *A Jacques Barzun Reader: Selections from His Works*. Edited by Michael Murray. HarperCollins, 2002.

Barzun, H.-M. *L'Ère du drame: essai de synthèse poétique moderne*. Figuière, 1912.

Barzun, H.-M. *Poème et drame*, vol. IV. Figuière, 1913.

Bedford, John Robert Russell. *The Duke of Bedford's Book of Snobs*. Coward-McCann, 1966.

Brett, Katharine. *Modesty to Mod: Dress and Underdress in Canada, 1780–1967*. Royal Ontario Museum, University of Toronto. Catalogue for exhibit May 17 to September 4, 1967.

Burke, Edmund. "On Conciliation with America (1775)," in *Oxford Essential Quotations*, 4th ed. Edited by Susan Ratcliffe. Oxford University Press, 2016.

Carpenter, Edmund. "Eternal Life." *Explorations: Studies in Culture and Communication* 2 (2016): 54–62. Originally published by University of Toronto, 1954.

Carpenter, Edmund. "Space Concepts of the Aivlik Eskimos." *Explorations: Studies in Culture and Communication* 5 (2016): 126–40. Originally published by University of Toronto, 1955.

Carpenter, Edmund. "That Not-So-Silent Sea." In *The Virtual Marshall McLuhan* by Donald Theall. McGill-Queen's University Press, 2001.

Carpenter, Edmund. *Two Essays: Chief and Greed*. Persimmon Press, 2005.

Carpenter, Edmund Snow, Frederick Horsman Varley, and Robert J. Flaherty. *Eskimo by E. Carpenter, Sketches and Paintings by F. Varley, and Sketches and Photos of R. Flaherty's Collection of Eskimo Carvings*. University of Toronto Press, 1959.

Carroll, Lewis. *Alice's Adventures in Wonderland*. Macmillan, 1865.

Cavell, Richard. *The Explorations of Edmund Snow Carpenter: Anthropology Upside Down*. McGill-Queen's University Press, 2024.

De Caro, Laura. "Moulding the Museum Medium: Explorations on Embodied and Multisensory Experience in Contemporary Museum Environments." *ICOFOM Study Series*, no. 43b (2015): 55–70. https://journals.openedition.org/iss/397.

Debicka, Elizabeth, and Avi Friedman. "From Policies to Building: Public Housing in Canada's Eastern Arctic 1950s to 1980s." *Canadian Journal of Urban Research* 18, no. 2 (2009): 25–39.

"Education: OK's Children." *Time*, November 7, 1960.

Empson, William. *Seven Types of Ambiguity*. Chatto & Windus, 1930.

Farber, M.A. "School Aid Body for World Seen: Educators Suggest Group Be Set Up to Channel Funds." *New York Times*, October 10, 1967.

Fisher, Helen V. "Children's Museums: A Definition and a Credo." *Curator: The Museum Journal* 3, no. 2 (1960): 183–92. https://doi.org/10.1111/j.2151-6952.1960.tb00632.x.

Gagnon, Monika Kin. "The Christian Pavilion at Expo 67: Notes from Charles Gagnon's Archive." In *Expo 67: Not Just a Souvenir*, edited by Rhona Richman Kenneally and Johanne Sloan. University of Toronto Press, 2010.

Gagnon, Monika Kin, and Lesley Johnstone. *In Search of Expo 67*. McGill-Queen's University Press, 2020.

Genosko, Gary. "Where the Youth Aren't." *Amodern*, 5. https://amodern.net/article/where-the-youth-arent/.

Giedion, Sigfried. *Space, Time and Architecture*. Harvard University Press, 1942.

Gombrich, Ernst H. *Art and Illusion: A Study in the Psychology of Pictorial Representation*. Pantheon Books, 1960.

Hall, Edward Twitchell. *The Hidden Dimension*. Anchor Books, 1966.

Hemingway, Ernest. *A Farewell to Arms*. Scribner, 1929.

Hemingway, Ernest. *Men Without Women*. Scribner, 1927.

Hugo, Victor. *The Hunchback of Notre-Dame*. Charles Gosselin, 1831.

Hurst, Willliam Arthur. "Vision and Reading Achievement." *Clinical and Experimental Optometry* 47, no. 5 (1964): 118–34.

Joyce, James. *Finnegans Wake*. Faber & Faber, 1939.

Lauder, Adam. "Clash of Spaces: Harley Parker's Reconceptualization of the Museum as a Communication System." *Amodern*, 5. https://amodern.net/article/a-clash-of-spaces/.

Leighton, Alexander H. *My Name is Legion: Foundations for a Theory of Man in Relation to Culture*. Basic Books, 1955.

Lovell, Jonathan, and AnnMarie Brennan. "The Labyrinth as Immersive Multimedia Environment: Marshall McLuhan at Expo 67." *Journal of Architecture* 26, no. 2 (2021): 147–73.

Lybyer, Albert Howe. *The Government of the Ottoman Empire in the Time of Suleiman the Magnificent*. Harvard University Press, 1913.

Malraux, André. *Museum Without Walls*. Translated by Stuart Gilbert and Francis Price. Doubleday, 1967.

Marchand, Philip. *Marshall McLuhan: The Medium and the Messenger*. Vintage Books, 1990.

McHale, John. "The Plastic Parthenon." In *Kitsch: An Anthology of Bad Taste*, edited by Gillo Dorfles. Studio Vista, 1969.

McLuhan, Marshall. "Address at Vision 65." *The American Scholar* 35, no. 2 (1966): 196–205.

McLuhan, Marshall. *Counterblast*. McClelland & Stewart, 1969.

McLuhan, Marshall. *Culture Is Our Business*. Ballantine Books, 1970.

McLuhan, Marshall. *The Gutenberg Galaxy: The Making of Typographic Man*. Routledge & Kegan Paul, 1962.

McLuhan, Marshall. "Marshall McLuhan to Barbara Ward, February 9, 1973." In *Letters of Marshall McLuhan*, selected and edited by Matie Molinaro, Corinne McLuhan, and William Toye. Oxford University Press, 1987.

McLuhan, Marshall. *The Mechanical Bride: Folklore of Industrial Man.* Vanguard, 1951.

McLuhan, Marshall. "The Southern Quality." *The Sewanee Review* 55, no. 3 (1947): 357–83.

McLuhan, Marshall. *Understanding Media: The Extensions of Man.* McGraw-Hill, 1964.

McLuhan, Marshall, and Quentin Fiore. *The Medium Is the Massage: An Inventory of Effects.* Bantam, 1967.

McLuhan, Marshall, and Quentin Fiore. *War and Peace in the Global Village: An Inventory of Some of the Current Spastic Situations That Could Be Eliminated by More Feedforward.* Bantam Books, 1968.

McLuhan, Marshall, and W. Terrence Gordon. *The Relation of Environment to Anti-Environment.* Marshall McLuhan Unbound 4. Gingko Press, 2005.

McLuhan, Marshall, Kathryn Hutchon, and Eric McLuhan. *City as Classroom: Understanding Language and Media.* Book Society of Canada, 1977.

McLuhan, Marshall, and Eric McLuhan. *Laws of Media: The New Science.* University of Toronto Press, 1988.

McLuhan, Marshall, and Barrington Nevitt. *Take Today: The Executive as Dropout.* Harcourt Brace Jovanovich, 1972.

McLuhan, Marshall, and Harley Parker. *Through the Vanishing Point: Space in Poetry and Painting.* Harper & Row, 1968.

McLuhan, Marshall, Wilfred Watson, and W. Terrence Gordon. *From Cliché to Archetype.* Gingko Press, 2011.

"McLuhan Will Study Twiggy on A.B.C.-TV." *New York Times*, June 9, 1967.

Miller, Wright Watts. *Russians as People.* Dutton, 1962.

Molinaro, Matie, Corinne McLuhan, and William Toye, eds. *Letters of Marshall McLuhan.* Oxford University Press, 1987.

More, Thomas, and Gilbert Burnet. *Utopia: Written in Latin by Sir Thomas More, Chancellor of England: Translated into English.* Richard Chiswell, 1685.

Nagel, Alexander. *Medieval Modern: Art out of Time.* Thames & Hudson, 2012.

"Obituary: Abraham Kirshner." *Globe and Mail*, October 28, 2004.

"Oral History Interview with Richard McLanathan." https://www.aaa.si.edu/collections/interviews/oral-history-interview-richard-mclanathan-12237.

"Our World 1967 Full Broadcast (First Worldwide Television Broadcast, BBC1 Version)." https://www.youtube.com/watch?v=s3LmQFt4pQc.

Parker, Harley. *The Culture Box: Museums as Media.* Edited by Gary Genosko. University of Alberta Press, 2025.

Parker, Harley. "New Hall of Fossil Invertebrates, Royal Ontario Museum." *Curator* 10, no. 4 (1967): 284–96.

Parr, A.E. "The Habitat Group." *Curator: The Museum Journal* 2, no. 2 (1959): 107–28. https://doi.org/10.1111/j.2151-6952.1959.tb01401.x.

Parr, A.E. "Habitat Group and Period Room 1." *Curator: The Museum Journal* 6, no. 4 (1963): 325–36. https://doi.org/10.1111/j.2151-6952.1963.tb01353.x.

Plato. *The Republic.* Translated with an introduction by Christopher Rowe. Penguin, 2012.

Post, Emily. *Etiquette: The Blue Book of Social Usage.* Funk & Wagnalls, 1922.

Poulet, Georges. *Studies in Human Time.* Translated by Elliott Coleman. Johns Hopkins University Press, 1956.

Pound, Ezra. *The ABC of Reading.* Cox & Wyman, 1934.

Raspe, Rudolf Erich. *Baron Muenchausen's Narrative of His Marvellous Travels and Campaigns in Russia.* 1785.

Schlack, Julie Wittes. "50 Years On, Remembering the 'Our World' Broadcast and What It Means Today." *WBUR.org.* June 26, 2017. https://www.wbur.org/cognoscenti/2017/06/26/satellite-tv-julie-wittes-schlack.

Schmidt, Dana Adams. "Cambridge Welcomes a Freshman: Prince Charles." *New York Times,* October 9, 1967.

Theall, Donald F. *The Virtual Marshall McLuhan.* McGill-Queen's University Press, 2001.

Thomas, W. Stephen. "How Do Museums Use the Mass Media? A Report from the United States." In *Museums, Imagination and Education.* UNESCO, 1973.

Thomas, W. Stephen. "The Museum of Arts and Sciences, Rochester, N.Y." *Museum International* 20, no. 3 (1967): 174–76.

Veatch, Henry Babcock. *Rational Man: A Modern Interpretation of Aristotelian Ethics.* Liberty Fund, 2003.

"Veteran Pioneered Learning Techniques." *York Region.Com,* November 9, 2011, https://www.yorkregion.com/news-story/1461034-veteran-pioneered-learning-techniques/.

Williams, D. Carleton. "Acoustic Space." *Explorations: Studies in Culture and Communication* 4 (2006): 54–62. Originally published by University of Toronto, 1955.

3

Postscript
Multi-Sensory Museology

DAVID HOWES

WHEN MARSHALL MCLUHAN AND HARLEY PARKER descended
on New York and stormed the Museum of the City of New York in
October 1967—at the invitation of then-Director, Ralph Miller—they
unleashed a maelstrom of ideas and special effects.

True to Canadian form,[1] the duo presented a mosaic approach to
the museum which consisted of diverse "probes" and an experimental
exhibition (curated by Parker) with a weltering array of media. The
juxtaposition of media created a "collideroscopic" surround that illuminated the Dutch and subsequent history of the city in a decidedly
nonlinear (anti-chronological, contrapuntal, multimodal) fashion.[2]

It is fitting that the invitation to the 1967 seminar took the form
of an audiotape of a dialogue between the two media iconoclasts,
and the event itself survives in the form of a transcript of McLuhan
and Parker riffing off each other's ideas and (im)moderating a discussion with the eighty or so participants.[3] Their whole purpose was to
disrupt the "visual space" of modern literate society (bounded, linear,
ordered, rational) with its "one-at-a-timeness" by superimposing
onto it the "acoustic space" (boundless, directionless, and charged
with emotion) or "all-at-onceness" of traditional oral societies and
the "tactile space" of the emergent post-literate society of electrical
circuitry.

Reading the transcript of the seminar with the benefit of hindsight
is an exhilarating and refreshing experience, since McLuhan and
Parker's probes have since become commonplaces or clichés of museum

discourse and practice. Multi-sensory museology is the new *Grundnorm* of the museum world, as evidenced by a series of groundbreaking shows, including *Tate Sensorium* (2015), *A Feast for the Senses* (2016), and *The Senses: Design Beyond Vision* (2018),[4] as well as increasingly widespread experimentation with so-called interactive display techniques in place of labels.[5]

The reviews of the seminar were ambivalent, as William Buxton brings out in his Introduction to this (re)publication, "a bit behind the times" according to one reviewer[6]: while other reviewers were bemused and professed to be unconvinced. This blasé reaction is particularly noticeable in Jacques Barzun's after-dinner speech (the closing event of the seminar), which sought to domesticate McLuhan's and Parker's uproarious barbs and un-museum-like comportment in the name of Barzun's father by quoting the latter at length.[7] McLuhan might have predicted this rearview mirror response to his and Parker's interventions, which bombarded the audience's senses with novel stimuli, but ultimately left many of them numb and defensive: "people hate this electronic all-at-onceness,"[8] they "deliberately refuse to perceive this in order to feel more comfortable."[9]

Nevertheless, one need not simply "turn off" or "tune out"; there is a way to handle such "information overload," according to McLuhan and Parker. The trick involves resorting to "pattern recognition." This "mosaical" technique of perception is at the antipode of the model of the text with its linearity and typographicality. It is multimodal in place of unimodal, attuned to evocation and (Baudelarian) correspondences in place of rational exposition, and participatory in place of planar or two-dimensional.

McLuhan's probes take the form of electric (and electrifying) aphorisms, such as "The medium is the message."[10] He perfected the sound bite, as such flashes of insight have since come to be known in our era of ever-diminishing attention spans. While invariably revelatory, the very brevity of the probes can also be obfuscatory. Consider the adage, "The book is an extension of the eye."[11] In point of fact, the book is not just that, as a 2022 exhibition at the Bodleian Library entitled *Sensational Books* amply testifies. Books have an odour,[12] a texture (the feel of parchment, the raised dots of Braille), a sound (the rustle of pages or, with the advent of the talking book, a voice), and they are susceptible to being chewed and tasted both by book worms and human toddlers alike (as with the copy of Dr. Seuss's *The Foot Book* in one of the vitrines, the corners of which are well gnawed and its contents presumably digested). There is more to the materiality of the book than meets the eye.[13]

McLuhan is to be lauded for expanding the definition of media to include *any* technological extension of the human body (clothing as an extension of the skin, the wheel as an extension of the foot, the telephone as an extension of the ear, etc.), and the idea that each new invention alters the "ratio" or balance of the senses. But his overarching theory may also be faulted on at least three grounds: first, for its essentialism; second, its technological determinism; and third, its failure to adequately address the full gamut of possible relations among the senses. For example, it is commonly assumed that vision is the most objective of the senses, taste the most subjective, hearing the most emotional, and smell the most memorable, but all these allegedly intrinsic sensory characteristics actually turn on how the senses have been *constructed* historically in the West. By contrast, in some non-Western societies, vision is associated with witchcraft (the evil eye), while touch (supposedly one of the proximity senses) may be understood to operate at a distance.[14] Similarly, the eye does not just see lines, it also perceives colour, and colours can be warm (orange, brown) or cool (blue); in some non-Western societies, select colours are even experienced as having an odour.[15]

The technological determinism of McLuhan's position is given in the notion that the onset of alphabetization resulted in the substitution of "an eye for an ear" and this visual bias was further intensified by the invention of the printing press.[16] This (alleged) substitution is at the core of his "Great Divide" theory of the evolution of human consciousness, which lumps the cultures of all nonliterate societies together in a single homogeneous category and opposes them to the visual culture of literate societies. By contrast, research in the anthropology of the senses has revealed that there are as many differences to the orchestration of the senses amongst so-called oral societies as there are between them and the class of literate societies. Furthermore,

there are important differences within each and every society, for the
division of the sensorium—or distribution of the sensible—also
varies along gender, class and/or racialized lines.[17]

By way of example, Constance Classen discusses the thermal
cosmology of the Tzotzil of Mexico and the visual-synesthetic
cosmology of the Desana of Colombia.[18] In each case, the priority
attached to one sense alters the relations amongst all the others.
Thus, according to the Desana "vision" of the cosmos (which is generated and sustained by the ritual ingestion of the hallucinogenic
Banisteriopsis caapi plant, or *yagé*, under the guidance of a shaman),
colours emanate from the light of the sun or moon and then combine
with heat to produce corresponding sets of odours and flavours.
Purple, for example, is said to come from the moon and is linked to a
rotten smell and an acid flavour. All of these hallucinogen-fuelled
percepts are encoded with moral precepts. For example, the drawn-
out sounds of a large flute played by men are said to have a strong
yellow colour, hot temperature, masculine odour, and trigger a
message that refers to child-rearing; or, again, different flavours are
identified with different kin groups and used to regulate marriage.
The *yagé* beverage thus performs much the same function as the
Bible—"The Great Code"[19]—in Western Christendom: it is a
cosmogony and moral code in the form of a sensory code.

Classen's essay underscores the importance of attending to the
"techniques of the senses"[20] or "ways of sensing"[21] unique to particular societies. Such techniques are *infra*technological and therefore
bound to escape notice when attention is restricted to the tech-
nologization of the sensorium. Her point is that each culture must
be approached on its own sensory terms. There can be no "natural
history of the senses,"[22] only cultural histories.[23]

The refinements to McLuhan's "Great Divide" theory, as suggested
by practicing cultural historians like Classen[24] and anthropologists
like Ruth Finnegan[25] and Sandra Dudley,[26] have many radical implications for museology. The question arises: If, as McLuhan and Parker
assert in the seminar, "artifacts create environments," how can museum
visitors be primed to sense things accordingly? What would it take to

reconstruct and convey something of the "historical sensations" of a period[27] or the social life of the senses (as of things) in an Indigenous society?

To their credit, McLuhan and Parker already floated many seminal suggestions in the course of their diatribe at the seminar, including:

- Abandon the model of the book—that is, dispense with labels, forget storylines, don't treat artifacts as illustrations.
- Liberate exotica from the glass boxes in which they are typically imprisoned—and, if conservation or security continue to concern you, then use air curtains in place of glass or create facsimile reproductions that can be handled.
- Make liberal use of multi-media to create "anti-environments."[28]
- Curate the odour of things—do not sanitize them.
- If you remain worried about visitors getting things wrong due to the muteness of objects (which cannot speak for themselves), then set up an orientation room and provide them with a tape machine with an array of answers to FAQs.
- Above all, de-departmentalize (i.e., abjure specialization) by juxtaposing objects from different cultures and different historical periods: "I would like to see Rembrandts juxtaposed to El Grecos in order that one thing can strike sparks off the other,"[29] or "an Aztec piece alongside a Chinese piece,"[30] says Parker; "You have to cross boundaries to make discoveries,"[31] says McLuhan.

Some of the above-mentioned suggestions have sunk in[32] even at such staid institutions as the Ashmolean Museum in Oxford. I recall being very much in my element (as a sensory anthropologist) when I toured the Asian Crossroads Orientation Gallery at the Ashmolean. It explored the contacts between cultures and the transmission of ideas, knowledge, and religion via the overland Silk Road and overseas trade routes between Europe and Asia in the early modern period, using interactive touch screens and a heterogenous assortment of objects.[33] My interest was also piqued by the label affixed to a vitrine of Chinese ceramics, which read, "Ceramics are experienced most directly through touch, yet various texts show how Tang dynasty (AD 618–906) wares appealed to other senses." There followed a series of quotations from the works of Chinese literati:

> Yue wares release the tea's fragrance.

> The ceramics of Yue resemble vessels of jade.

> The master of ritual music at the Taichang temple excels at percussion: taking twelve vessels of Xing and Yue ware containing different levels of water, he strikes them with a chopstick. The sound is wonderful.

> Xing (white) ware is like silver, Yue (green) ware is like jade, this is the first reason Xing is not as good as Yue; Xing ware is like snow, Yue ware is like ice, this is the second reason; the white of Xing ware makes the tea a red colour, the green of Yue ware makes the tea a fresh green colour, and this is the third reason Xing is not as good…Green colour enhances tea while red, yellow brown and black are not appropriate colours.

These literary allusions to the multi- and inter-sensory qualities of Yue and Xing ceramic ware might not seem all that stimulating, but the mere fact that they are registered speaks volumes about the sensory turn in museology.[34]

The main stumbling block to the total overhaul of the museum proposed by McLuhan and Parker is that museum specialists have long been trained to rely exclusively on considerations of chronology and typology to determine how artifacts should be displayed rather than concentrate on what McLuhan and Parker called "the training of perception."[35] Enter the idea of "sensology"[36] or "sensitive mediation."[37] Sensology leads with the senses in the investigation of material culture; it privileges percepts over concepts, and directs attention to apprehending "the sensori-social life of things"[38] both in their source communities and in the museum. In what follows, I would like to review some of what I consider to be the best, most promising practices for inculcating *uncommon sense* (or "environmental awareness," as McLuhan and Parker would put it)[39] in museum visitors, building on the legacy of Classen, Finnegan, and Dudley, and, behind them, McLuhan and Parker.

Museum Materialities and *Museum Objects*, both edited by Sandra Dudley, are exemplary of the sensory turn in museology. Dudley directs our attention to "experiencing the properties of things" rather than confining our attention to their form. One of the many fine chapters in *Museum Materialities* that I especially admire is "Dancing pot and pregnant jar? On ceramics, metaphors and creative labels," written by Wing Yan Vivian Ting. In it, Ting describes the *Creative Spaces* community outreach program that she ran at the Schiller Gallery of the Bristol City Museum in 2006–07. The participants were all students at two local teachers' colleges. The aim of the project was to facilitate a "robust and reflective object-human relationship" with items (mainly bowls) in the museum's collection of Chinese porcelain by empowering the participants "to listen to the sensual, tactile language of Chinese ceramics."[40] One sensory activity involved the students handling the bowls while wearing blindfolds to sensitize them to the tactile qualities of the ceramics, and then comparing these with their visual impressions when the blindfolds were removed. Another involved the participants looking at a ceramic piece while listening to a piece of music, such as the third movement of Bach's Harpsichord Concerto in D major. The titles of the musical pieces were withheld so as not to distract attention from the transcendent and engaging qualities of music (music being the most abstract, intangible form of art) and incite the participants to "explore the inner value of ceramic wares" through the formation of "perceptual syntheses."[41]

In effect, Ting's *Creative Spaces* project enabled the participants to "see" feelingly, musically, personally, and creatively by engaging the whole sensorium in the work of art interpretation, playing one sense off against another, and conjoining the senses in fun and unexpected ways. The associations the participants forged (e.g., between a big wine jar and "a pregnant woman with a softly swelling belly") could be described as metaphors following George Lakoff and Mark Johnson,[42] but they are more than mere figures of speech or conceptual bridges, they are *perceptual* through and through. The activities Ting proposed are best understood as exercises in "inter-sensoriality"[43] designed to feed the aesthetic imagination, infuse the perceptual with the personal, and make the object-human relationship that much more meaningful and hence fulfilling. Forget metaphor theory. Furthermore, in place of the emphasis on disinterested contemplation in the conventional definition of the aesthetic experience (following Kant), Ting's experiments are all about *participant sensation*—or recanting Kant, as it were. The *coup de grâce* of Ting's approach consisted in democratizing the curatorial function by inviting the participants to pen their own labels for the objects in the collection based on their intimate (albeit uneducated) engagement with them. The labels were then affixed alongside those authored by the curators.

On a recent trip to Paris, I made a pilgrimage to the Musée de Cluny, which is a mecca for sensory studies scholars like myself. It has a room dedicated to the world-famous *Lady and the Unicorn* tapestries, which present an allegory of the six senses. I must have visited this room at least a dozen times since my first visit in 1981, and every time I like to test my memory for the symbolism of each of the elements in the tapestries *without* reading any labels or using an audio guide (e.g., tray of sweets + monkey stand for taste, portable organ + hare stand for hearing, etc.) and contemplate the meaning of the majestic sixth tapestry, which accords pride of place to a treasure box and is embroidered with the phrase "*À mon seul désir*": does this tapestry stand for the will (which must subjugate the senses, control the desires) or does it reference the heart (conceived as the portal of the soul, which invests each sensation with emotion and discloses its spiritual significance)?

On this occasion I was scheduled to meet with Anne Sophie Grassin, Cheffe adjointe du Service de la médiation et de la politique des publics. Grassin is responsible for finetuning cultural mediation by augmenting its practice with "sensitive mediation."[44] The latter technique represents her solution to the crisis of attention and the overemphasis on cognition (or conveying "information") in conventional museology through engaging the senses. Since the museum reopened in 2022, Grassin's initiatives have included commissioning a singer to sing different objects in the collection (*La visite chantée*) and a dancer to interpret the *Lady and the Unicorn* tapestries through bodily movement (*La visite dansée*). She is also the genius behind a podcast series entitled *Sans les yeux*, which foregrounds the corporeal *savoir-faire* of contemporary artisans:

> Il propose de donner la parole à des artisans, spécialistes des savoirs-faire et les invite à s'exprimer sur les œuvres de la collection du musée à partir de leur expertise, de leurs gestes afin de donner à entendre de nouvelles résonances contemporaines. L'idée de ce nouveau format de médiation est de proposer un complément au discours scientifique par un éclairage à partir des savoirs-faire contemporains liés aux œuvres. L'artiste-artisan parle d'une œuvre à partir de son métier, de son regard et de ses gestes.[45]

> It proposes to give the floor to artisans, specialists in know-how, and invites them to discourse on the works of the museum's collection based on their own expertise, their gestures in order to enable us to hear new contemporary resonances. The idea behind this new format of mediation is to propose a complement to scientific discourse by casting light on contemporary know-how linked to the works. The artist-craftspeople speak about the work from the standpoint of their practice, their gaze and their gestures [author's translation].

Grassin's sensitive approach to the Musée de Cluny collection privileges the gestural over the visual, the percept over the concept, and mediation over (academic) interpretation. It is above all concerned with enhancing the *relationship* between visitors and objects by promoting sensory interaction (in place of mere viewing), addressing the "whole person" of the visitor.[46]

Another major impetus for the sensory turn in museology comes from Indigenous communities who had their material culture "collected" in the past and now either demand its repatriation or, in the alternative, that their treasures be treated as "sensitive material."[47] By way of example, consider the *Sacred Materials Programme* at the Canadian Museum of History (CMH). The CMH has a fine collection of Iroquois False Face masks. Twice yearly, medicine men from the Six Nations Confederacy are invited to come to the museum to chant, to smudge (with sage smoke), and to feed the masks (with corn meal mush). The way the masks are treated by the shamans flies in the face of the longstanding distinction between persons and things in the Western tradition. The masks are hailed as living, sentient beings—and as having sensory appetites—by the medicine men, who treat them as kin. These subject-objects not only exhibit diverse sensory proper-ties, they sense back.[48]

Marie-Pier Gadoua, a research assistant attached to the *Hands-On Museum* project directed by Constance Classen, describes a project in "collaborative archaeology" that she ran at the McCord Museum of Canadian History in Montreal.[49] It involved inviting Inuit elders to share their knowledge about traditional Inuit material culture (hunting implements, a model kayak, oil lamps, and some items that had no known use) through participating in handling sessions. The sessions were lively occasions, particularly once the gloves came off, both for the participants (on account of the social relations and storytelling the objects prompted) and for the objects, which were temporarily brought back to life through being handled. The work-shops led to the recovery and occasional discovery of affordances that the professional archaeologists and museum curators had never suspected, and the realization that, in the final analysis, the meaning of an object is in its use, not its label. Videoclips of the workshops were to be integrated in the McCord Museum's exhibitions and website, thereby constituting an "archive of the immaterial"[50] along-side the collection itself. Gadoua records that the workshops had many emotional benefits for the participants, such as evoking pride at the ingenuity of their ancestors, or alleviating stress—especially for those Inuit who were in Montreal on medical visits.

A third major impetus for the sensualization of the museum stems from diverse domestic laws (UK, US, France, Canada) stipulating that public institutions, like museums, must render their collections accessible to all sectors of the public, including the disabled.[51] Initiatives include the *Stimulating the Senses* program at the National Gallery in Ottawa, which offers touch tours for the visually impaired[52] and the work of the philanthropic organization Art Education for the Blind (AEB) based in New York. In an effort to render the masterpieces of Western art accessible to people with low vision, in 1998 the AEB produced the diagram manual, *European Modernism: 1900–1940*, created in association with OpticalTouch Systems™. It features colour reproductions of famous paintings overlaid with lines of varying boldness and differently textured patterns (dots, smooth patches, crosshatch). This permits the formal arrangement of the works to be felt. But what about the colours of the paintings? Their teinture is left untouched by the designers of the AEB manuals.

This blind spot regarding colour has proved a major stumbling block due to the enduring influence of the five-sense model of the sensorium, which assumes that each of the modalities are structurally and functionally distinct channels, or silos. By way of example, John Locke, the father of empirical psychology, was alerted to the report of a blind man who professed to understand "what scarlet signified"—it was "like the sound of a trumpet," the man claimed. How ingenious you might think, but not Locke. He rubbished it: "To hope to produce an *idea* of light or colour by a sound, however formed, is to expect that sounds should be visible, or colours audible; and to make the ears do the office of all the other senses. Which is all one as to say, that we might taste, smell, and see by the ears."[53] Any suggestion that it might be possible to form ideas about one sense in or by means of another was out of the question for Locke.

But not for Patricia Bérubé, a recent graduate of the PHD program in Cultural Mediation at Carleton University. In the participatory action/research-creation project that formed the basis of her doctoral thesis, Bérubé succeeded at breaching the firewalls between the senses decreed by Locke. The project unfolded in a series of phases that involved interviews and co-design sessions with six visually impaired participants (two of whom were blind since birth), and culminated in the co-production of "multisensory translations" or "transpositions" of two paintings: a naturalistic representation of a hilly landscape with rain showers and a relatively abstract representation of boats in a harbour. The first phase involved the production of tactile prototypes using wooden guidelines to delineate shapes and a tactile palette (whorls, straight lines, and smooth surfaces of moulded silicone) to encode the colour schemes. The second phase involved imbuing the tactile-colour fields with synthesized sounds of wind, rain, waves, etc., augmented by clips of music, verbal descriptions, and instructions for use to evoke the mood (affective tone) and atmosphere of the two artworks. The resulting multi-sensory translations of the two paintings are a sight to feel and listen to, not just behold. No less engrossing are Bérubé's detailed descriptions and thematic analyses (using NVivo) of the conversations that went on during the co-design sessions and all the technologies that were used and technical experts she engaged in order to produce the desired effects.[54] The excitement generated by the whole process and final products is palpable in the following testimonial by one of the visually impaired participants in the study:

> If I could go to a museum and feel stuff like this...I'd probably go back some other time. But up until this point, museums have just not been a place of interest to me at all—like zero interest. Like if you wanted to punish me for something you know, take me to a museum basically...But now this project is alive. This is fun.[55]

Sensology, or sensitive mediation *à la* Grassin, leans in with the senses in its approach to the material culture of the museum. As such, it qualifies (in more senses than one) the focus on the materiality of things in conventional material culture studies and is in keeping with the increased importance attached to the recognition and preservation of the "intangible cultural heritage" of humanity.[56] These approaches still use artifacts (or "cultural property") as supports, but shift the onus onto visitor-object interaction, the training of perception.

As noted previously, McLuhan and Parker were strong advocates for transforming museums into environments for the training of perception. This made their approach post-scriptural, and, in the estimation of some critics, anti-intellectual. But it is not anti-intellectual; rather it is imbued with the "wisdom of the senses"[57]—that is, with wit (an archaic term for sense).

McLuhan also opined that "one of the most important things that museums can do today is to help solve one of our biggest problems: our incapacity for intercultural dialogue."[58] This brings us to the final example of McLuhanism to be treated here, though it will take us beyond the walls of the museum. It is given in the work of Chris Salter, holder of the Concordia University Research Chair in New Media, Technology, and the Senses from 2010 to 2022. Salter is the inventor of the "performative sensory environment," or PSE.[59] PSEs are like museum exhibitions but without any objects, only qualia, only effects.

One of Salter's earliest installations was called *Displace (v. 1.0)*, a sound-and-light, and gustatory-and-olfactory, and thermal as well as textured and kinetic show—or "fugue of the five senses"—which sought in part to evoke the synesthetic cosmology of the Desana.[60] *Displace (v. 1.0)* was first shown at the annual meeting of the American Anthropological Association in Montreal in 2011. It was billed as "a flight simulator for anthropologists." In effect, it offered a training ground for the senses that—through opening a crack in the Western sensorium by experimenting with diverse alternative arrangements and transpositions of the senses—would enable ethnographers to attune themselves to the sensoria of other cultures that much more readily and deeply.

Salter's latest research-creation project is called *Sensory Entanglements* (SE). The SE team is made up of Indigenous and non-Indigenous artists and scholars from Canada and Australia. Its realizations take the form of a series of PSEs including the interactive sound installation *Heart Band* (2021) by the Métis artist-researcher David Garneau and the fragrant light sculpture with powerful sonic and proprioceptive dimensions called *Yahkâskwan Mîkiwhap*, or "Light Tipi" (2016) by interdisciplinary performance artist Cheryl L'Hirondelle in association with Cree elder Joseph Naytowhow.[61] As Salter states,

The team is attempting to explore the productive tension in how the "newness" of emerging technologies (despite their colonial origins and structures) might enable an "Indigenizing" of sensorial artistic experiences that disrupts historical boundaries, challenges entrenched borders, creates potent forms of culturally specific empathy, and potentially may de-colonize the representation of otherness.[62]

I suspect that McLuhan and Parker would have been much taken by these experiments in crossing sensory and cultural borders. The whole purpose of these artworks is to forge a new common sense and a new consensus regarding the terms of the relationship between Indigenous peoples and mainstream Canadian society going forward.[63] In these works, the "message" is one of intermediation.

Author's Note

My place of work, Concordia University, is located on unceded Indigenous lands. The people of the Kanien'kehá:ka Nation are recognized as the custodians of the lands and waters of Tiohtiá:ke/Montreal. Historically known as a gathering place for many First Nations, today this city is home to a diverse population of Indigenous and other peoples. At Concordia, we respect the continued connections with the past, present, and future in our ongoing relationships with Indigenous and other peoples within the Montreal community. Part of the research on which this paper is based was made possible by a grant from the Social Sciences and Humanities Research Council of Canada (no. 435-2020-1279). I wish to thank Bill Buxton for the invitation to write this chapter, and for his many insightful comments on an earlier draft.

Notes

1. For a discussion of the mosaic structure of the Canadian imaginary, see http://canadianicon.org/.
2. On McLuhan's notion of the collideroscope of the sensorium, which he borrowed from James Joyce, and which has certain affinities with Claude Lévi-Strauss's "fugue of the five senses" and the way in which Glenn Gould played Bach, see Howes, "Collideroscope (Intersensoriality)" and Howes, *Sensory Studies Manifesto,* 69–70.
3. McLuhan and Parker pointedly refused to present written papers at the seminar. They wanted to keep things oral.
4. I reviewed these three shows in Chapter 7 of *The Sensory Studies Manifesto.* I would add that these groundbreaking exhibitions actually represent a restoration of the

Umwelt of the early museum as documented by Constance Classen in "Museum Manners" and *The Museum of the Senses*, with particular reference to the Ashmolean Museum (est. 1683) and the British Museum (est. 1753). See further Jones, *Sensorium*.

5. Classen, *Museum of the Senses*; Bielo, "Experiential Design."

6. Battcock, "Failure of McLuhan."

7. *Museum Communication* seminar report in the present volume, 200–01.

8. *Museum Communication* seminar report, 96.

9. *Museum Communication* seminar report, 155. Of course, the resistance to McLuhan and Parker's electronically suffused brainstorming shown by Barzun and the reviewers is completely outmoded now, and (if anything) we need a new McLuhan to awaken our senses to the environment created by the proliferation of sensor technologies and ubiquitous computing (see Salter, *Sensing Machines*).

10. McLuhan himself never really got a handle on the import of this probe: its meaning kept on shifting chimerically. See Gordon, *Marshall McLuhan*, 173–79.

11. McLuhan and Fiori, *The Medium is the Massage*, 36–37.

12. A section of the *Sensational Books* exhibition was devoted to the smell of books. It included a series of cylinders which one could sniff to experience, for example, the faded tobacco smell of a book from J.R.R. Tolkien's personal library (Tolkien was an inveterate pipe smoker), or the buttery smell of the Duke Humfrey reading room at the Bodleian, as well as a copy of the "Historic Book Odours Wheel" which is used in the olfactory archaeology of old libraries.

13. Howes, "*Sensational Books* Exhibition Review."

14. Howes, *Sensual Relations*.

15. Young, "Smell of Greenness"; Young, "Colours of Things."

16. McLuhan, *Gutenberg Galaxy*.

17. Classen, "Foundations for an Anthropology"; Classen, *Colour of Angels*; Howes, *Varieties of Sensory Experience*; Howes, *Sensual Relations*; Howes, *Sensory Studies Manifesto*.

18. Classen, "McLuhan in the Rainforest."

19. Frye, *The Great Code*.

20. Howes, "Les techniques des sens."

21. Howes and Classen, *Ways of Sensing*.

22. Ackerman, *Natural History of the Senses*.

23. Classen, *Colour of Angels*; Classen, *Cultural History of the Senses*.

24. Classen, "Foundations for an Anthropology"; Classen "Senses."

25. Finnegan, *Communicating*.

26. Dudley, *Museum Materialities*; Dudley, *Museum Objects*.

27. Ankersmit, "Huizinga on Historical Experience," 23–29.

28. See further McLuhan and Parker, *Through the Vanishing Point*.

29. *Museum Communication* seminar report, 111.

30. *Museum Communication* seminar report, 147.

31.   *Museum Communication* seminar report, 104.

32.   Many of McLuhan's (and McLuhan and Parker's) catchphrases and concepts have become part of the *lingua franca*, so that they are used by contemporary scholars without the latter being aware of their source.

33.   I sought to flesh out the sensory dimensions of these conjunctures in Howes, *Sensorial Investigations*, 190–207.

34.   Howes, "Introduction to Sensory Museology"; Levent and Pascual-Leone, *Multisensory Museum*.

35.   *Museum Communication* seminar report, 71. See also, Gordon, *Marshall McLuhan*, 100; Friesen, "Vision and the 'Training of Perception.'"

36.   Newhauser, *Cultural History*.

37.   Grassin, "Le tournant sensible."

38.   Howes, "Scent, Sound, and Synaesthesia."

39.   McLuhan and Parker, *Through the Vanishing Point*.

40.   Ting, "Dancing Pot and Pregnant Jar?," 189.

41.   Ting, "Dancing Pot and Pregnant Jar?," 197.

42.   Lakoff and Johnson, *Metaphors We Live By*.

43.   Howes, *Sensory Studies Manifesto*.

44.   Grassin, "Le tournant sensible."

45.   Grassin, "Écouter les oeuvres."

46.   Grassin, "Le tournant sensible," 15–16.

47.   See Howes, "Sensitive Material."

48.   Howes, *Sensorial Investigations*.

49.   Gadoua, "Making Sense Through Touch."

50.   Leahy, "Incorporating the Period Eye."

51.   Candlin, *Art, Museums and Touch*.

52.   Clintberg, "Where Publics May Touch."

53.   For contextualization and discussion of this quote, see Howes, *Sensorial Investigations*, 129.

54.   Experts included Robert Gagnon of Lezar3D for the 3D printing (who also collaborated with Bérubé on her Master's thesis project), and the American digital artist Henry Lowengard, developer of the iOS version of the Adaptive Use Musical Instrument (AUMI) software that allows users to play musical phrases and sounds through movement and gestures. At the suggestion of one of the blind co-researchers, there was talk of multiplying the modalities further by devising and incorporating a thermal colour palette, but this was not pursued for safety reasons. On all this see Cho, "Study of Multi-Sensory Experience."

55.   Bérubé, "Towards a More Inclusive Museum," 135.

56.   UNESCO, *Intangible Cultural Heritage*.

57.   Classen, "Other Ways to Wisdom."

58.   *Museum Communication* seminar report, 104.

59.   Howes and Salter, "Meditations of Sensation."

60. Salter, *Alien Agency.*

61. For a description of these artworks see Howes, *Sensory Studies Manifesto*, 195–203, and for a glimpse see *Explorations in Sensory Design*, https://www.sensorydesign.ca/.

62. Quoted in Howes, *Sensory Studies Manifesto*, 195.

63. Garneau, "Imaginary Spaces of Conciliation and Reconciliation."

Bibliography

Ackerman, Diane. *A Natural History of the Senses.* Random House, 1990.

Ankersmit, Frank. "Huizinga on Historical Experience." In *Senses and Sensation: Critical and Primary Sources*, vol. 2, *History and Sociology*, edited by David Howes. Routledge, 2018.

Battcock, Gregory. "The Failure of McLuhan: Or the Whites Won." *Westside News*, October 19, 1967.

Bérubé, Patricia. "Towards a More Inclusive Museum: Developing Multi-Sensory Approaches to the Visual Arts for Visually Impaired Audiences." PHD diss., Carleton University, 2022.

Bielo, James S. "Experiential Design and Religious Publicity at D.C.'s Museum of the Bible." *The Senses and Society* 15, no. 1 (2020): 98–113.

Candlin, Fiona. *Art, Museums and Touch.* Manchester University Press, 2010.

Cho, Jun Dong. "A Study of Multi-Sensory Experience and Color Recognition in Visual Arts Appreciation of People with Visual Impairments." *Electronics* 10, no. 4 (2021): 470.

Classen, Constance. *The Colour of Angels: Cosmology, Gender and the Aesthetic Imagination.* Routledge, 1998.

Classen, Constance, ed. *A Cultural History of the Senses in the Age of Empire.* Bloomsbury, 2014.

Classen, Constance. "Foundations for an Anthropology of the Senses." *International Social Science Journal* 49, no. 153 (1997): 401–12.

Classen, Constance. 2005. "McLuhan in the Rainforest: The Sensory Worlds of Oral Cultures." In *Empire of the Senses: The Sensual Cultural Reader*, edited by David Howes. Routledge, 2005.

Classen, Constance. 2007. "Museum Manners: The Sensory Life of the Early Museum." *Journal of Social History* 40, no. 4 (2007): 895–914.

Classen, Constance. *The Museum of the Senses: Experiencing Art and Collections.* Bloomsbury, 2017.

Classen, Constance. "Other Ways to Wisdom: Learning Through the Senses Across Cultures." *International Review of Education* 45, no. 3–4 (1999): 269–80.

Classen, Constance. "The Senses." In *Encyclopedia of European Social History: From 1350 to 2000*, vol. 4, edited by Peter Stearns. Charles Scribner's Sons, 2001.

Clintberg, Mark. "Where Publics May Touch: Stimulating Sensory Access at the National Gallery of Canada." *The Senses and Society* 9, no. 3 (2015): 310–22.

Dudley, Sandra, ed. *Museum Materialities: Objects, Engagements, Interpretations.* Routledge, 2010.

Dudley, Sandra, ed. *Museum Objects: Experiencing the Properties of Things.* Routledge, 2012.

Finnegan, Ruth. *Communicating: The Multiple Modes of Human Interconnection.* Routledge, 2002.

Friesen, Norman. "Vision and 'the Training of Perception': McLuhan's Medienpädagogik." In *Senses and Sensation: Critical and Primary Sources*, vol 3, *Biology, Psychology, and Neuroscience*, edited by David Howes. Routledge, 2018.

Frye, Northrop. *The Great Code: The Bible and Literature.* Penguin Random House, 1981.

Gadoua, Marie-Pierre. "Making Sense Through Touch: Handling Collections with Inuit Elders at the McCord Museum." *The Senses and Society* 9, no. 3 (2014): 323–41.

Garneau, David. "Imaginary Spaces of Conciliation and Reconciliation: Art, Curation, and Healing." In *Arts of Engagement: Taking Aesthetic Action in and Beyond the Truth and Reconciliation Commission of Canada*, edited by Dylan Robinson and Keavy Martin. Wilfrid Laurier University Press, 2016.

Gordon, W. Terrance. *Marshall McLuhan: Escape into Understanding.* Stoddart, 1997.

Grassin, Anne Sophie. "Écouter les oeuvres par les gestes: Podcast "Sans les yeux."" *Laboratoire du geste*, 2021. http://www.laboratoiredugeste.com/spip.php?article810.

Grassin, Anne Sophie. "Le tournant sensible de la médiation culturelle." *La Lettre de l'OCIM*, no. 202–03 (2022): 10–17.

Howes, David. "Collideroscope (Intersensoriality)." Sensory Studies Picture Gallery. https://www.sensorystudies.org/picture-gallery/collideroscope1-erik-adigard/.

Howes, David. "Introduction to Sensory Museology." *The Senses and Society* 9, no. 3 (2014): 259–67.

Howes, David. "Scent, Sound and Synaesthesia: Intersensoriality and Material Culture Theory." In *Handbook of Material Culture*, edited by Chris Tilley, Webb Keane, Susanne Kuechler, Mike Rowlands, and Patricia Spyer. Sage, 2006.

Howes, David. "*Sensational Books* Exhibition Review." *The Senses and Society* 18, no.1 (2023): 81–84.

Howes, David. "Sensitive Material." https://centreforsensorystudies.org/sensitive-material/.

Howes, David. *Sensorial Investigations: A History of the Senses in Anthropology, Psychology, and Law.* Penn State University Press, 2023.

Howes, David. *The Sensory Studies Manifesto: Tracking the Sensorial Revolution in the Arts and Human Sciences.* University of Toronto Press, 2022.

Howes, David. *Sensual Relations: Engaging the Senses in Culture and Social Theory.* University of Michigan Press, 2003.

Howes, David. "Les techniques des sens." *Anthropologie et sociétés* 14, no. 2 (1990): 99–115.

Howes, David, ed. *The Varieties of Sensory Experience: A Source Book in the Anthropology of the Senses.* University of Toronto Press, 1991.

Howes, David, and Constance Classen. *Ways of Sensing: Understanding the Senses in Society*. Routledge, 2013.

Howes, David, and Chris Salter. "Mediations of Sensation: Designing Performative Sensory Environments." *NMC Media-N* 11, no. 3 (2015). https://median. newmediacaucus.org/research-creation-explorations/mediations-of-sensation-designing-performative-sensory-environments/

Jones, Caroline A., ed. *Sensorium: Embodied Experience, Technology and Contemporary Art*. The MIT List Visual Arts Center and The MIT Press, 2006.

Lakoff, George, and Mark Johnson. *Metaphors We Live By*. University of Chicago Press, 1980.

Leahy, Hellen. "Incorporating the Period Eye: Spectators at Exhibitions of Exhibitions." *The Senses and Society* 9, no. 3 (2014): 284–95.

Levent, Nina, and Alvaro Pascual-Leone, eds. *The Multisensory Museum: Cross-Disciplinary Perspectives on Touch, Sound, Smell, Memory, and Space*. Rowman and Littlefield, 2014.

McLuhan, Marshall. *The Gutenberg Galaxy*. University of Toronto Press, 1962.

McLuhan, Marshall, and Quentin Fiori. *The Medium is the Massage: An Inventory of Effects*, produced by Jerome Agel. Gingko Press, 1967.

McLuhan, Marshall, and Harley Parker. *Through the Vanishing Point: Space in Poetry and Painting*. Harper Colophon Books, 1969.

Newhauser, Richard, ed. *A Cultural History of the Senses in the Middle Ages, 1000–1400*. Bloomsbury, 2014.

Salter, Chris. *Alien Agency: Experimental Encounters with Art in the Making*. The MIT Press, 2015.

Salter, Chris. *Sensing Machines: How Sensors Shape Our Everyday Life*. The MIT Press, 2022.

Ting, W.Y.V. "Dancing Pot and Pregnant Jar? On Ceramics, Metaphors and Creative Labels." In *Museum Materialities: Objects, Engagements, Interpretations*, edited by Sandra Dudley. Routledge, 2010.

UNESCO. *What Is Intangible Cultural Heritage?* 2003. https://ich.unesco.org/en/what-is-intangible-heritage-00003.

Young, Diana. "The Smell of Greenness: Cultural Synaesthesia in the Western Desert." *Etnofoor* 18, no. 1 (2005): 61–77.

Young, Diana. "The Colours of Things." In *Handbook of Material Culture*, edited by Chris Tilley, Webb Keane, Susanne Kuechler, Mike Rowlands, and Patricia Spyer. Sage, 2006.